written and researched
by Hope Caton

www.purpleguide.com

Turin & Piedmont: The Purple Guide
Credits

Writer: Hope Caton
Editor: Robin Bell
Design: Sharon Platt
Cartography: Anderson Geographics Ltd
Sub-editor: Jon Stanhope
Contributors:
Neil English (Mountains section), Patricia Cleveland-Peck (Lakes gardens),
Catherine McCormack (Turin galleries), Donna J. Macdonald, Sharon Platt
Website design: Mark Parker at Escape Media www.escape-media.com
Photography: All photographs by Hope Caton, except:
Neil English 135, 139; GAM 82 (Galleria d'Arte Moderna e Contemporanea Torino);
Scala Archives 54, 61, 79; Turismo Torino: 43, 45, 64, 70, 75, 87, 91, 98, 118, 149, 202,
206, 207, 214, 238, 239; Scans: Bobbett Creative

With many thanks to …
The Italian Tourist Board in London and their associates in Piedmont. **Special
thanks to**: Damir Biuklic (Mailander), Paola Musolino (Turismo Torino), Sonia
Bartoletti (Distretto Turistico dei Laghi), Enrica Gaia (Ente Turismo Langhe Roero)
Amin Momen (Momentum Ski: 020 7371 9111) www.momentumski.com

Publishing Information

Published in the United Kingdom in January 2006 by:
The Purple Guide Ltd
Teddington Studios
Broom Road
Teddington Middlesex
TW11 9NT

ISBN 0954723430
Printed and Bound by J.H. Haynes & Co. Ltd., Sparkford
Maps © 2006 Anderson Geographics Ltd. Used by permission.
Poem p.195 © Gabriel Griffin. Used by permission.

Sales and PR

For information, telephone our sales department on 020 8614 2277
or email: **sales@purpleguide.com**
Public Relations: Sue Ockwell at Travel PR: 020 8891 4440
Distibuted in the UK and EU by NBN International: 01752 202327

Write to us

We welcome the views and suggestions of our readers. If we include your
contribution in our next edition, we will send you a copy of the book, or any other
Purple Guide that you would prefer. Please write to us at the address above or
email: **feedback@purpleguide.com**

The publishers have done their best to ensure that the information found in
Turin & Piedmont: The Purple Guide is current and accurate. Some information
may be liable to change. The publishers cannot accept responsibility for any loss,
injury or inconvenience that may result from the use of this book.

thepurpleguide
the inside story

'a winning formula' The Sunday Times

Unlike most traditional guide books, The Purple Guide provides a wealth of surprising and entertaining stories and secrets, anecdotes and facts, adding a whole new dimension to your travel experience that might otherwise be missed.

We aim to make your holiday relaxed and fun. As well as offering valuable tips and advice, we give you the inside story on the best that Piedmont has to offer:

- **Turin** with its art nouveau cafés, aperitivo bars, art galleries and the mysterious Shroud
- **Mountains** with details on Olympic improvements for skiiers
- **Lakes** with Lago Maggiore and Lago d'Orta
- **Langhe** one of the world's premier food and wine regions

We concentrate on the most interesting sights, knowing that you want to see what's important and still have enough energy left in the evening for a delicious meal. We include:

- a 43 page **food and drink** section
- 26 pages of personally researched **shopping** listings
- **introductory maps** and advice on the main sights so you can choose your own itinerary.

Updates
We constantly update our website with useful information to support each guidebook we publish. Before you leave for Piedmont, be sure to visit our *Updates* page for new information on special events, restaurants and shopping. You can also find out about other titles and buy your guidebooks online.

www.purpleguide.com

CONTENTS

PIEDMONT

VIEW FROM BAROLO

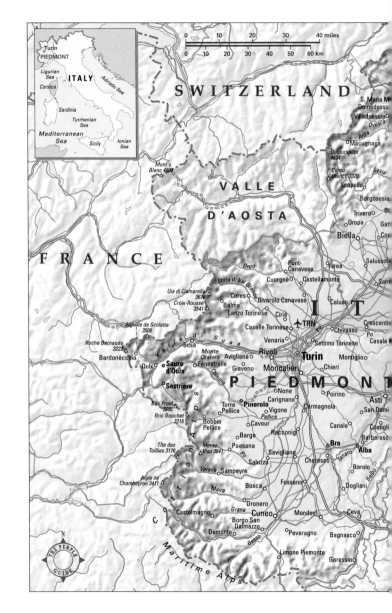

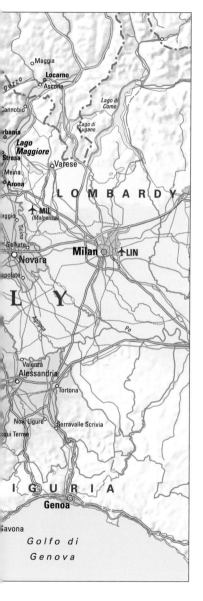

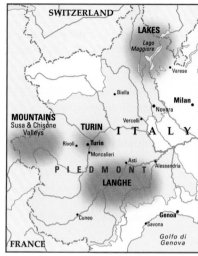

In Italian the name is *Piemonte*, and means 'foot of the mountain'. Piedmont borders France to the west; Switzerland is to the north. The Italian region of Lombardy is to the east, and Liguria is to the south. One of 20 regions in Italy, Piedmont encompasses an area of 9,807 square miles (25,400 km).

There are four destinations in Piedmont that are popular with holiday-makers: **Turin**, **Mountains** (Susa and Chisone Valleys), **Lakes** (Lago Maggiore) and **Langhe.** These are covered extensively in this book.

PIEDMONT

Turin

Renowned as the capital of Fiat, the city has not received many plaudits for its looks, but it really is much prettier than most people would imagine. Hosting the 2006 Winter Olympics has helped to shake off the old image. This is a small and manageable city for the tourist. There is something for everyone here: good food, interesting art, friendly people and a great nightlife.

Shopping is 30 per cent cheaper than in Rome or Milan, and there's plenty of choice. Food and speciality shops abound, especially those selling chocolate. The café scene is marvellous, with beautiful art nouveau and Baroque interiors that are like museums in themselves. Modern art lovers will appreciate what's on offer, and those on a spiritual quest can visit the Turin Shroud. Some say the city is also home to the Holy Grail.

Mountains

All the lifts and runs in the Susa and Chisone Valleys were upgraded for the Olympics. The area is one of the best ski regions in the Italian Alps. With added snow-making facilities, Olympic investment has extended the winter season. The moment temperatures drop below zero, snow is produced in vast quantities. Other seasons have their rewards: hiking, mountain-biking and golf are just some of the recreational activities on offer. As always in Piedmont, the food and wine is extraordinarily good.

Lakes

Lago Maggiore is famous for its alpine scenery and the beauty of its gardens. Bordered by granite mountains in the north and rolling hills to the south, the bright blue lake is fed by two main rivers: the Ticino from Switzerland and the Toce in Italy. Where fresh water enters from the Alps, the lake takes on a shimmering, turquoise glow. There are other lakes to explore, most notably Lago d'Orta with the lovely island of San Giulio.

Visit in the summer, as it rarely gets too hot on Lago Maggiore and there is usually a cool, fragrant breeze. Around the lake, the pace of life is leisurely. This is a perfect holiday destination if you're travelling with your mother, or if you just want to relax. Those seeking an active nightlife should look elsewhere in Piedmont.

Langhe

This area is gaining a reputation as the 'new Tuscany'. Only an hour southeast of Turin, Langhe is a region of rolling, vine-covered hills. Famous for being the source of the elusive white truffle, and the home of the so-called King and Queen of wines (Barolo and Barbaresco), the Langhe region is all about food and wine. The author's favourite meal of all time was found in the small town of Canale. Visit in the autumn, when you can see solitary truffle hunters walking the roads at dusk with their specially-trained dogs.

There is evidence that people lived in the Alpine valleys of Piedmont 100,000 years ago in the Paleolithic age. Nothing much is known about their lives until the Neolithic period (8000 BC) when villages were established and settlers engaged in hunting and farming. Iron age rock paintings (dated 4000 BC) have been discovered in Valle di Susa. By this time Alpine passes were being used to transport goods (especially copper and tin) south to the Mediterranean at Genoa and west to France and Iberia. Around 2000 BC there was an influx of peoples from Iberia (modern Spain) who merged with the locals and became known as Ligurians.

Celts & Romans

Bands of Celts arrived in Piedmont around 700 BC from present-day France and Switzerland. Although they were fierce warriors, they managed to assimilate peacefully into the Ligurian culture. The Celts brought their language, *Occhitano,* which is still spoken in the mountains, where it is also called *Provençal Alpine*. The language is closely related to *Catalan* in Spain and also to the *Languedoc* dialect in France.

Turin was established by Celt-Ligurians in around 500 BC and was originally named *Taurasia*. After a terrifying winter journey through the Alps during the Punic wars of 212 BC, Hannibal rested here with his exhausted troops and his one remaining elephant. But before leaving, he burned the village to the ground. In 58 BC, Julius Caesar declared Taurasia a Roman city and renamed it *Colonia Giulia*. Caesar granted valuable Roman citizenship to all its inhabitants. In the Langhe, *Alba Pompea* (modern Alba) became the centre of Roman life and as such offered all the expected amenities, including

opulent public baths and an amphitheatre that held gladiator games. The warm sulphur-rich waters of *Aquae Statiellae* (Acqui Terme) became a popular spa.

Medieval Piedmont

Like much of Europe, Piedmont was subject to barbarian invasions for hundreds of years following the decline of the Roman Empire. On Christmas day in the year 800, the region came under French domain when Charlemagne was crowned Holy Roman Emperor. Independent in spirit, the Piedmontese did not make docile subjects and – after 88 years of struggle – they managed to evict the French armies from their territory. The area then became a prize fought over by a number of Italian duchies and families until 1046 when the first member of the Savoy family (p.65) gained a foothold in Turin.

By the 13th century, the Savoy controlled the province of Turin and the Borromeo family ruled Lago Maggiore from Milan. An independent republic was formed in the Susa and Chisone valleys. It was called *Republique di Escartons* with Oulx appointed capital. The alpine passes were key to the wealth and security of Turin and Piedmont. A line of fortifications was built at the most strategic points in the mountains. The impressive fortresses of Fenestrelle and Exilles survive as examples today. Langhe was caught up in the Guelph and Ghibbiline wars – conflicts between the Pope and the Holy Roman Emperor. At that time Alba had more than 100 defensive towers.

The Savoy

In 1559, the Savoy were granted dominion over all of Piedmont. The Savoy court moved from Chambéry (France) to Turin, together with the Holy Shroud (p.54). Italian was declared the official language of the realm but the Piedmontese dialect, a mixture of French and Italian, became the court vernacular. It is still spoken today. Piedmont was again besieged by French troops in 1706 who this time were allied with Spain. Pietro Micca blew up a tunnel in Turin that prevented a French advance and turned the tide to victory. The conflict ended in 1713 and the Savoy king,

The Waldensians

Three hundred years before the Protestant Reformation, the mountains of Piedmont became a refuge for a persecuted Christian sect: the Waldensians. The movement began in Lyons in about 1170. Legend has it that the founder's name was Peter Waldo, but historians now recognise that he was not called Peter until 150 years after his death and his original surname was most likely Valdes. He was a wealthy merchant who had a life-changing religious experience: one that led him to renounce wealth, interpret the bible literally and take up a life of preaching. Valdes did not want to separate from the church, instead he sought to reform it and as a result he and his followers were driven out of Lyon. They were excommunicated in 1184, pronounced heretics in 1215 and then persecuted under the Inquisition of 1231. Some fled to Piedmont's mountains where they established permanent settlements. Their knowledge of alpine passes and their bravery in combat made the Waldensians useful to the Savoy. They were tolerated until 1655 when, under French and papal influence, the Savoy began a campaign against the Waldese. Oliver Cromwell sent a mission of protest, but to no avail. Many Waldese were forced to flee to Protestant Switzerland. They returned to the valleys in 1689 and were granted full religious and civil rights in Piedmont in 1848.

Vittorio Amedeo II acquired the Kingdom of Sicily. But Savoy rule over Sicily was short lived: the Spanish, now allied with Piedmont, exchanged the island for Sardinia seven years later. To this day, Sicilians resent the Piedmontese for onerous taxes initiated under Savoy rule.

It wasn't only troops and goods that made the arduous journey through the Alps to Piedmont. Between the 17th and 19th centuries, thousands of British aristocrats braved the snow and winds for eight long days to reach Turin on the first leg of the Grand Tour, an extended journey that would include Florence, Rome, Naples and Venice. These sons of wealthy men, used to warmth and pampering, were carried up and over the mountain passes in rickety chairs borne by short, muscular men, smelling of sweat and alcohol. Grand Tourists unable to cope with the chairs often finished the climb on their knees. The ultra-modern court at Turin was a welcome sight for these exhausted travellers.

Italian Unity

Napoleon was the first leader to establish political unity in Italy. His armies exiled the Savoy, conquered the Venetians, ousted the Pope from lands in Emiglia Romana, and removed the dukes of Ferrara and Milan. All of northern Italy was united in a territory named the Cisalpine Republic, which was renamed the Italian Republic in 1802. The independent state endured until Napoleon's defeat in 1815 when the Congress of Vienna returned papal lands, restored the Duchy of Milan and handed Piedmont back to the Savoy.

Italians who had tasted independence were reluctant to return to the old system. A nationalist movement was born in Turin (p.73) and named after a news publication called *Il Risorgimento*, which was published by Camillo Benso Cavour who later became Prime Minister. In 1861 the Kingdom of Italy was declared a new country governed by a parliamentary monarchy, with Turin as its capital. King Vittorio Emanuele II became the nominal head of state. After four years the capital was moved to Florence and then, in 1870, the centre of national government moved to Rome. Turin's economy, deprived of income from monarchy or government, was modernised. Giovanni Agnelli founded Fiat in 1899; Lancia began production in 1905. Turin became a centre of newspaper and book publishing, as well as film-making, producing 562 films in 1915.

Artisans, factory-workers and peasants organised themselves through guilds and societies, who would provide minimal financial aid to members during times of illness. By the 1880s these societies were shaking off wealthy patrons in favour of self-sufficiency through members' dues. In newly industrialised Piedmont, workers began to strike for better conditions. The first strike was held by wool-workers in Biella, near Lago Maggiore. The Italian trade union movement was formed on Fiat factory floors in Turin.

Wars and Fascism

When World War I broke out, Italy stayed neutral at first but was persuaded by the Allies to enter the conflict, with the expectation of receiving tracts of land in Slovenia and Dalmatia. These turned out to be false promises as these same territories had also been pledged to the Serbs and Greeks. Italy had to settle for a small part of south Tyrol.

After the war, the cost of living spiralled and food shortages intensified as hungry peasants flooded into the cities. Politics evolved into extremes of left and right, with the divide widest in the north: Turin on the left, Milan on the right. In 1919, the Fascist Party was formed in Milan as a reaction to the Socialists who had taken Italy into war. Trade union membership soared in Turin. Strikes and protests became commonplace. This served to increase support for the fascists among ruling industrialists, including the Agnelli family. In 1921, Benito Mussolini was elected to power and the Fascist Party ruled Italy.

The outbreak of World War II in 1939 led to a boom at Fiat. Production was increased to fulfill military orders. The new assembly line at Mirafiori employed 22,000 workers. Italy entered the war in June 1940 allied to Germany, but support from Nazi forces was non-existent and Italian casualties were heavy. In 1941 Mussolini sent his ill-equipped troops to Russia. Most died as they attempted to walk home through the Russian winter after defeat at Stalingrad. In March 1943, a strike against appalling working conditions in a Turin factory grew into a massive anti-fascist, anti-war protest. Mussolini was arrested and an armistice with the Allies was declared on September 1943. Nazi forces invaded Piedmont from the north and sent Panzer divisions to Naples and Monte Cassino. Mussolini was returned as head of a puppet state called the Italian Republic. Turin was severely bombed. The damage was so great that in 1943 many parents loaded their children onto trains bound for La Foce near Montepulciano. This was a war for national liberation as well as a civil war. Communists, Socialists and Catholics took up arms to fight

Nazism and Fascism. Partisan resistance fighters in Alba held off the Nazis for 23 days. When the war ended in 1945, Mussolini tried to flee the country, probably heading for Austria. He was stopped by partisans who promptly shot him.

Modern Turin

Giovanni Agnelli was forced to retire from Fiat because of the company's ties to Mussolini's government. Vittorio Valletta ran Fiat's operations and Turin benefited from a post-war boom, which saw many impoverished southerners moving north for work. The city became a company town; its population soared along with the output of Fiat cars. When Giovanni died, his grandson Gianni became head of the family and in 1963 Gianni took over as General Manager of Fiat. He became CEO in 1966, holding the post until 1996. Gianni famously said: 'What's good for Fiat is good for Italy'. During his time the company expanded and bought Ferrari and Lancia. But as the century progressed changes in the auto market, combined with high labour costs, caused Fiat to go into decline. By the time of Gianni Agnelli's death in 2003, Turin had long ceased to be a company town.

Piedmont Today

With an eroding industrial base Piedmont faced a crisis of economics. The solution has been to encourage high-tech businesses, invest in service industries, and develop the region as a tourist destination. Hosting the 2006 Winter Olympics has certainly revitalized Turin and the resorts in the mountains, with millions of euros spent on urban regeneration projects and improvements to the transportation infrastructure.

With some of the best wine and food in the world, agricultural exports are seen as very important. This is, after all, the home of the 'king of wines' and the famous white truffle, and so 'gastro-tourism' is being promoted heavily, especially in the Lange. Turin has dropped the Fiat baggage and re-styled itself as a fun destination for short breaks and for longer holidays. The good news is that both the city and the region are living up to expectations.

The Piedmontese

They can be summed up as hard-working, responsible, serious, ambitious, reliable and – above all else – intensely passionate about food. A distinctly northern people, some Piedmontese feel closer ties with their Swiss and French neighbours than with other Italians. The antipathy is mutual: in southern Italy there is a great deal of enmity towards them and the term *Piemontese* is used as an insult. The lingering resentment dates back to a short period in the 18th century when the Kingdom of Sicily was ruled from Piedmont and Sicilian taxes went north. Today, the Piedmontese are resentful that their taxes go south to pay for services in Sicily and other areas populated by people they consider less hard-working than themselves.

For the past three hundred years Turin's thriving café culture has been a breeding ground for authors, anarchists, publishers and socialists. The Italian independence movement, the *Risorgimento,* was born in Torinese cafés. The left-leaning *La Stampa,* published in Turin, is one of Italy's most read papers. In the post-war period several prominent younger novelists were on the editorial team of *Einaudi* newspaper in Turin, including Cesare Pavese, Elio Vittorini, Natalia Ginzburg and Italo Calvino. Distinguished authors Umberto Eco and Primo Levi are from Piedmont.

The Piedmontese love all things new and exciting, especially in the arts. Italian cinema was born in Turin and this is a city that honours contemporary art in other fields. Unlike many other Italian cities which venerate the old, this is a place to see sculptures and paintings by new artists.

The writer Giovanni Arpino best sums up the Piedmontese attitude towards food and wine in a story about an old man who lay dying. Unable to open his eyes, he asked for a piece of gorgonzola cheese and a specific bottle of Barolo from his own cupboard. The cheese appeared, the man smiled. Then the bottle arrived and was uncorked. As the wine's aroma wafted past his nose, his eyes still closed, the man shouted loudly that this was most certainly not *his* Barolo.

TURIN

A relatively small city that is easy to navigate, Turin is laid out in a grid pattern. This is a legacy from the city's beginnings as a Roman outpost. Troops rested in Turin before embarking on the hazardous journey north through the Alps, and recuperated here on their long march south to Rome.

Turin's main sights are to be found in the centre, or *Centro*, which is bordered on three sides by broad avenues and the Po river on the east side. The Roman grid pattern is obvious, with Via Po and Via Pietro Micca the only streets set at an angle. The 17km of colonnaded streets in the centre are a pleasure to walk along, whatever the weather.

Lingotto is an up-and-coming district located south of the centre. This was the birthplace of Fiat and where the factory workers lived. Turin's hosting of the 2006 Winter Olympics has resulted in the construction of new stadiums and sports facilities in the industrial heart of the city. The district takes its name from the original factory, the *Lingotto*, now a shopping mall, exhibition space and the location of the Agnelli art collection.

Torino Card

48 hours €15
72 hours €17

This plastic card permits one adult and child to travel on all public transport, including trams and buses, in any consecutive 48 or 72 hour period. The card also allows free entrance to Turin's museums and attractions including the Mole lift, the funicular railway to Basilica di Superga, and boats on the River Po.

Purchase the card from any tourist office or ask your hotel concierge. The date, time and your name are written on the card by the seller so you can decide exactly when you want to activate it.

The Torino Card is a bargain and very convenient to use. Present it at any ticket desk to receive free entry. Keep it with you on public transport as proof that you have paid the fare. An inspector may ask to see your pass.

Tourist Office

Atrium Torino
Piazza Solferino
011 535 181
09.30-19.00 daily
info@turismotorino.org

It is worth stopping by this centrally located office for information on local and cultural events. They give out free maps, sell the ChocoPass (p.39) and they will also book walking tours on your behalf.

Weather permitting, public skating is held here during the winter.

Tickets

Turin's efficient bus and tram network is run by GTT (Gruppo Torinese Trasporti). Bus and tram routes are clearly indicated on large signs at the stops. Trams serve the centre, buses go further afield.

Tickets are valid across the network and can be purchased at bars and newsagents or at the GTT office at Porta Nuova – the central bus and train station located on Corso Vittorio Emanuele II (map 1, D5). A detailed route map can be bought there.

A single ticket is 90 cents and a *carnet* of 15 tickets €12.50. Tickets must be stamped in the machines on board and are valid for 70 minutes.

Other than the Torino Card, three additional transport passes are available:

• all-day pass (*giornaliero*) €3
• a shopping (*negozio*) pass valid for a four-hour period while shops are open, €1.80
• a group card (*viaggiare insieme*), valid for up to four people to travel between 14.30-20.00 Saturdays and public holidays, €4

SEE TRAVEL BASICS (P.286) FOR MORE INFORMATION.

Useful tram routes

4
(north-south)
Porta Nuova • Corso Vittorio Emanuele II • Via XX Settembre • Piazza San Giovanni • Piazza della Repubblica • Via Milano (travel north on Via XX Settembre and south on Via Milano)

9
(northwest-southeast)
Corso Alessandro Tassoni • Piazza Lorenzo Bernini • Corso Vittorio Emanuele II • Corso Massimo D'Azeglio • Parco del Valentino

13
(east-west)
Madre del Dio • Piazza Vittore Veneto • Via Po • Piazza Castello • Via Cernaia • Piazza Statuto • Via Cibrario • Corso Alessandra Tassoni • Via Fabrizi

15
(southwest-northeast)
Piazza Sabotino • Corso Vittorio Emanuele II • Porta Nuova • Via Milano • Piazza Castello • Via Po • Via Bava • Ponte di Sassi • Sassi-Superga funicular

Mountains and Valleys

Two mountain ranges form a crescent shape along Turin's horizon. The Alps lie to the west and north, the Apennines to the south. A third less prominent range, the Monferrato, rises to the east of the city. At the base of the mountains is a vast plain comprising 17,500 square miles. Turin is located at a narrow point between the Alps and Monferrato hills.

A great view of the snow-capped peaks is seen from the top of the Mole (p.48). The pyramid-shaped peak to the south-west is Monviso. At 3841m above sea level it is Piedmont's highest peak and the origin of the river Po. To the west lies the pointed triangle of Monte Rocciamelone (3538m), the tallest mountain in Valle di Susa. The smaller peak in front is Monte Pirchiriano (920m) where Sacra di San Michele stands guard over the entrance to the valley. Other mountains on the western horizon are Monte Rognosa (3280m), Monte Albergian (2996m) and Roc del Boucher (3285m).

Turin stands at the edge of the Valle di Susa, the main valley and historic access road through the Alps to France. The scene of many battles, control of this mountain pass has been very important to the history of Piedmont. The fortresses and castles along the route are beautiful reminders of past struggles. Today the valley carries a motorway (E70) to speed skiiers to the alpine resorts. Bardonecchia is the last town in Italy before entering France. South of Valle di Susa is Valle del Chisone, a smaller valley popular with skiiers who favour the resort of Sestriere. All roads and ski facilities were upgraded for the 2006 Winter Olympics.

Looking southwest from the Mole you can see the equestrian town of Pinerolo. Five smaller valleys spread southwards towards Cuneo: Vale Pellice, Valle Po (named for the river) Val Varaita, Valle Maira and Valle Grana. Directly south of Turin are the Ligurian Apennines and the towns of Cuneo and Mondovi. This area is growing in popularity with hot-air balloon enthusiasts.

The Basilica di Superga (p.100) is set high in the hills on the east side of Turin. The view from the front of the Basilica takes in Turin and the entire Alpine range. You can also see the Mole and the Po river as it winds its way through the city. Wealthy Torinese make their homes in these hills which undulate towards the wine provinces of Langhe where both the King (Barolo) and Queen (Barbaresco) of wines are produced.

The Po river flows out of Turin in a northeast direction towards Milan. The flat valley along the river is the centre of rice-growing in Italy (some say all of Europe) and fields of rice paddies shimmering with water is all the eye can see. The town of Vercelli is known as the capital of rice.

Turin's airport is located to the north of the city at Caselle. Further north is Parco Nazionale del Gran Paradiso and the Italian region of Valle D'Aosta. The A5 is the route to the Mont Blanc tunnel into Switzerland. Mont Blanc is 150km away from Turin, too far to be seen from the top of the Mole.

Po River

The source of the river Po is 6,500 feet (1981m) above sea level on Monviso in the Alps, near the French border. High on the mountain in the Rio Martino cave, water gushes forth in a 60 foot-high waterfall. In the river's first ten miles, the rushing water descends 500 feet. The Po flows down through the valley before it opens into the flat plain near Saluzzo, southwest of Turin. Here the river slows and gently meanders through the south of Turin before heading north-east in the direction of Lombardy and Milan. Throughout the remainder of its course the Po flows more or less due east, winding along the 45th parallel for 405 miles (652 km) to its vast delta near Venice where it empties into the Adriatic.

Called *Padus* by the Romans, the Po is Italy's longest river. Two and a half miles across at its widest point, the Po's mean flood is 53,000 cubic feet per second. The fast moving water accumulates silt, a fine-grained sandy sediment, which creates an unstable riverbed. This silt once emptied into the Venetian lagoon, causing havoc in Venice for centuries. Canals were built to divert the river and its tributaries away from the lagoon and prevent the build-up of silt deposits. Constant dredging is required to keep the canals free-flowing. Movement and instability of the river-bed means the Po is only navigable at certain points.

The Po is Italy's most economically important river. Along its banks are farms and businesses that produce most of the country's food and industrial exports. The cities along the river have long been engines for the Italian economy: Turin, Milan, Parma, Mantua, Ferrara, Verona, Padua and Venice.

But the Po isn't only about industry. There are many green spaces in Turin located along its banks. *Parco del Valentino*, closest to the city centre, is where locals take their Sunday *passeggiata*. There are two sights to visit in the park: *Castello Valentino*, the palace of Maria Cristina of France, and *Borgo Medioevale,* a reconstruction of a medieval Piedmont village built for the Turin Exposition in 1884.

Baroque

The term Baroque often evokes images of lavish decoration, gilding and over-the-top ornamentation, but Baroque actually refers to the post-Renaissance period of the 17th and 18th centuries (roughly 1600-1750), the time when many of Turin's palaces and colonnaded streets were built. This means that a baroque building in Piedmont is very different from a baroque building in Rome. Roman baroque architecture is ornamental and decorative, whereas Piedmontese baroque tends to have much cleaner lines and precise geometrical proportions.

The development of Turin is closely connected to the establishment of the Savoy monarchy. In 1578, Emanuele Filiberto made Turin the capital of the Savoy duchy. To ensure the city was a proper showpiece worthy of the monarchy, he began a programme of planned urban development. A new town plan was created with a strict layout that included the addition of

squares, buildings and monuments. Architects came from all over Italy to contribute their talents to the new buildings. The result was a city of a stately and cohesive character, reminiscent of Paris. However, this meant that much of medieval Turin had been sacrificed. What remains is found in the narrow lanes of *Il Quadrilatero*, the Roman Quarter.

The Savoy owned all the land in the centre of Turin. They granted tracts to nobles and court dignitaries for villas and palaces on the condition that the exterior design of any building conformed to a master plan. With luxurious ornamentation forbidden on the outside, nobles showed their wealth by commissioning grand interiors, with marble staircases, elaborate reception rooms and ornamented courtyards. Straight paved roads were built to accommodate royal carriages, and these were lined with colonnades.

Rebuilding involved three principal architects: Ascanio Vitozzi designed Palazzo Madama at the end of the 16th century, to revitalize the centre of Turin; Guarino Guarini was a Theatine monk from Modena who built the church of San Lorenzo in 1665; Filippo Juvarra was a court favourite who arrived in Turin around 1715. Juvarra's first commission was the Basilica di Superga, built to fulfil a vow made by Vittorio Amedeo II during the siege of Turin in 1706. Juvarra circumvented rules forbidding exterior ostentation by building large windows to highlight the lavish interiors.

Art Nouveau

Towards the end of the 19th century, Turin was ready for a new style of architecture. Recent industrial expansion had led to the growth of a wealthy middle class, who were keen to invest in property in the city centre. In 1885, extensive plans were made to redevelop the historical centre, and expand the city further. These plans coincided with a new international movement in decoration and architecture, developed in the 1880s and 1890s and centred in western Europe, called *art nouveau*.

In 1896, an interior design gallery opened in Paris under the name Maison de l'Art Nouveau. Although the English would adopt the label *art nouveau*, the French used the English term 'Modern Style', in deference to the English origins of the movement. Art nouveau was actually a further development of the Arts and Crafts movement, begun in Britain in the mid-18th century. The art nouveau style took its decorative inspiration from the natural world, using curves and sinuous forms derived from plants, flowers and insects. The old Paris métro entrances are an example of art nouveau, as is glassware by Lalique, buildings by Gaudì, paintings by Gustav Klimt, and illustrations by Aubrey Beardsley.

The 1902 Turin Exhibition of Decorative Art introduced art nouveau to Italy. Raimondo D'Aronco and Annibale Rigotti designed elaborate pavilions for the Parco Valentino. Many of the objects on display came from Liberty & Co in London. As a result, art nouveau became known as *stile Liberty* (Liberty style) in Italy. The pavilions no longer exist and all that remains of D'Aronco's work in Turin is the Casa D'Aronco in nearby Via Petrarca.

After the exhibition, many buildings inspired by art nouveau were constructed on the new Via Pietro Micca.

Known locally as *la Diagonale*, this was the first street in the centre to break from the old Roman grid. Although few government buildings were commissioned in the art nouveau style, it was taken up enthusiastically by the new class of entrepreneurs and professionals in Turin.

The best-known exponent of Liberty style in Turin was Piero Fenoglio. His Casa Fenoglio-La Fleur, at the junction of Corso Francia and Via Principi d'Acaja, was a family house named after his wife. A little further out and south of GAM is the chic area of La Crocetta, with many art nouveau buildings.

Art Nouveau walk

Begin at Caffè Platti (Corso Vittorio Emanuele II, 72) and stroll under the colonnades to Largo Vittorio Emanuele. Turn right on Corso Galileo, then left on to Corso G. Matteotti. You will see a distinctive art nouveau balcony on the corner of Via Papacino. Walk along Via Papacino and explore. Beautifully decorated buildings line both sides of the road and the side streets. When you've had enough, turn right at Via Promis and continue along Via Meucci until you reach Piazza Solferino. At the north end, take Via Pietro Micca to Piazza Castello where you can stop at *Mulassano* or *Baratti e Milano* for chocolate. Both are Torinese institutions with sumptuous art nouveau interiors.

33

Cafés

The historic cafés of Turin are stunning works of gilt, marble, tiles and frescoes, decorated with chandeliers and mirrors. These sumptuous interiors were the backdrop when Italy's fate was decided during the Risorgimento of the 19th century. Political plans were exchanged between statesmen and the intelligentsia, while artists, generals and intellectuals played their part in the movement for national unity and independence. Heroes of the Risorgimento such as Garibaldi and Cavour plotted in Caffè Florio on Via Po, while nobles and stars of the nearby Teatro Regio populated Caffè Mulassano in Piazza Castello.

Mulassano
Piazza Castello 15
011 547 990
07.30-21.00 daily
map 1-2, D2
The bar in this miniature jewel-box café (designed by Antonio Vandone) is made of onyx, the coffered ceiling is gilded mahogany and a palm is planted in a Chinoise vase. It's tiny but perfect. Mulassano claims to have been the first (in 1920) to serve *tramezzini*, filled sandwiches made with very thinly sliced bread.

Baratti & Milano
Piazza Castello 27
011 547 990
09.00-21.00 Tues-Sun
map 1-2, D2
Founded in 1873 and named after the owners, the café was designed by Giulo Casanova who used walnut for the panelling and the bar. It was immediately patronised by the Savoy family and members of the Court. Baratti & Milano are one of the best chocolatiers in Turin and are also known for their fine selection of tiny cakes.

Caffè San Carlo
Piazza San Carlo, 156
011 532 586
08.00-24.00 daily; 01.00 Fri, Sat
map 1-2, D3
San Carlo first opened its doors
in the early 1800s, but proved
so popular with left-leaning
intellectuals that it was closed in
1837 for promoting subversive
activities. The gold gilt interior
is dominated by a large murano
glass chandelier. In 1837, San
Carlo became the establishment
which first introduced gas
lighting to Turin. The adjacent
room, mysteriously known as the
gabinetto cinese is decorated with
Grecian columns and sculptures
set against French style frescoes
by Petro Spintz and Giacomo
Beltrami.
San Carlo offers a fixed price
menu for lunch that is good
value, or you can select items
from the buffet. The food is
well-prepared and the service
is prompt if a bit perfunctory.
Beware, the waiter likes to flirt
with all the young ladies and he
can be grouchy if you arrive
at opening time.

Caffè Torino
Piazza San Carlo 204
011 545 118
07.30-01.00 daily
map 1-2, D3
Located under a neon Martini
sign, this elegant café contains
original furnishings dating from
1903. It was a favourite with the
literary set: writers Cesare Pavese
and Luigi Einaudi regularly met
here. Step on the bronze bull in
the pavement by the entrance to
guarantee your good luck.
Caffè Torino is famous for its
delicious cakes and is *the*
place to come for your early
morning coffee.

Caffè Fiorio
Via Po 8
011 817 0612
08.00-01.00 daily; 02.00 Fri, Sat
map 1-2, F2
Established in 1780, Fiorio is
perhaps the oldest café in Turin.
In the days of the monarchy,
the ruling elite made political
decisions here over a dish of ice
cream. The old nobility have been
swept away but Fiorio still serves
an excellent gelato. Sit inside
with the original baroque decor,
outside under the porticoes, or
purchase a take-away cup or
cone from a window at the side
of the building.

Al Bicerin

Piazza della Consolata 5
011 436 9325, www.bicerin.it
08.30-19.30 daily, closed Wed
closed 13.00-15.30 Sat, Sun
map 1-2, C1

A *bicerin* is a hot drink made with espresso, hot chocolate and cream. The name means 'small glass', and bicerin is traditionally served in one. There is a dispute as to whether the drink was invented here or at Caffè Fiorio but the bicerin made here is the best in Turin. Chocolate cake is another speciality.

Fortunately this tiny café has a large outdoor area, otherwise you'd never get a table. Prepare to wait to sit down on a Sunday.

Caffè Platti

Corso Vittorio Emanuele II 72
011 506 9056, www.platti.it
07.30-21.00 daily
map 1-2, C4

Platti is a beautiful restaurant and popular with wealthy Torinese. It is decorated in a French baroque style and its original furnishings date back to its opening in 1870. Rumour has it that Gianni Agnelli developed plans for the formation of the Juventus football club at one of Platti's tables.

In 1910 the adjacent confectionery was panelled in walnut and ornamented with gilt putti by Valabrega. Platti makes excellent chocolate, creamy and smooth. The south-facing tables under the porticoes, often bathed in sunlight, are a pleasant place to while away the hours. Come here for *aperitivo*; Platti offers an abundant selection of snacks.

Café Lavazza

Via San Tommaso 10
011 534 201 www.lavazza.it
08.00-19.00 Mon-Fri; 22.30 Sat
map 1-2, D3

Turin is renowned for Italy's most famous brand of coffee. Back in 1895, Luigi Lavazza bought a grocery shop in the commercial district of the city for a paltry sum and created the famous blend now drunk by three-quarters of all Italians. Lavazza coffee has become synonymous with style and their renowned advertising campaigns are on display in the chic surroundings.

Coffee

Despite being an Italian institution, coffee originated in the Middle East and the first ever coffee shop was in Istanbul. Legend has it that Mohammed was visited by the archangel Gabriel one day when he was feeling ill. The angel brought a black potion from Allah, which reinvigorated the prophet and inspired him to perform great deeds. Another legend tells the story of an Arabian shepherd called Kaddi, who noticed that his goats became excitable after eating the berries of a certain plant. Kaddi mentioned this phenomenon to the abbot Yahia who went on to make a bitter, dark drink that reinvigorated the body.

Coffee followed the spread of Islam across the Middle East after it escaped from a ban under Islamic law (unlike alcohol). The drink arrived in Venice in the 1570s at a time when the city relied heavily on trade with the Muslim East. Coffee was originally consumed in Italy for medicinal purposes and was a luxury item. It only became a popular refreshment in the 1640s when Venice opened its first coffee house. Two hundred cafés appeared along the canals of the city and before long the craze spread to Milan and Turin. In 1600, Pope Clement VIII was urged to consider coffee part of the infidel threat, given that it was the favourite drink of the Ottoman Empire. However, he decided to 'baptise' rather than ban it and coffee became an acceptable Christian beverage. The Pope is reported to have cried: '*It is so delicious that it would be a sin to let only misbelievers drink it! Let's defeat Satan by blessing this drink, which contains nothing objectionable to a Christian!*'

Achilles Gaggia perfected his coffee machine in 1946. Today Italian bars sell an average of 230 cups of coffee per day, 60 per cent are espresso, otherwise known as *un caffè*, while 14 per cent are sold as cappuccino. Beware of the incredulous stare you will receive if you order a cappuccino after dinner. This is a breakfast drink for Italians, who believe it is bad for the digestion to fill the stomach with hot milk after an evening meal. To maintain your credibility, drink cappuccino only until 11am. Afterwards, order a macchiato (p 228).

Chocolate

Turin and Piedmont have been famed for their confectionery industry since ancient times. Pliny wrote about the Roman settlers of Turin and how they used the seeds of the alpine fir tree mixed with honey to make a sweet called *aquicelus*, which resembles Turin's present day nougat. Today twenty percent of Italy's industrial confectionery production comes from the region, and it's claimed that there are more master chocolatiers in Turin than in all of Belgium and France combined.

Chocolate was introduced to Italy in 1606 by the Florentine explorer Francesco Antonio Carletti, following his travels in the New World. It did not gain popularity until the 1660s, when influential scientist Francesco Redi developed luxurious recipes for drinking chocolate, including concoctions perfumed with musk and jasmine. In 1678, a royal decree was issued authorizing chocolate production, at first mostly for export, but chocolate soon beguiled many Italians on their own soil. It is said that Casanova had a fondness for the stuff, reputedly naming it the 'elixir of love' and indulging in chocolate's supposedly aphrodisiac properties before bedding his many conquests. In the 19th century chocolate was considered a good medium for administering poison and it is rumoured that Pope Clement XIV perished from a poisoned cup of drinking chocolate, in revenge for his suppression of the chocolate-drinking Jesuit order.

Turin's most famous chocolate product today is *gianduja,* a combination of cocoa, milk, sugar and hazelnuts from Piedmont, developed in 1852. The mixture was originally shaped in the form of a little boat called a *gianduiotto*, but was then renamed after Gianduja, the Piedmontese masked character found in *commedia dell'arte*. It became so popular that it was served at the wedding of Grace Kelly and Prince Rainier of Monaco in 1956 and is enjoyed internationally today, in the guise of Ferrero Rocher chocolates and Nutella chocolate spread, both exported from Piedmont.

Chocolate makes a star appearance in Piedmontese cuisine, and not only in ice cream. It is also served with pears, game, in dessert ravioli, and it is commonly drunk in liquid form. Turin is famous for its chocolate drinks: *bicerin* (espresso and chocolate) and hot chocolate which was made fashionable in the 18th century as a way of keeping out the alpine cold. Enjoy authentic examples in any of the historic cafés around Piazza San Carlo, or if you want to gorge on gianduja head to Peyrano, one of the best chocolatiers in the city, at Corso Vittorio Emanuele 76.

The ChocoPass is a book of coupons for tastings at participating shops and cafés, available from the tourist office. The type of tasting offered, whether ice cream, cake or bon-bon, is marked on the coupon. Purchase ten tastings in 24 hours for €10 or 15 in 48 hours for €15. It's good value if you love chocolate, but you may find you buy the right to try more chocolate than you can sample. Also, it is a challenge to get round to all the shops within the time allotted.

The best chocolate

Confetteria Avvignano
Via Carlo Felice 50
09.00-13.00, 15.30-19.30
closed Mon am
map 1-2, D4

Caffè Platti
Corso V. Emanuele II 72
07.30-21.00 daily
map 1-2, C4

Cioccolato Peyrano
Corso V. Emanuele II 76
09.00-12.30, 15.00-19.30
closed Sun, Mon
map 1-2, C4

Baratti & Milano
Piazza Castello 27
09.00-21.00 Tues-Sun
map 1-2, D2

Passeggiata Torinese

The Italian tradition of taking an afternoon walk, or *passeggiata*, has little to do with exercise. The purpose is to meet friends, share the latest gossip, show off new shoes and perhaps have an ice cream or do a little window shopping. Passeggiata occurs in the late afternoon, from 4-6pm when shops reopen after siesta and before aperitivo.

Turin's colonnaded streets offer miles of covered shop-lined walkways that are popular for passeggiata. Though there is no prescribed walk in Turin, you will find many locals taking a stroll along the river Po towards Piazza Vittore Veneto and Via Po. A walk along the Via Po is especially favoured because you can stop for a cone or cup of Fiorio's excellent ice cream.

Cross Piazza Castello to pick up Via Garibaldi, a pedestrian-only shopping street in the Roman quarter. The road runs due west and was once the central street of the old Roman settlement. Now it is full of shops and cafes and you can often see the Alps in the distance.

Aperitivo

The word *aperitivo* goes back to the Latin verb *aperire* meaning 'to open'. It is thought that the tradition of stimulating the appetite with small morsels of food began in ancient Egypt. The very agreeable Piedmontese custom of *aperitivo* occurs daily between the hours of 6-9pm. During the early evening bars, cafes and restaurants serve wine, beer and cocktails accompanied by glorious buffets of hot and cold food. There is no extra charge for the food and you may help yourself to as much or as little as you desire, but drinks can cost up to €2 more than at other times of the day.

The traditional aperitivo in Turin is a sweet vermouth. The word vermouth comes from the German *wehrmut*, meaning bitter-sweet (or nostalgic). The beverage was invented in Turin in 1786 by Benedetto Carpano who blended white wine with an infusion of herbs. A Turin speciality is a *Carpano Punt e Mes*, vermouth with a half-dose of bitters. The name was coined when an addled stock exchange agent mistakenly called out the trading floor term for 'point and a half', *punt e mes* in the Torinese dialect, while ordering a drink at Carpano's bar.

Martini, the global leader in the production of vermouth, was established in 1863. The company makes four different types of vermouth: *rosso* (red), *bianco* (white), dry and rosé. Rosso is made from wine mixed with an aromatic extract of herbs soaked with distillates of raspberry, orange and juniper. Caramel is added to give the liquor its distinctive amber colour. Martini vermouths and Cinzano are made from longstanding secret family recipes. The history of the families and their beverages can be found at the Martini Museum of the History of Wine in Pessione.

The aperitivo ritual is so much a part of Piedmontese life that it often substitutes for the evening meal – an Italian version of the after-work drink in the pub, but with much better food. The best buffets are found along Via Po, especially Caffè Roberto, which was once a favourite haunt of the artist Giorgio de Chirico.

Nightlife

I Murazzi

The name for the strip of discos and dance clubs located side by side along the banks of the river, *I Murazzi* stretches from Ponte Umberto to Ponte Vittorio Emanuele. The area really comes alive in summer when clubs open their outdoor terraces and the entire riverfront becomes one long party until dawn. Most clubs don't open until at least 11pm, but it's usually 1am before things really get going. Some clubs close at 4am, some stay open longer. Admission is free to most clubs but drinks are expensive and credit cards are not generally accepted.

Beach, **Pier 7-9-11**, **Alcatraz** and **Jammin** are the best known clubs along the river. If you're hungry, Jammin opens its outdoor tables for aperitivo and there is a bona fide restaurant tucked between the clubs called Bokaos.

YOU WILL NEED MOSQUITO REPELLENT IN SUMMER MONTHS.

Borgo Dora

Just north-west of the Roman quarter is an area known as *Borgo Dora*, an abandoned industrial district that has been taken over by all-night clubs and discos. The surrounding neighbourhood is a bit rough, but most places are clustered together in the same complex: Via Valprato 68 houses **Docks Home**, **Docks8**, **On-Gaia** and **Café Blue**.

If you are asked for a membership card at the door, show your passport and you will most likely gain free admittance. Credit cards are not accepted. Buses 12, 46 and 77 stop nearby, but be prepared to take a taxi both ways because service to the area is infrequent. Buses stop running before the clubs have really got going.

Locals usually begin their evenings by meeting with friends at bars and restaurants in the Roman quarter, before heading off to dance till dawn in Borgo Dora.

SEE PAGE 238-40 FOR FURTHER LISTINGS

CENTRO

Turin has three main squares: Piazza San Carlo, Piazza Castello and Piazza Vittorio Veneto, all connected by colonnaded streets lined with cafés and shops.

The city is home to the mysterious Turin Shroud. Authentic or not, the cloth has an interesting past. Film fans will want to visit the outstanding cinema museum housed in the Mole, Turin's disitinctive landmark. Ride the lift to the top for a superb view of the city and the mountains.

Be sure to stop at one of Turin's many luxurious cafés. Once places of politics and intrigue, they are now an elegant setting for coffee. Leave your diet at home and indulge in the fine chocolates and pastries on offer. Tasting several types in one go is made easier by their small size.

Turin is a centre for modern art and a mecca for young artists. Each Christmas there is a brilliant show of lights by contemporary artists.

North of Via Giuseppe Garibaldi, The Roman Quarter comes alive at night. A large student population means there are some good nightclubs. In summer, the narrow lanes are filled with people.

ROMAN QUARTER

Map Labels

RONDO DELLA FORCA · CORSO · PIAZZA DELLA REPUBLICA · REGINA · MARGHERITA · LARGO BELGIO

P. EUGENIO · CORSO VALDOCCO · Porta Palatina · PIAZZA CESARE AUGUSTO · Giardino Reale · CORSO SAN MAURIZIO · LUNGO PO MACHIAVELLI

Museo della Sindone · VIA SAN DOMENICO · CORSO PALESTRO · Duomo · Palazzo Reale

PIAZZA STATUTO · CORSO SICCARDI · PIAZZA PALAZZO DE CITTA · S.Lorenzo · PIAZZETTA REALE · Teatro Regio · Mole

VIA GIUSEPPE GARABALDI · Palazzo Madama · PIAZZA CASTELLO · VIA GUISEPPE VERDI

Centro · VIA PIETRO MICCA · VIA ROMA · PIAZZA CARIGNANO · VIA PO · VIA PO · PIAZZA VITTORIO VENETO

Giardino Cittadella · Giardino Lamarmora · Palazzo Carignano · PIAZZA CARLO EMANUELE II · Gran Madre di Dio · PTE VITTORIO EMANUELE I

VIA CERNAIA · Museo d. Marionetta · Museo Egizio · PIAZZA SAN CARLO

VINZAGLIO · C. GALILEO FERRARIS · VIA RE UMBERTO I · VIA ALFIERI · VIA GIOVANNI · PIAZZA CAVOUR · GIOLITTI · Monte dei Cappuccini · S. Maria del Monte

CORSO GIACOMO MATTEOTTI · C. G. MATTEOTTI · PIAZZA CARLO FELICE · PIAZZA BODONI · Aiuola Balbo · Fiume Po · CORSO CASALA

CORSO · VITTORIO · EMANUELE II

GAM

Mole Antonelliana
• Turin's distinctive landmark contains a cinema museum
Duomo • home of the Turin Shroud
San Lorenzo
• gorgeous baroque church
GAM • modern art gallery
Palazzo Reale • the royal court of the Savoy dynasty
Museo Egizio
• largest Egyptian collection outside Cairo
Gran Madre di Dio
• location of the Holy Grail?

Porta Palazzo
Europe's largest outdoor market located in Piazza della Repubblica

Did you know that..?
Turin was the first stop on the Grand Tour and the place where aristocrats learned their manners.

Il Quadrilatero
A lively area known as the Roman Quarter

nightlife p.238
shopping p.266
restaurants p.232

CENTRO

La Mole Antonelliana

Via Montebello 20
011 812 5658
museonazionaledelcinema.it
10.00-20.00 Tuesday-Sunday
10.00-23.00 Saturday
closed Monday
admission with Torino card or
lift and museum €6.80
lift only €3.62, museum €5.20
children free
map 1-2, F2

Turin's distinctive landmark
was commissioned as
a synagogue and was
intended to reach a height
of 47m (154ft). The architect
Alessandro Antonelli had
his own ideas and the
structure got ever taller,
finally reaching a height
of 167m (530ft). Jewish
leaders finally pulled out of
the project and ceded the
Mole to Turin city council.
Take the lift to the top for
panoramic views of the city.

The lift

Ascending through the
centre of the cinema
museum, the lift takes
59 seconds to reach the
viewing platform. The car
holds nine people. The wait
is usually 30-45 minutes but
if the queue extends outside,
your wait could be longer
than 90 minutes.

Museo Nazionale del Cinema

Don't miss the cinema museum: it is one of the best in the world. The imaginative interior was designed by François Confino in 2000 to house the collection begun by Maria Adriana Prolo in 1940. Films are shown on the walls of the cavernous central atrium where you can stretch out on the orange 'fish' chairs. Every half hour the window coverings rise to showcase the architecture and structure of the Mole interior, accompanied by dramatic soundtrack music.

Exhibits are arranged around three themes: the history of cinema (*archaeologia del cinema*), the making of cinema (*macchina del cinema*) and the genres in cinema (*sala del tempio*). To illustrate the most popular categories (horror, romance, science fiction, fantasy, comedy, drama, thriller) rooms on the ground floor are decorated like film sets for the genre. For example, the romance set is a pink bedroom dominated by a round 60s style bed. Exhibits are interactive so there are often children having pillow fights on the bed, or couples lying side by side watching a film screen located under the bed's canopy.The fantasy room is fronted by a huge fridge with giant carrots and an enormous celery. Walk through the fridge and you'll discover cinema seats shaped like toilets – these are favourites with young children.

A ramp leads up to the second and third floors where exhibits illustrate how films are made and what each department does, from makeup to wardrobe and on to special effects. The museum has priceless collections of props and memorabilia, including the robes worn by Peter O'Toole as Lawrence of Arabia, Darth Vader's caped costume, Alien monster suits, and one of Federico Fellini's hats.

Further up the ramp, there are historical exhibits from European and Hollywood cinema. The museum also has an enormous collection of more than 5,000 magic lanterns and magic lantern slides that date from the 18th and 19th centuries, 100,000 photographs and daguerrotypes, and over 300,000 movie posters and playbills. Fun for every age group.

Cinema in Turin

The golden idol dominating the central hall of the cinema museum is taken from *Cabiria,* a film directed by Giovanni Pastrone in 1914.

In 1908 Pastrone co-founded Itala Film with Carlo Sciamengo. This was the year *The Last Days of Pompeii (Gli ultimi giorni di Pompeii)* was made, the first Italian film to be noticed abroad. Global success came in 1912 with *The Fall of Troy (La Caduta di Troia)* directed by Pastrone. The film was a hit in America and influenced a number of legendary filmmakers. Italian cinema had arrived.

Turin was at the heart of Italian film in the formative days: the city has always been a magnet for writers, poets, thinkers and inventors, full of cafés perfect for long discussions and the working out of creative ideas and partnerships. Pastrone had another hit with his next historical epic, *Cabiria,* set in the Punic wars and co-written with celebrated author Gabriele d'Annunzio. In a time of five-minute comic shorts, *Cabiria* was three hours long, with a cast of thousands. Pastrone invented a system to mount the camera on a dolly so he could follow the action. He also invented a process that would add colour to black and white film stock.

FERT, an independent studio and production facility, was founded in 1919. The studio complex was a busy place in the 1920s and again during the 1950s. Michelangelo Antonioni set his classic *Story of a Love Affair (Cronaca di un Amore)* in Turin. Fellini's bizarre film crew were also to be found on the streets of the city. FERT closed down in the 1970s but has been resurrected as a multimedia complex and the headquarters of the Virtual Reality and Multimedia Park.

The *Cinecittà* studio complex was built in Rome in the 1930s and today is the centre of the Italian film business. With the recent success of films like *Gladiator* and *Troy,* epics have returned to popularity. These new Hollywood examples of the genre owe a great debt to Giovanni Pastrone and his colleagues – the inventors of this style of cinema.

The Italian Job

In cinema, the number one most important asset is the producer's contact list. Michael Deeley, producer of *The Italian Job*, knew Lord Harlech who knew Gianni Agnelli (the Fiat boss) who more or less owned Turin. Agnelli read the script, liked it and agreed to help with the film as a favour to his friend Lord Harlech. Agnelli probably appreciated the ironic plot twist that had a band of cockney crooks steal four million pounds worth of gold from Fiat and escape in six British-built Mini Coopers.

In the 1969 film Michael Caine plays Charlie Croker, who devises a scheme to steal gold by creating a traffic jam. Turin did in fact have a traffic computer, an item central to the plot. It was used to create the actual chaos needed in the film. Streets were also blocked with a canteen van and a camera vehicle. The resulting traffic mayhem was filmed from a nearby roof. Douglas Slocombe, director of photography, said: *'It was incredible – the authorities in Turin really let us create those jams.'*

The famous getaway scenes with the Minis racing, jumping and spinning over Turin's roads and rooftops were choreographed by Remy Julienne. He had the cars rumble down the 40 steps of Gran Madre di Dio – narrowly missing a wedding-party – and then drive under the arcades of Via Po and around Piazza Castello. The action then jumps to the racetrack at the top of Lingotto, far south of the centre. The rooftop where the Minis seem to disappear is the Palavela, recently renovated for the Winter Olympics. Turin authorities authorised the damming of the river Po to film the final getaway through the weir. Some say the film's cliffhanger ending was because the production ran out of money; others blame the 1960s censors for not allowing criminals to be seen to get away with a crime. Director Peter Collinson hated the idea so much he refused to shoot it, and the scene was filmed by the assistant director.

The Italian Job flopped on release. Showings on television have helped the film rise to its current status as one of the best caper movies of all time.

Duomo

Duomo di San Giovanni Battista
Piazza San Giovanni
011 436 1540
07.00-12.30,15.00-19.00 Mon-Sat
open 08.00 on Sunday
map 1-2, D1

Turin's cathedral is home to one of Christendom's most holy relics: the Turin Shroud (*Sacra Sindone*).

The Duomo was not originally planned to hold the Shroud. It was begun in 1491 by Meo del Caprino for Cardinal Domenico della Rovere, who is buried in the church. It was the height of the Renaissance, a time when the papacy was at its most powerful and many churches were being commissioned. The Duomo follows the typical Renaissance structure of a long central nave flanked by two side aisles with individual chapels. Carrara marble was the building material of choice during the Renaissance. It was the only marble that Michelangelo thought to be truly worthy of his talent. Marble conveyed status: many churches could only afford a front facade. In the Duomo, marble was also used to build the interior.

When the church was built, the Shroud was the property of the Savoy dynasty, and was lodged at their palace in Chambéry, France. In the mid-1500s they established Turin as their capital and it became necessary to build a special chapel to house the Shroud. The *Capella della Sindone* was commissioned in 1611. The Shroud's importance meant the dome of the Capella had to be higher than the Duomo, because it stood between the spiritual power of the Duomo and the temporal power of Palazzo Reale, at the centre of Turin.

The Capella is situated at the end of the Duomo's central nave. In the centre of the chapel is an altar by Antonio Bertola, which sits on a black marble floor with gilded stars. The black marble was specifically chosen by architect Guarino Guarini to express mourning and also to contrast the white marble of the central nave. The effect is one of extreme darkness and there is a definite chill in the air. On 1 June 1694 the Shroud was moved to the Capella. It was wrapped in gold cloth and stored in an asbestos-lined casket, and later installed inside a bullet-proof display case.

Shortly after 11pm on 11 April 1997, fire broke out in the Capella, seriously damaging the walls and dome. Fireman Mario Trematore hacked into the chapel through the roof of the Palazzo Reale and used a sledgehammer to break open the display case to rescue the Shroud. That the artifact emerged unscathed was called a miracle by both believers and sceptics. Arson was suspected as the cause of the fire but the case was never proven. The exterior of the chapel dome is still undergoing repairs, but the interior has now been restored.

Today the Shroud is stored flat in a sealed, fireproof, atmosphere-controlled container behind bullet-proof glass in a chapel at the end of the north aisle, left of the altar. The container is covered with a cloth. It is not possible to view the actual Shroud but a two-thirds sized copy is on display. The Shroud was taken out for public viewing during the Jubilee of 2000 and will not be brought out again until the Jubilee of 2025. You will be asked to be silent when viewing the container.

Also worth seeing in the Duomo is the *Capella dei Santi Crispino and Crispiniano,* commissioned by the shoemakers guild. A Renaissance altarpiece by Defendente Ferrari and Giovanni Martino Spanzotti shows the *Madonna and Child* flanked by a further 18 panels that narrate the story of Crispino and Crispiniano, the patron saints of cobblers. Guarino Guarini also lined the walls of the Duomo's rear wall with black marble. Above the door is a replica of Leonardo da Vinci's *Last Supper*.

IL VERISSIMO RITRATTO DEL SANTISSIMO SVDARIO
DEL NOSTRO SALVATORE GIESV CHRISTO

OREMVS
DEVS QVI NOBIS IN SANCTA SINDONE, QVA CORPVS TVVM SACRATISSIMV
E CRVCE DEPOSITVM A IOSEPH INVOLVTVM FVIT, PASSIONIS TVÆ VEST GIA
RELIQVISTI, CONCEDE PROPITIVS, VT PER MORTEM, ET SEPVLTVRAM TVAM AD
RESVRRECTIONIS GLORIAM PERDVCAMVR QVI VIVIS, ETC.

The Turin Shroud

The Shroud is a single piece of linen measuring 14.3 feet (4.3m) long by 3.6 feet (1.1m) wide. Imprinted into the cloth is a negative image of a male corpse who was beaten and crucified. To date there has been no definitive answer to the question of the man's identity, or how the image came to be imprinted on the linen. Debate rages whether this was the burial shroud used to wrap the body of Jesus Christ.

Faint, brownish, full-length front and back images of a man 5 feet 11 inches tall are visible on the cloth's surface. Discernible wounds within the images suggest that the man was scourged and crucified with spikes through his wrists and feet. The human image is not a painting. Computer processing has shown three dimensional properties not consistent with paintings or photographic imaging. Colour is completely absorbed into the fabric, a result of chemical change rather than the application of coloured materials.

The linen was spun with a Z twist and woven in a three to one herringbone twill on a primitive loom with an irregular technique. The cloth is 350 micrometres thick, about half the thickness of common newsprint. The weaving is consistent with first century methods described by Pliny.

Pollens have been found on the cloth that support the view that the Shroud originates in the Middle East. Red bloodstains confirm the locations of visible wounds. That bloodstains have remained red when they should normally turn black continues to puzzle scientists. Chemical analysis of the stains confirm that the blood is human type AB.

The fire of 1532 left two dark parallel lines of scorches running along the entire length of the Shroud. These are intersected by 29 triangular patches of a different fabric which were sewn on by the Poor Clares. These patches cover the holes made by a drop of molten silver from the Shroud's casket. Most water stains date from the fire, but others suggest the cloth was folded and stored in an earthenware jar similar to those that held the Dead Sea Scrolls.

The story of the Shroud

There was a man by the name of Joseph. His hometown was the Jewish village of Arimathea. He went to Pilate and asked for the body of Jesus. Taking him down, he wrapped him in a linen shroud and placed him in a tomb chiselled into the rock where no one had ever been laid. Luke 23:51-54

At early dawn, they came to the tomb, taking the burial spices they had prepared. They found the stone rolled away from the tomb, but when they went inside they did not find the body. While they were perplexed about this suddenly two men in dazzling clothes stood beside them. Luke 24:1-4

But Peter got up and ran to the tomb, stooping and looking in, he saw the linen cloths by themselves. Luke 24:12.

It is said that the Apostle Peter picked up the cloth and carried it with him on his travels through Turkey. Legends of the Shroud's continued existence persisted, but were circumstantial until a French knight, Geoffrey de Charny, found it in Constantinople. Apparently, the Shroud was hidden in a crevice underneath a stone bridge.

De Charny's letter to Pope Clement VI in 1349, asking for permission to build a church in Lirey, France, marks the beginning of the undisputed history of the Shroud. Pilgrims flocked to see the first public showing of the Shroud in 1355, an exposition complete with souvenirs – a single medallion still survives from that exposition. These festive showings were halted and the Shroud was hidden by Bishop Henry who refused to believe the cloth was genuine. But opportunities presented by the Shroud in attracting pilgrims and selling souvenirs meant it couldn't remain hidden for long. In 1390 a Papal bull granted new indulgences to those who visited the Shroud at St Mary of Lirey.

The Savoy acquired the Shroud from Margaret de Charny in 1453, in exchange for a castle and the estate revenues of Miribel (near Lyon). Margaret was threatened with excommunication if she did not return the Shroud to St Mary of Lirey, but the clerics agreed to accept the Savoy offer of annual compensation for their loss of revenue and forever renounced any claims to the Shroud.

The Shroud was installed at the Savoy chapel in Chambéry: *'enveloped in a red silk drape, and kept in a silver casket covered with crimson velvet, decorated with silver-gilt roses, and locked with a golden key.'* The casket was deposited behind the high altar in a special cavity hollowed out of the wall and secured by an iron grille with four locks, each opened by separate keys, two of which were held by the Duke.

When fire raged through the church in 1532, precious time was lost while a blacksmith was summoned to prise open the grille. The fire had melted the silver casket but miraculously the Shroud was intact. Chambéry's Poor Clare nuns repaired the Shroud, sewing it onto a backing cloth and sewing patches over the worst of the damage.

In 1578 the Shroud arrived in Turin. It was carried in procession from the Duomo to Piazza Castello where it was hung from the wall of the castle for forty hours and viewed by forty thousand pilgrims. The Shroud continued to be exhibited from the castle walls on feast days, royal weddings and other special occasions. During the Turin Exhibition of 1898, Secondo Pia made a photograph of the Shroud using a glass negative. It is said he almost dropped the plate when he saw a the positive figure of a man.

Over the next century many scientific and religious bodies were formed to study the Shroud. In 1978, the cloth was submitted to five days of rigorous testing by a team of American-based scientists known as STURP. The verdict was unclear and the team itself was divided about its conclusions.

The Shroud was bequeathed to the Pope and the Holy See by Umberto II upon his death in 1983, with the proviso that the cloth remain in Turin. Scientists then appealed to Pope John Paul II for permission to take samples from the Shroud for carbon dating. John Paul believed the Shroud to be genuine. When he viewed the cloth he knelt and kissed the hem.

Three radiocarbon dating laboratories took samples in secret on 21 April 1988. Six months later the results established an approximate date of 1325 for the Shroud. The British Museum dated it between 1260 and 1390.

In 1998, a public Exposition of the Shroud was held to commemorate the centenary of Secondo Pia's first photograph of the cloth. Over two million pilgrims visited the Shroud during the eight week exhibition. In addition the Turin Shroud official website was launched (www.sindone.org) with information in four languages. The website receives 30,000 hits per month.

In 2005, just before his death, Raymond N. Rogers, Fellow of the Los Alamos Laboratory, published an article in which he claimed: '*the sample used to test the age of the Shroud of Turin in 1988 was taken from a rewoven area of the Shroud. Pyrolysis/mass spectrometry results from the sample area coupled with microscopic and microchemical observations prove that the radiocarbon sample was not part of the original cloth of the Shroud of Turin. The radiocarbon date was thus not valid for determining the true age of the Shroud.*' And so the debate continues.

The chapel in San Lorenzo contains a permanent exhibit with full-size reproductions of the Shroud.

Museo della Sindone

Confraternita dei Santi Sudario di Torino
Via San Domenico 28
011 436 5832
www.sindone.it (Italian only)
09.00-12.00, 15.00-19.00 daily, closed Monday
admission with Torino card or €5.50
map 1-2, C1

The museum was founded in 1936 to gather together all the historical and scientific information about the Shroud, together with artifacts collected over the centuries.

The foundation that runs the museum also conducts further research into the Shroud, in addition to hosting conferences and seminars.

San Lorenzo

Via Palazzo di Citta
011 436 1527
7.30-noon, 15.30-19.30 daily
map 1-2, D2

The church was begun in 1668 for the Theatine Order, of which Guarino Guarini was a member. It was the architect's first commission for the Savoy in Turin. For a time it was their Royal chapel. Guarini's design is based on the work of Borromini (1559-1667), with a round inner space and curved chapels lining the perimeter. Each chapel has a curved stone pediment supported by slender rose-coloured marble columns.

As with all of Borromini's work, there are few straight lines or hard edges in San Lorenzo. Borromini was a master of optical illusion, and Guarini studied his work carefully. The dome is a luminous cage of slender intersecting ribs forming the shape of an eight-pointed star. This *motif* is repeated in luminous gold at the centre of the ribbing. Rays of light stream in through curved windows between the points of the star. As this 'heavenly light' fills the dome, it creates the illusion that the structure is higher than it really is.

A **side chapel** dedicated to the Shroud contains full-size photographic replicas of the front and back of the relic, in both positive and negative versions. In addition, there are small but useful displays about the history of the Shroud.

Guarino Guarini (1624-1683)

Born in Modena, Sicily, Guarini was a student of the Theatine Order. He was educated in mathematics, philosophy, theology, and astronomy. Guarini also studied Islamic architecture because he admired its mathematical symmetry. It was his love of mathematics that led him to an architectural career.

Guarini is known for four buildings: *San Vicenzo* in Modena, *Ste Anne-la-Royale* in Paris, and *San Lorenzo* and *Capella della Sindone* in Turin. He was also the published author of literary works and treatises about mathematics and architecture, and the connections between the two disciplines.

SAN LORENZO: INTERIOR OF THE DOME

Optical illusions were an important part of religious architecture in the Baroque period. Guarini's talent in this regard made him widely known and respected. He was expert at making a dome appear larger and deeper through the use of false perspective and trompe l'oeil. Previously, most illusions had been achieved through the skilful application of paint applied to the interior of a dome to create the impression that the structure was receding into space. Guarini's innovation was to design a diaphanous, 'openwork' dome where the optical illusion was created by the dome's structure as opposed to using paint to achieve the desired effects.

In San Lorenzo, kneel before the altar and look up, as if taking mass. There above you is one of Guarini's most endearing illusions: two gilded angels have pulled back the sky to reveal the layer beyond, heaven itself.

Palazzo Reale

Piazzetta Reale
011 436 1455
08.30-19.30 Tuesday-Sunday
closed Monday
Entrance is by guided tour (in Italian) every 30 mins (lasting 45 mins)
Gardens open November-March: 09.00-16.00 Tuesday-Sunday
April, May, September, October: 09.00-17.30
June-August 09.00-19.00
admission with Torino card or €6.50
map 1-2, D2

Palazzo Reale was built in 1563 when Emanuele Filiberto
transferred the capital of the Duchy of Savoy to Turin. He set
about fortifying the city and built a splendid royal residence
for the Savoy dynasty. The fact that the dukes of Savoy had,
in the previous century, gone to great lengths to acquire the
Shroud reflects the court's ambitions in politics, which at the
time were the politics of the Catholic church. This sumptuous
palace in the heart of the city was the official residence of the
dukes and the House of Savoy, the kings of Sardinia, and
later of Vittorio Emanuele II, the first king of Italy.

Because it is connected to the *Cappella della Sindone*, the roof
on the west wing of the Palazzo was also damaged in the fire
of 1997. Unfortunately, due to ongoing restoration work there
is no given schedule as to which rooms will be open on any
visit, but you should see some of the following on a tour of
the first floor. The second floor is currently being restored.

The first part of the visit is to one of the newest sections of
the palace. The grand **Staircase of Honour** with its ornate
motifs and imposing portraiture was constructed in 1862
following the unification of Italy. It celebrates the Savoy
dynasty.

In the **Salone degli Svizzeri**, on the upper part of the walls
are frescoes which illustrate the genealogical history of the
house of Savoy. There is also a marble bust of Julius Caesar.

The **Council Room** has the original table where, in 1848,
Carlo Alberto signed the decree agreeing to constitutionalism

in Italy, thereby capitulating to the demands of Count Cavour and the Risorgimento movement. His bust appears alongside in the style of a Roman emperor.

Galleria del Daniel is named after the painter Daniel Seiter who was brought in from Rome to renovate the palace's decorations. The vaulted ceiling shows a fresco of Vittorio Amedeo III being received by the gods on Mount Olympus. The set of mirrors opposite the windows is a reminder of the galleria's former life as a ballroom.

The **Throne Room** is unmistakable as it overflows with gilt. The luxuriant velvet on the throne derives its texture from being bathed in liquid gold.

Gabinetto Cinese displays a new taste for exoticism, with original Chinese panels framed in gold. It showcases the work of Claudio Francesco Beaumont, who was the court artist of Carlo Emmanuele III. On the ceiling is a fresco of the *Judgment of Paris*.

The **Alcove Room** contains decorative caryatids with swollen bellies to symbolise fertility. This was an appropriate choice for the bedroom of Carlo Alberto's French princess. This room also contains a copy of Anthony van Dyck's portrait of Charles I, King of England, with his children.

Of particular interest is the royal architect Filippo Juvarra's playful Baroque 'scissor staircase' which seems to hover precariously between the first and second floors like the open blades of a pair of scissors. Look for the laughing face of Juvarra, mocking those who doubted his abilities to realise such an ingenious piece of architecture.

At one time, a corridor connected the palace to the Palazzo Madama but this was destroyed in another fire.

Giardini Reali

The gardens were designed by French architect Andre Le Notrê, who also designed the gardens of Versailles. Plantings are arranged with basins and walkways resembling the spokes of a wheel.

Palazzo Madama

Museo Civico di Arte Antica
Piazza Castello
011 442 9912
Closed for restoration. Due to reopen in 2006

The Palazzo is an architectural hodge-podge. The east façade is the red brick Roman gate of Porta Pretoria between two 13th century medieval towers. The west façade is a pale cream coloured baroque palace designed by Filippo Juvarra. The two sides of the Palazzo appear to the casual observer to belong to two separate buildings.

Palazzo Madama has served many uses during its 2,000 year history. It became the residence of the royal *Mesdames* in 1721 and the museum's collection includes their paintings, furniture, objects and illuminated manuscripts. Court architect Juvarra converted the medieval battlement into a grand palace by adding a façade and a monumental staircase, which is rumoured to be haunted by one of two ghosts in the palace. The other spirit stalks the dungeons.

Turin is reputedly haunted by a selection of ghostly shrouded ladies, including the Russian princess Barbara Beloselski who died in 1792 at the age of 28. She is said to appear in the coffee houses of the city, in search of men to escort her to the San Lazzaro graveyard where her body was buried.

The Savoy Dynasty

Counts of Savoy

Umberto I (1003-48)
First Count of Savoy

Amedeo I (1048-51)
son of Umberto I

Oddone (1051-57)
son of Umberto I

Pietro I (1057-78)
son of Amedeo I

Amedeo II (1078-80)
son of Oddone

Umberto II (1080-1103)
son of Amedeo II

Amedeo III (1103-1148)
son of Umberto II

Umberto III (1148-89)
son of Amedeo III

Tomasso I (1189-1233)
son of Umberto III

Amedeo IV (1233-53)
son of Tomasso I

Bonifacio (1253-63)
son of Amedeo IV

Pietro II (1263-68)
brother of Amedeo IV

Filippo I (1268-85)
brother of Pietro II

Amedeo V (1285-1323)
nephew of Amedeo IV

Edoardo (1323-29)
nephew of Amedeo V

Aimone (1329-43)
son of Amedeo V

Amedeo VI (1343-83)
son of Aimone

Dukes of Savoy

Amedeo VIII (1391-1434)
son of Amedeo VI

Ludovico (1434-65)
son of Amedeo VIII

Amedeo IX (1465-72)
son of Ludovico

Filippo II (1472-97)
brother of Amedeo IX

Filiberto II (1497-1504)
son of Filippo II

Carlo II (1504-53)
brother of Filiberto II

Emanuele Filiberto (1553-80)
son of Carlo II

Carlo Emanuele I (1580-1630)
son of Emanuele Filiberto

Kings of Piedmont & Sardinia

Vittorio Amedeo I (1630-37)
son of Carlo Emanuele I, King of Sicily, King of Sardinia

Francesco Giaciato (1637-38)
son of Vittorio Amedeo I

Carlo Emanuele II (1638-75)
son of Vittorio Amedeo I

Vittorio Amedeo II (1675-1730)
son of Carlo Emanuele II

Carlo Emanuele III (1730-73)
son of Vittorio Amedeo II

Vittorio Amedeo III (1773-96)
son of Carlo Emanuele III

Carlo Emanuele IV (1796-1802)
son of Vittorio Amedeo III

Vittorio Emanuele I (1802-21)
brother of Carlo Emanuele IV

Carlo Felice (1821-31)
brother of Vittorio Emanuele I

Kings of Italy

Vittorio Emanuele II (1849-78)
Cousin of Carlo Felice

Umberto I (1878-1900)
son of Vittorio Emanuele II

Vittorio Emanuele III (1900-46)
son of Umberto I

Exiled

Umberto II (1946-83)
son of Vittorio Emanuele III

Savoy Dynasty

Their origins lie in the alpine region of Maurienne in France, a region once known by the Romans as *Sabaudia*. At first they were feudal lords who made their money from guarding strategic mountain passes and by acting as guides. The progenitor of the dynasty, Umberto Biancamano (980-1047) also known as Humbert, may have been the great-grandson of Holy Roman Emperor Otto II. In 1003, in gratitude for military service rendered to Emperor Conrad II, Umberto was granted the title Count of Savoy. The Count brokered a marriage between his youngest son Oddone and Adelaide of Turin, daughter of the Marquis of Turin. By the 11th century, the Count of Savoy ruled much of the French and Italian Alps and the Turin valley.

The title was handed down from generation to generation, sometimes passing to brothers and nephews but always to progeny of Umberto I. As was common in the Middle Ages, the Savoy had their own private army of knights and warriors. It was the time of chivalry and Christian crusades, a time when jousting tournaments were held and knights gave love-tokens to their ladies. Amedeo VI was known as the 'Green Count' after the signature colour of his liveries at tournaments. He founded the Order of the Annunciation in 1362, which survives as one of the oldest dynastic orders of chivalry. Amedeo VIII was very pious but was also a warrior-knight whose faithful service to the Emperor earned him the title Duke of Savoy in 1416. In 1434, Amedeo ceded the Duchy of Savoy to his son Ludovico and retired to a monastery. In 1439, he was elected as the anti-Pope Felix V, but resigned in favour of the true Pope ten years later.

Ludovico acquired the Shroud for the Savoy family. His son Amedeo IX installed the relic at Chambéry, a French town located east of Lyon and north of Grenoble. Chambéry was the home of the Savoy until the 1500s, when Piedmont was engulfed in wars between French, Spanish and Austrian monarchs. When Amedeo's nephew Carlo II lost against the French in 1536, he retreated into the mountains and to all appearances the Duchy of Savoy was finished. But Carlo had a brave son, Emanuele Filiberto, who succeeded to the title in 1553 at the age of 25. Emanuele served as a general in the Spanish army and, with Spaniards as backup, he appeared in full armour at the battle of Saint Quintino and defeated the French. The treaty of Cateau-Cambrésis guaranteed self-rule to the Duchy of Savoy while ceding the Spaniards' hegemony over the rest of Italy. Emanuele established Turin as the capital and initiated a building programme. Medieval Turin was demolished to create palaces worthy of the Savoy. Palazzo Reale was completed in 1658, the Carignano Palace in 1680, and Madama Reale was completely refurbished to house Savoy widows. A new chapel was commissioned to house the Turin Shroud, the possession of which gave the Savoy a respectability and status far above other Italian duchies.

In the complicated chessboard that was 18th century Europe, Emanuele's grandson, Duke Vittorio Amedeo II, was a master player who finished the game as a king. The Savoy had to be cunning in order to avoid becoming mere pawns of those more powerful and Vittorio was extremely slippery with a reputation for duplicity. He was married to Louis XIV's niece and was a faithful ally of France in the early years. As war clouds gathered over Europe, Vittorio supported the Spanish and Austrian Hapsburgs against the French. However, when the Spanish objected to Piedmont's takeover of Milan, a separate treaty was made with Austria against the interests of Spain. In the War of the Spanish Succession, Piedmont was allied with France in the opening phase of the conflict but then switched to the Hapsburgs. In 1713, Vittorio Amedeo II emerged from the Treaty of Utrecht negotiations as King of Piedmont and of Sicily.

The wealth of Sicily far exceeded that of Piedmont and Palermo was more prosperous than Turin. The new king began taxing his subjects immediately but never visited the island. Seven years later, he accepted a Spanish offer to trade Sicily for Sardinia. And it was to Sardinia that Vittorio Amedeo III escaped when Napoleon invaded Piedmont in 1797. Napoleon abolished the last vestiges of feudalism and the corresponding rights to property. The Congress of Vienna restored Piedmont to the Savoy, with the addition of Genoa. In 1831 the Crown passed from Carlo Felice to his fifth cousin once removed, Carlo Alberto. Alberto was descended from Tommaso Francesco, grandson of Emanuele Filiberto.

Carlo Alberto was compelled to abdicate in 1848 after military defeat in Milan. Alberto had ordered troops in to quell revolutionary disturbance only to be defeated by Austrian forces. He was succeeded in 1849 by his son, Vittorio Emanuele II.

The Risorgimento was a complex and controversial movement with origins in Turin. The ultimate result – a united Italy – was long overdue, and brought in a new democratic system with a two-chamber parliament. Vittorio Emanuele II was declared King of Italy in 1861, albeit following a referendum riddled with corruption. It was unbelievable to the average Italian that 98 per cent of eligible voters had cast their ballot in favour of the Savoy. The kingdom may have been won, but the loyalty of the Savoy's subjects had been lost. Taxes and prices rose and the standard of living fell. Workers protested in the streets and the government introduced martial law. In 1900, King Umberto I was assassinated by the mysterious anarchist Gaetano Bresci who had been living in New Jersey, USA. Umberto's son and successor Vittorio Emanuele III was to be the last genuine King of Italy.

Mussolini's Fascists marched on Rome in 1922. The frightened king acceded to Fascist demands for power and his surrender was later confirmed by parliament. A degree of stability followed. Mussolini established food programmes and negotiated the Lateran Treaties of 1929 which brought the Kingdom of Italy a much-needed diplomatic rapport with the Vatican. But as the Fascist powerbase grew, censorship and police brutality, including torture, were commonplace. King Vittorio became subject to Mussolini and signed a series of repressive and racist laws, including those restricting the rights of Jews. Italy's brutal invasion of Ethiopia in 1935 – only to be expelled by the British five years later – did little to enhance its reputation at the League of Nations. The conquest of an exotic foreign land earned Vittorio Emanuele a short-lived Imperial title; it also earned his country the world's wrath and, after World War II, the first United Nations citation for crimes against humanity.

The declaration of war against the Allies was another serious mistake, one that would lead to the slaughter of thousands of Italian civilians. When the Allies invaded Sicily in the summer of 1943, they were welcomed by the population as liberators from the Fascist yoke. Resentment against the regime ran so deeply that it seemed not to occur to the cheering crowds that these soldiers were enemy invaders. King Vittorio quickly removed Mussolini and declared war against Germany.

The House of Savoy's retreat from Rome during the war was widely viewed as an act of cowardice which led to a profound questioning of the monarchy's role, and its future in Italy. King Vittorio Emanuele III abdicated in 1945. He was succeeded briefly by his son King Umberto II, who campaigned to preserve the monarchy. In early June 1946, another referendum was held, during which Italian women voted for the first time. The vote was decided narrowly in favour of a republic. Umberto and the Duchy of Savoy went into exile.

Umberto died in Geneva in 1983, prevented by a constitutional provision from ever returning to his homeland. He was succeeded by his son and heir, Prince Vittorio Emanuele, who lives in Switzerland with his wife, Princess Marina of Savoy, née Ricolfi Doria. As Duke of Savoy, Vittorio Emanuele is the 44th head of the dynasty. Intended as a provisional measure, the exile law forbade the male descendants of the last King of Italy from entering the country for decades. It was abolished in 2002 and the Savoys revisited Italy in December of that year. As guests of the Vatican, their first, brief (one-day) visit to Italy allowed them the diplomatic honours usually accorded to heads of state. It was the first time that Vittorio's son Emanuele Filiberto had set foot in Italy.

Piazza Carignano

This large rectangle was the centre of Risorgimento Turin. Italy's first parliament convened in the Palazzo Carignano, which now houses the Museo Risorgimento. Opposite the Palazzo is the Accademia delle Scienze which houses the Museo Egizio, Turin's outstanding Egyptian collection. The Galleria Sabauda, strong on Flemish painting, is located on the floors above the Museo Egizio.

Teatro Carignano, located next to the Accademia, was built in 1787. It is the city's only remaining 18th century theatre and is still in use today for performances of the *Teatro Stabile di Torino,* Turin's premier theatre company. The bust on the façade is of Vittorio Alfieri who put on his first tragedy, *Anthony and Cleopatra,* in this theatre.

FOR TICKET INFORMATION SEE PAGE 88.

Next to the theatre, is Turin's oldest restaurant **Del Cambio**, so called because this was where stagecoach teams were changed. The restaurant was a favourite of Cavour who regularly dined here, and Vittorio Emanuele II would wander across for his aperitivo. It was in the piazza's restaurants and bookshops that unification was plotted. The **Luxembourg Bookshop** sold papers and books published by Cavour including a draft constitution.

Gelateria Pepino was established in 1884 by Domenico Pepini, an ice cream maker from Naples who invented something similar to a Magnum: vanilla ice cream on a stick, covered in a thin coat of chocolate.

Palazzo Carignano

The imposing red brick Baroque façade dominates the square. Designed by Guarino Guarini, it was built between 1679-84 at the height of the Baroque period. The influence of Borromini is evident in the curved frontage. Like Palazzo Madama, this palace has two different personalities: the façade on the other side of the palace, facing Piazza Carlo Alberto, dates from the 19th century and was designed by Gaetano Ferri.

The Palazzo was the birthplace of Kings, both Carlo Alberto and Vittorio Emanuele II were born here.

Museo Risorgimento

Via Accademia delle Scienze 5
011 562 1147
www.regione.piemonte.it/cultura/risorgimento
09.00-19.00 Tuesday-Sunday
admission with Torino card or €5
map 1-2, E2

The idea of founding a museum dedicated to the Risorgimento was first conceived in 1878, but it took until 1908 before it opened in the Mole. The museum was moved to Palazza Carignano 30 years later.

The movement is detailed in a chronological history which runs through 26 rooms. The exhibition begins well before the events of 1848, and continues to beyond World War II. The process of national unification is explained from a Piedmontese point of view with an emphasis on the contribution of the Savoy. Several large paintings are on show which were commissioned by the Savoy to commemorate great Risorigimento battles, as well as others portraying notable Savoy victories.

The collection begins with the epic *Battle of Turin*, which celebrates Vittorio Amedeo's victory over the French. This eventually netted him the Crowns of Piedmont and Sicily. The museum holds rare items from the Napoleonic period, Cavour's cabinet study and Garibaldi's shirts and poncho.

Fifty years of the Kingdom of Italy are chronicled with references to social unrest and the assassination of the monarch in 1900. World War I and II are given ample space and there is a large gallery devoted to the trade union movement and partisan resistance to Mussolini's fascists.

The first Parliament of Piedmont convened here in the **Chamber of the Piedmontese Parliament**, also known as the Subalpine Parliament. The first parliament met in 1848; the clock in the hall is frozen at the time of the last session in October 1864. The gilded hall was built for the parliament of a united Italy but it had little use: Italy's capital was moved to Florence in 1864 and then to Rome in 1870.

Risorgimento

The Risorgimento movement aimed to unite Italy under one flag and one government. For many Italians struggling under the yoke of foreign rulers, the movement meant more than unity: it promised a better standard of living and a new control over their future.

The Risorgimento had two distinct phases. The first was idealistic and romantic, beginning with unrest in 1815 and climaxing in the revolutions of 1848-49. The second stage was more pragmatic and diplomatic, carrying on during the 1850s and culminating in the creation of a united Italy.

The revolution itself began in Sicily in January 1848 and quickly spread along the peninsula. People took to the streets against their rulers, be they Austrians, Spanish or even popes. But soon cracks began to show. Italian leaders disagreed about whether the unified country should be a confederation, a republic, a monarchy or under papal rule. The revolution foundered. King Carlo Alberto was twice defeated by the Austrians and the papacy united with the French against Garibaldi. By summer 1849 the Italian insurgency had collapsed.

Count Camillo Benso di Cavour (1810-1861), Prime Minister of Piedmont-Sardinia, used the threat of revolutionary resurgence to persuade conservative opinion that an Italy united under the House of Savoy would be a force for stability. The only Italian state with a constitution and an elected parliament, Piedmont-Sardinia exerted a powerful attraction for the large majority of Italian nationalists.

By 1859 Cavour achieved victory against Austria, and a successful campaign in southern Italy by Garibaldi unseated the Bourbons. The Kingdom of Italy was proclaimed by parliament in Turin on March 12, 1861. All of Italy was represented except Venice, which remained under Austrian rule until 1866, and Rome which was under papal control until the city was liberated in 1870.

Museo Egizio (Egyptian Museum)

Via Accademia delle Scienze 6
011 561 7776
08.30-19.30 Tuesday-Sunday
Closed Mondays and 25th December, 1st January, 1st May
admission with Torino card or €6
map 1-2, E3

Founded in 1824, Turin's Egyptian Museum is the single most important collection outside Cairo. It is housed in the Collegio dei Nobili, which started life in 1679 as a Jesuit college for young noblemen. The collection is spread over three floors, with main exhibits found on the ground and first floors. The basement holds lesser exhibits of funerary urns, beer-making and writing implements. Unfortunately, exhibits are not labelled with explanatory information in English, but the bookshop is well stocked with inexpensive guides.

Italian interest in Egypt developed in the 18th century when Carlo Emanuele III sent Vitaliano Donati on a scientific mission along the Valley of the Nile. He returned to Turin having found statues of Rameses II and the goddesses Isis and Sekhmet. Between 1798-99 Napoleon Bonaparte was commander-in-chief of the Italian army. He led his troops into Egypt with a view not only to conquer, but to record and scientifically catalogue the remnants of the ancient Egyptian civilization.

The museum was created out of the collection of Bernadino Drovetti, the French Consul in Egypt and a Turin native. In 1824, Carlo Felice bought his collection of Egyptian artifacts. Ernesto Schiaparelli was a director of the museum and he was able to expand the collection, helped by his links with the Italian Archaeological Mission, which launched a number of excavation campaigns along the Nile between 1903 and 1920.

Ground Floor

The figure in the centre of **room 1** is an example of natural mummification dating from 4000 BC, preserved in the dry heat of the Egyptian desert. The deceased were buried with their personal effects to take with them into the after-life.

Here, these include a boomerang for hunting ducks, a pair of sandals and some arrows.

Room 2 holds a cast of the Rosetta stone (the original is on permanent display in the British Museum). The tablet was discovered by an official in the French army in the small town of Rosetta in 1799. Inscriptions appear in hieroglyphics, demotic and Greek: the first two being Egyptian scripts and the latter the language of Egypt's rulers at the time it was carved (196 BC). The text was written by Egyptian priests and is a song of mourning for the pharaohs of Egypt. The stone was the key to the deciphering of ancient Egyptian hieroglyphics.

Room 3 contains some of the Schiaparelli excavations from the Giza necropolis. Note the statue with sunken eyes standing guard outside the tomb. The eyes were stolen by superstitious thieves looking for gold, afraid that the stone statue would be able to witness their deeds.

The **Temple of Ellesyia** was found in Nubia, a strip of

land between Egypt and Sudan. It is made from 16,000 stone blocks, and frescoed inside with a pharaoh seated with two divinities on either side. Crosses in the stonework suggest that this temple was used as a church in a later period, and holes indicate the historic presence of an attached awning or canopy to protect the congregation from the heat of the Egyptian sun.

The **statuary collection** contains examples from the 18th and 19th dynasties (1750-1185 BC). The Egyptians believed that a statue was not merely a commemorative object, but was an actual personification of the deceased that could assume the soul once it had left the defunct body. Many have the head of a divinity, such as the lioness goddess Sekmet who was the deity of medicine and protector of the Pharaoh. On the left is King Sethi II, in a posture typical of Egyptian statuary, with left foot in front of right, a primitive way of suggesting movement. A cobra also appears as a symbol of knowledge.

The statue of *Rameses II* is from the 19th dynasty. It has been termed the 'Egyptian Apollo Belvedere' because it is as influential in understanding Egyptian plastic arts as the Greek bust of Apollo (now in the Vatican Museums) was for Renaissance artists. Rameses is shown wearing a long pleated tunic and pleated mantle, with the warrior's helmet on his head – known as the blue crown, because of its covering of blue faience appliqués. His wife and son appear on either side.

First floor

The most touchingly human exhibit in the collection is the fully intact **Tomb of Kha**. An architect to the Pharoah, Kha's tomb dates from 3500 BC. It was discovered by archaeologist Ernesto Schiaparelli in 1906. The sarcophagus is displayed with Kha's personal effects, including underwear embroidered with his initials, and summer and winter tunics. His wife's sarcophagus is displayed alongside and includes all of the female paraphernalia one would expect today, even down to her eyeliner pen and cosmetics case.

Room 5 houses the tomb of Nefertari, the wife of Rameses II, also discovered by Schiaparelli in the Valley of the Queens near Luxor. Despite being a woman her funerary celebrations were similar to that of a pharaoh.

Room 7 contains bronze statues of animals sacred to the Egyptians. They believed that the gods could assume the identity of an animal as well as a person and even went as far as mummifying the more important animals, the most celebrated being the cat.

There is a room of mummified corpses on the first floor. Those with an eye for the macabre will note the long hair and fingernails that continued growing even after death.

The Schiaparelli Family

The Schiaparellis were one of Turin's most illustrious families. Ernesto Schiaparelli (1856-1928) discovered the tomb of Queen Nefertari in 1904. Giovanni Schiaparelli (1835-1910) was an esteemed astronomer and director of the Milan Observatory. He is most famous for his observation of apparent patterns of straight lines on the surface of the planet Mars. He named these *canali*, the Italian word for 'channels', which unfortunately became mistranslated as 'canals' – implying that there was indeed life on Mars, and prompting a flood of study and speculation.

Elsa Schiaparelli (1890-1973) together with Coco Chanel dominated the world of Parisian fashion between the two world wars. Elsa collaborated with the artists and writers of the Surrealist Movement, notably Salvador Dali, with whom she created her famous *Lobster Dress*, worn by Wallace Simpson. Elsa invented the colour *shocking pink* and introduced eccentric prints, buttons and accessories to the world of fashion. Her spirit of flamboyance was captured in the perfume *Shocking*, created in 1937 and made using 500 ingredients. It was bottled in a crystal flaçon inspired by the curves of Mae West.

Galleria Sabauda

Via Accademia delle Scienze 6
011 547 440
08.30-14.00 Tues, Fri-Sun, 14.00-19.30 Wed and Thurs
closed Monday
admission with Torino card or €4
map 1-2, E3

Sabauda is Piedmontese for Savoy. The gallery is so called
because it was founded on the Savoy collection, with later
additions from the Palazzo Ducale in Genoa, the Gualino
bequest and ongoing acquisitions by the Italian state.

The Galleria Sabauda was originally established in Palazzo
Madama in 1832, with paintings from Palazzo Reale and
Palazzi Carignano. In 1865 the collection was moved to
its current location on the second and third floors of the
Accademia. There are plans to transfer the entire collection
in 2007 to Manica Nuova in the Palazzo Reale.

The gallery contains works from Italian, Flemish and Dutch
masters from the 14-19th centuries. On the second floor
paintings are hung chronologically, while on the third
floor they are arranged in three separate Savoy dynastic
collections. The Gualino collection is displayed in its own
suite of seven rooms on the third floor. Paintings are hung
fairly close together due to a shortage of wall space so it is
easy to wander from room to room and miss some of the
highlights.

Second floor

The first five rooms are dedicated to Piedmontese paintings
of the Renaissance. A further six rooms display works of
Italian masters and these include a *Madonna and Child* by
Beato Angelico and another by Giovanni Bellini. Filippino
Lippi's *Three Archangels and Tobias* depicts the young
traveller with his three angelic companions, while in *Tobias
and the Angel* by Antonio Pollaiolo, the artist has dressed
the young Tobias in a jaunty hat with a red velvet cape
and matching hose, looking more as if he's returning home
from all-night revelry than setting out on a long journey.

PAUL DE VOS: *STUDY OF A LAWYER*

The Angel too is bedecked in red velvet, wearing slouchy chamois boots that wouldn't be out of fashion today.

The remaining rooms on the second floor are dedicated to Flemish and Dutch masters that originally belonged to Prince Eugenio of Savoy-Soissons. In **room 8** Hans Memling's *Passion of Christ* is an unmissable painting and was commissioned for Santa Maria Novella in Florence. Here too are portraits by Rembrandt and the powerful *Vanity of Human Life* by Jan Bruegel the Elder.

Third floor

The dynastic collections continue the theme of Italian and Flemish works. Venetian painters Andrea Mantegna, Tintoretto and Paolo Veronese are displayed together with Rubens' *The Raising of Lazarus,* and *Study of a Lawyer* by Paul de Vos. Look out for a Botticelli *Venus* in the rooms of the **Gualino collection**.

GAM

Galleria Civica d'Arte Moderna e Contemporanea Torino (GAM)
Via Magenta 31
011 442 9550
www.gamtorino.it
09.00-19.00 Tuesday-Sunday, closed Monday
admission with Torino card or €7.50, free entry on Tuesdays
map 1-2, B5

Italy's first modern art gallery was founded as a response to an 1863 constitutional act stipulating that Turin museums should no longer confine their collections to Old Masters, but should be responsible for representing contemporary work. The collection was originally housed in pavilions erected for the 1880 National Fine Arts Exhibition, but these were entirely remodelled by architects Carlo Bassi and Goffredo Boschetti in 1955 following the destruction caused by World War II bombing.

The collection comprises more than 15,000 paintings, sculptures, installations and photographs of which 700 pieces are on permanent exhibit. The works span the late 19th to late 20th centuries and are mostly Italian in origin, with only a handful of international works represented. One of these is the outstanding *Red Girl* by Modigliani, and there are also paintings by Paul Klee and Otto Dix.

GAM is arranged over four floors: temporary exhibits are held in the basement and on the ground floor, which also has a conference hall. Permanent exhibits are spread over two floors: 19th century paintings are hung on the Victorian red walls of the second floor, while 20th century work is displayed in the modern white galleries on the first floor.

First floor

Room 1 contains works from the early 20th century, characterized by beautiful displays of light. These are achieved by the use of pure colours. One of the most emotive paintings in the collection is *The Mirror of Life (where one goes, the others follow)* by Giuseppe Pellizza da

Volpedo. This was one of the most significant paintings of its time, a work of art distinguished by the composition and the symbolism of the subject matter, taken from Dante.

Room 2 is dominated by Giacomo Grosso's *la Nuda,* an incredibly sensuous work, wholeheartedly devoted to the pleasures of looking. The influence of post-Impressionist French painting is clear in **room 4**, especially in Felice Carena's *Peasants in the Sun*, in which Gaugin's Tahitian arcadia is transposed into the rural idyll of Anticoli Corrado, a small town in Lazio that became a haven and commune for artists during the war.

Otto Dix, Modigliani and Paul Klee are exhibited together in **room 5**. Modigliani's *Red Girl* is typical of the artist's portrait style, wherein he captures the personality of his subject but adds an element of cubism. Klee's *Troubled* depicts a magical world which draws its inspiration from a natural landscape.

Room 10 has some rich pickings from Italian art between the two world wars. These include Gino Severini's portrait of his daughter, who was a skilled bookbinder, hence the book in her hands. The style is testament to a return to craftsmanship inspired by classical Rome.

Italian Abstraction is the theme of **room 11** including Luigi Veronesi's graphic protest against the Fascist regime. Josef Alber's *Homage to the Square* is also in this gallery. *Execution of the Partisans* by Renato Guttuso depicts a gruesome scene of execution, made all the more chilling by the everyday suits and ties worn by the dead.

Janis Kounellis's work is displayed in **room 19**. He was a key member of the Italian *Arte Povera* movement that used references to road signs and advertising in an attempt to reconnect painting with the public and the world outside of the rarified atmosphere of galleries and museums.

In **room 23** Andy Warhol's *Orange Car Crash* is printed multiple times on silk. Any element of tragedy in the event depicted is lost as it becomes an article of mass production, reflecting and critiquing the era in which it was made.

Second floor

Room 2 exhibits Romantic works produced under the rule of Carlo Alberto. Francesco Hayez reveals his love for *Carolina Zucchi (The Invalid)* in his portrayal of her vivacity despite the illness which has confined her to bed.

A number of heroic paintings are displayed in **room 7**, including Eugenio Agneni's impassioned *Ghosts of Florentines,* a protest against the rule of foreigners depicted through scenes of occupation that occurred in Renaissance Florence. Dante appears in the foreground with the poet's crown of laurel leaves. The cupola of the Florentine Duomo and the Piazza della Signoria are also recognizable.

Room 8 has a most intriguing portrait by Andrea Gastaldi of the legendary Pietro Micca who sacrificed himself to prevent the French entering Turin in 1706. His heroism is remembered in many paintings and poems, and one of Turin's two diagonal streets is named after him.

One of the most striking paintings in **room 13** is Francesco Mossi's *The Adultress*. The figure embodies lust and gluttony and is made all the more provocative by the subject's direct gaze and burning sensuality. Little wonder the painting sparked an outcry when first exhibited in Turin in 1887. Don't miss Giacomo Ginotti's sculpture *The Incendiary*, inspired by the bloody events in Paris of 1871 when women were the fiercest fighters in resistance to the Prussians.

A more peaceful image of women is depicted in **room 14**. The charming *Tailor Shop,* by Giacomo Favoretto, shows women chatting at work surrounded by fabric in a riot of colours and textures. This subject matter is reminiscent of the paintings of modern life in Paris in the 1880s.

In **room 16** is the sinister *After the Duel* by Antonio Mancini, which depicts a boy dressed in a bourgeois suit drawing back from the bloodied clothes and sword of an unexplained encounter. The painting's theatricality is amplified by the appearance of a shadow on the left-hand side of the canvas.

Gran Madre di Dio

Piazza della Gran Madre di Dio 4
011 819 3572
07.30-12.00, 15.30-1900 daily
map 1-2, H3

This neoclassical church was built to honour the return of Vittorio Emanuele I to Turin in 1814, after the downfall of Napoleon. The architect Ferdinando Bonsignore's design for the church was inspired by the Pantheon in Rome. Napoleon fancied himself as a new Roman Emperor and his passion for ancient Rome made it fashionable to model new buildings after those built 2,000 years ago. The trend continued throughout the early part of the 19th century, long after Napoleon was defeated and exiled.

In Rome, the visitor walks down sloping ground to enter the Pantheon through a portico of columns, which due to a shortage of granite in Egypt were made 10 feet lower than the architect planned. No such errors were made here: the Gran Madre is set high above the Po river, and the visitor must climb a substantial stairway to reach the portico whose perfectly proportioned columns support the gilded pediment.

Magic and the Holy Grail

The exterior statues represent *Faith* and *Religion*. Legend says they were erected by Masons and each holds the key to a secret regarding the hiding place of the Holy Grail. The Gran Madre is regarded as a centre of magic. In the folklore of Turin, the city is said to be one of a triangle of white magic cities (Turin, Lyon, Prague) and, even more mysteriously, one of a triangle of black magic cities (Turin, London, San Francisco). The church is said to stand on a point of magical energy and to guard the Holy Grail, which is hidden in its foundations. Rumours have circulated around the existence of the Grail for centuries, but the popularity of Dan Brown's books has refuelled modern interest.

Monte dei Cappuccini

The wooded hilltop is a favourite for Sunday passeggiata and it is an excellent place to take photographs of Turin. Atop the hill, illuminated atmospherically at night, is the church of Santa Maria del Monte.

Santa Maria del Monte
Via Giardino 35
011 660 4414
08.30-12.00, 15.00-19.30
map 1-2, H4

A monastery was commissioned in 1584 for the local Capuchin monks, the brown-robed clerics who give the name to the *cappuccino.* Designed by Ascanio Vitozzi, the church took many years to finish and was not consecrated until 1656. The building was begun by Vitozzi but completed by Amedeo di Castellamonte. Inside is a lovely octagonal dome. Each year the church is decorated with small blue lights called *Piccoli Spiriti Blu* (Little Blue Spirits) designed by Rebecca Horn, a perennial exhibit in the annual *Luci d'Artisti* festival of light.

Museo Nazionale della Montagna
Via Giardino 39
011 660 4104
www.museomontagna.org
09.00-19.00 daily
admission with Torino card or €5
map 1-2, H4

As the name implies, this museum focuses on the mountain heritage of the people of Turin. It was built in 1863 to honour the explorer Prince Luigi di Savoia, Duke of Abruzzo, who launched an expedition to the North Pole. The museum houses a collection of photographs and momentos of the expedition along with other mountaineering exhibits.

Exhibits on the ground floor detail the everyday life and traditions of alpine peoples. The first floor has displays on exploration, mountain sports and climbing equipment. The second floor offers an observation post with stunning views of the Alps.

Performing Arts

Founded in 1681, Teatro Regio was Turin's only public theatre until the 19th century. During the Savoy reign the performing arts existed only to please the monarchy. Public concerts were rare and a circuit developed, a musical tour of Savoy, Hapsburg and Borromeo palaces by composers such as Vivaldi or Handel. Concerts were a regular after-dinner feature in sophisticated residences.

In Piedmont, puppet theatre became extremely popular. It began with Commedia dell'Arte and evolved considerably. Well-known artists were commissioned to create elaborate theatres complete with stage, moveable backdrops and carved furniture. Marionettes were stars in plays written for them – they even had their own costume designers and face painters.

Teatro Regio Torino

Piazza Castello 41
011 881 5241
www.teatroregio.torino.it
box office: 10.30-18.00 Tuesday-Friday, till 4pm Saturday
€17.00 and up
map 1-2, E2
The opera house has an annual season from September to June with ballet and concerts by the Philharmonic and RAI symphony.

Teatro Stabile di Torino

www.teatrostabiletorino.it
box office 12.00-19.00 daily
showtime usually 20.45
Sunday matinee 15.30
Turin's premier theatre company. Performances are staged in one of three theatres:
• Teatro Carignano
Piazza Carignano 6 (011 517 6246)
• Teatro Gobetti
Via Rossini 8 (011 815 9132)
• Teatro Alfieri
Piazza Solferino 2-4 (011 562 3800)

Puppet theatre

Marionette Grilli

Teatro Alfa
Via Casalborgone 16, Collina
011 819 3529
www.marionettegrilli.com
show 16.15 Sunday
box office: 11.00-13.00 Sunday
€5-6
The company performs original operetta-style pieces in Italian every Sunday afternoon and in summer at Borgo Medioevale.

Marionnette Lupi

Museo della Marionetta
Via Santa Teresa 5
011 530 238
museomarionettelupi@tin.it
shows 16.00 and 17.00 Sunday
€6.50
map 1-2, D3
The Lupi family donated their collection of marionettes to start this museum, which now has 5,000 hand-painted puppets. The museum is open for half an hour before the show and one hour after.

Festivals

Turin hosts festivals, concerts and special events throughout the year. Perhaps the most special is the winter festival of lights – *Luci di Artisti* – when all of Turin is lit up during Christmas and New Year. This is followed by Biennale Internazionale Arte Giovane (BIG) which brings 300 promising young artists from around the world, to give the public a glimpse of the art stars of the future. CiccolaTO, held in March, is but one of the many food fairs at Lingotto during the spring.

Torinodanza is followed by the Blues Festival in July, and the prestigious Settembre Musica series of classical music performances in September. Turin's film festival in November is second only to Venice in Italy, and in the same month ladies sing the blues at Feminine Blues.

Luci di Artisti Nov-Feb
Piazza San Carlo, Piazza Carignano, Monte dei Cappuccini and others
Founded in 1997, this event brings together impressive light installations by contemporary artists. New artists are added each year, and the best installations from previous shows are retained.

Big Torino Apr-May
Via Maria Vittoria 18
011 443 0010
Every two years Turin hosts this event showcasing young artists.

TorinoDanza Feb-May
011 881 5557
Contemporary dance festival held in venues around Turin.

Torino Blues Festival July
Rivoli-Maison Musique Folkclub
Piazza Solferino 3
011 537 636
Paired with the Amsterdam Blues Festival to bring in the world's best blues musicians, mostly from the US.

Torino Settembre Musica
Sep-Oct
Via San Francesco da Paola 6
011 442 4703
box office open 10.30-18.30 Mon-Sat
Classical music is played in churches and other unusual venues around Turin. Established in 1977, the festival attracts premier players and recently began adding jazz, contemporary and ethnic music.

Torino Film Festival mid-Nov
www.torinofilmfest.org
Via Monte di Pietà 1
011 562 3309
Turin's film festival has been going since 1982 and screens many Italian films not accepted in Venice.

Blues al Femminile Nov-Dec
Associazione Culturale Centro Jazz
Via Pomba 4
011 884 477
Blues concerts, photographic exhibits, projection shows and talks.

Parco Valentino

Italy's first public gardens were established here in the 1850s. The park stretches for several miles along the Po river parallel to Corso Massimo d'Azeglio from the Ponte Umberto I in the north to the Ponte Balbis in the south. It is easily reached on the number 9 tram.

There are two castles in the park, **Castello del Valentino** and **Rocca Medioevale**, a replica that includes a village. The Viale Cagni is a nice riverfront promenade between Castello del Valentino and Ponte Umberto. Behind the Castello del Valentino is the **Orto Botanico**, a botanical garden which features an exhibit of plant species described in the Bible.

Boating trips
Via Murazzi 65
011 5786 4733
€4.00 or Torino card
A one-hour return boat cruise on the river Po begins at the Murazzi dock just below Piazza Vittorio Veneto. The boats *Valentino* and *Valentina* travel slowly along the river beside Parco del Valentino, to the Borgo Medioevale where you may disembark for a walk or a visit before returning.

Borgo and Rocca Medioevale
Viale Virigilio 107
011 443 1701
09.00-20.00 daily in summer, closing time 19.00 in winter
village free, Rocca admission with Torino card or €3
map 3-4, H2

The Borgo and Rocca are a 19th century reconstruction
of a medieval Piedmont village and castle built for the
Turin exposition of 1884. Medieval Turin was completely
destroyed to build the baroque city of the Savoy and this
replica is complete with drawbridge, narrow alleyways and
old-style frescoes. Artists recreated authentic Piedmontese
shops and houses, using over forty villages as source material.
It's a charming tableau set in an idyllic location along the
banks of the Po. There is a free puppet theatre on summer
Sunday afternoons.

Castello del Valentino
Corso Massimo d'Azeglio
011 669 4592
map 1-2, G6

This was once the favourite
palace of Maria Cristina,
Queen of France. It has been
restored and today hosts
special art and photographic
exhibits by artists such as
Robert Mapplethorpe.

LINGOTTO
& BEYOND

Once the centre of Fiat production, the Lingotto has been transformed into a multi-purpose complex with an art gallery and a concert hall.
At Stupinigi, the Savoy hunting lodge is actually a grand palace set in a large park.

A visit to the Pinacoteca on top of the Lingotto is essential for art lovers. The nearby Museo dell' Automobile contains the first car made by Fiat. A visit to Basilica di Superga will take an afternoon, but there is an excellent restaurant in the vicinity. Those who appreciate contemporary art should make the journey to Rivoli. If your taste is more traditional, see the Palazzina di Stupinigi.

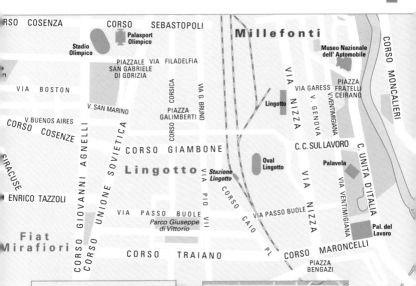

CORSO COSENZA CORSO SEBASTOPOLI **Millefonti**

Stadio Olimpico Palasport Olimpico

PIAZZALE VIA FILADELFIA
SAN GABRIELE DI GORIZIA

VIA BOSTON

V. SAN MARINO

V.BUENOS AIRES
CORSO COSENZE

SIRACUSE

ENRICO TAZZOLI

VIA CORSICA

VIA G. BRUNO

PIAZZA GALIMBERTI

CORSO GIAMBONE

Lingotto

VIA PASSO BUOLE
Parco Giuseppe di Vittorio

Fiat Mirafiori

CORSO GIOVANNI AGNELLI

CORSO UNIONE SOVIETICA

VIA PIO VII

CORSO CAIO

VIA PASSO BUOLE

CORSO TRAIANO

PL

Museo Nazionale dell' Automobile

CORSO MONCALIERI

VIA GARESS

VIA NIZZA

PIAZZA FRATELLI CEIRANO

V. VENTIMIGLIANA

Lingotto

V. GENOVA

C. C. SUL LAVORO

Oval Lingotto

Stazione Lingotto

Palavela

VIA NIZZA

VIA VENTIMIGLIANA

C. UNITA D'ITALIA

Pal. del Lavoro

CORSO MARONCELLI

PIAZZA BENGAZI

Pinacoteca Agnelli
• Gianni Agnelli's private art collection
Basilica di Superga
• grand baroque church in a magnificent setting
Palazzina di Stupinigi
• Turin's Versailles
Rivoli • contemporary art in an old castle

restaurants p.240
shopping p.266
nightlife p.238

Tranvia Sassi-Superga
Period-style funicular train that takes you up to the Basilica di Superga.

Lingotto shopping
A mall with lots of shops that are open late.

Did you know that..?
Gianni Agnelli said he loved the wind because it was the one thing he couldn't buy.

Lingotto

Via Nizza 280
Otto gallery shopping centre
12.00-22.00 Mon 10.00-22.00 Tues-Sun
map 5-6, G2

Lingotto was built by Giacomo Trucco to house Fiat's production line and management staff. It was the year 1914, and the automobile was the hot new invention. In the course of a few years Fiat came to be considered Europe's most efficient car manufacturer.

The complex is actually two parallel buildings, each 500m (1,640 feet) long, connected at various points by passageways. The large internal courtyards were gradually filled in by offices as Fiat's workforce continued to grow. The demand for cars outstripped supply and in 1939 Fiat built another production line in nearby Mirafiori. As the speed of the cars increased the rooftop testing track became obsolete, as did the production facility itself.

Although Fiat's car production was outsourced to Poland in the 1990s, Lingotto is still the administration centre for the company, employing a staff of 6,000 (down from 13,000 in 2000). In 1986 Renzo Piano was commissioned to convert the press offices into art galleries, beginning what was to become a complete rebuilding of the entire complex. Piano kept the rooftop track but designed a glass bubble meeting room, *La Bolla,* in the centre. He also created the distinctive shape of the Pinacoteca Agnelli. The cherry-wood lined Renzo Piano auditorium was completed in 1994. It has a ceiling that can be raised or lowered to adjust the acoustics. Currently, the RAI orchestra performs twice a week.

Otto Gallery

Lingotto now holds a large convention centre, a shopping mall, cinemas, a Meridien hotel and several cavernous exhibition halls. In 2002, the Otto Gallery was opened in the north wing. Shops and restaurants line three internal courtyards, each with a sliding glass roof to allow daylight in and offer protection against inclement weather.

Pinacoteca Agnelli

Via Nizza 230
011 006 2008
www.pinacoteca-agnelli.it
10.00-19.00 Tues-Sun
admission with Torino card or €6
map 5-6, G2

On top of the Lingotto is the *Scrigno,* a glass annex with 25 of the most precious paintings from the collection of the late Gianni Agnelli. The Fiat chairman and art lover claimed that the spirit of his collecting was to offer 'pleasure, beauty and joy' to his fellow citizens. This pleasure in looking is the only theme that binds the disparate works together. Agnelli was so fond of the collection that his body lay in state here after his death in 2003.

The collection has paintings dating from 1724 to 1948, each arguably a masterpiece. Those with classical tastes, who prefer to view their art in manageable doses rather than dispersed across vast museums, will enjoy a visit here. Enter either from inside the mall next to the superb bookshop, or from the glass lift on the building's exterior.

Matisse is the best-represented artist in the Pinacoteca collection. His paintings are rarely seen in Italy's galleries – perhaps because his work deviated so far from the traditions of Italian painting. The works on display were painted during Matisse's time in Nice during World War II and are made up of complex interiors, still lifes and studies of women. Two notable pieces are *Tabac Royal* and *Women with Anemones.*

Renoir's voluptuous *Baigneuse* once belonged to English critic Kenneth Clarke, who sold it to Agnelli to finance the purchase of his country house. The painting portrays Aline Charigot at the tender age of 22, before she became Renoir's wife and mother of his children. The setting is the island of Capri, visited by the couple after a brief time in Rome. Renoir's style was greatly influenced by seeing Raphael's paintings at the Villa Farnesina in Rome during that trip.

The collection traces the development of Canaletto through six of his paintings from 1726 to 1738. In *Il Canal Grande da Santa Maria della Carita,* Canaletto uses extremes of light and dark in his depiction of Galleria Accademia when it was a monastery. Gino Severini's *Les Lanciers Italiens en Galop* captures the decisive moment of a cavalry charge, which may have evoked personal memories for Agnelli, who served as a cavalry officer in Russia and Africa. Although painted in 1915 it was inspired by Paolo Uccello's *Battle of San Romano,* painted 500 years ago.

Modigliani's overtly sensual *Nu couche* was once owned by the Banca d'Italia, before entering Agnelli's collection. It is said that the artist's tangled love affairs are reflected in this portrait. Picasso is another artist whose complicated relationships influenced his paintings. One lovely example from his blue period, *L'Hetaire* was painted in Paris and inspired by a demi-mondaine beauty known as 'la Belle Otero'. Picasso's use of colour is reminiscent of playing cards and cabaret posters popular at the time. *Homme appuye sur une Table* is a more mature cubist work in which the human body is abstracted almost beyond recognition.

Other artists represented in Agnelli's collection are Canova, Bellotto, Balla and Tiepolo.

Basilica di Superga

Strada della Basilica di Superga
011 899 7456
Basilica:
08.00-19.00 in summer
08.00-18.00 in winter
dome and tombs:
09.30-12.00, 15.00-18.00 daily
open through lunch Saturday
closed Sunday mornings
closed at 17.00 in winter
dome or tombs €3
dome and tombs €5

Tranvia Sassi-Superga
Funicular at Stazione Sassi
011 576 4733
9.00-12.00, 14.00-20.00 daily
closed Tuesday
Torino card or €3

The Basilica di Superga stands high on a hill above Turin
and offers stunning views of the entire Po valley. To reach
the church, take the number 15 tram to Stazione Sassi and
board the charming 1930s funicular, Tranvia Sassi-Superga,
for a ride through the forest to the top of the hill. From the
funicular station it's a short walk up to the Basilica. The
church can also be reached by road.

Vittorio Amedeo II dedicated the Superga to the Madonna
in gratitude for victory against the French in 1706, marking
a turning point in Savoy fortunes. A marble relief over the
high altar commemorates the battle, and a chapel in the
left transept commemorates the vow made by the King of
Piedmont to the Madonna.

Court architect Filippo Juvarra built the church using stones
quarried at the base of the hill – the site of the funicular
station today. The Superga is meant to be imposing and it
succeeds. This gigantic structure is Turin's Pantheon: Italy's
Savoy kings and and dukes are buried underneath the
church, except for Vittorio Emanuele II whose remains are
in the Pantheon in Rome.

In 1949 a plane crash wiped out the entire Turin football
team after the players had won a key victory. The tragedy
broke the heart of a city recovering from World War II.
A museum dedicated to the team is entered via the cloister.

Palazzina di Stupinigi

Piazza Principe Amedeo 7
from Turin take SS23 south towards Pinerolo, exit Stupinigi
011 358 1220
09.00-12.30, 14.00-18.00 daily (17.00 in winter)
closed Mondays
admission €6.20, no credit cards

The once tree-lined Corso Unioni Sovietica runs in a perfectly straight line for 10km from the gates of Turin to the Savoy hunting lodge, *Palazzina di Stupinigi*. This grand palace was begun in 1729 by court architect Filippo Juvarra. Work was carried out quickly and, two years later, the mansion had its first hunt. One hundred years later, King Vittorio would hunt here twice a week. In 1766 Francesco Ladetto installed the bronze deer on top of the copper and bronze dome above the central gallery. The sculpture was later replaced by an iron copy, and the original is now housed in the ticket office.

Set in 1,700 hectares of wooded parkland, the palace is the Savoy equivalent of Hampton Court or Fontainebleau. When a young 18th century English aristocrat visited here while on the Grand Tour, he was completely astonished and awestruck by the sheer luxury of the palace, so unlike anything seen in Britain. Until then, an English hunting lodge was a cold draughty place with little thought for gilt or decoration. In 1919, the land became a public park and ownership of the Palazzina was transferred to the Italian state.

In February 2004, thieves broke into the palace and made off with over 10 million euros worth of paintings and objets d'art. To date the culprits have not been apprehended.

The palace

Juvarra's design was based on a Saint Andrew's cross: four diagonal wings that branch off a large elliptical central ballroom. Juvarra called on the best painters and artisans (most were from Venice) for the internal decoration. The most interesting areas are the eastern apartments, the King's apartments and the rooms of the equerries. Begin the tour through the courtyard at the library where there is a collection of 18th century French blue lacquer furnishings. Panels in the gaming room were painted by the Viennese painter Christian Wehrlin. Paolina Bonaparte and Camillo Borghese took up residence here during the Napoleonic era and former's marble bathtub was the first in Turin. In the east wing are large paintings of another Savoy hunting lodge at Mirafiori.

The oval ballroom was designed to be the showpiece of the palace and is the highlight of the tour. The walls are decorated with a beautiful series of frescoes: *The Triumph of Diana* by Giuseppe and Domenico Valeriani. In the centre of the room hangs a bronze and crystal chandelier, a wedding gift for Maria Teresa Savoy and Count Filippo d'Artois in 1773.

Museo di Arte Ammobiliamento (Museum of Furniture)
09.00-11.50, 14.00-17.20 daily
closed Monday
A collection of furniture, paintings and high quality objects coming from the palace and other royal mansions. These include two complete Empire sitting room suites, the bathtub of Paolina Bonaparte and a carriage that once belonged to Napoleon.

The mistress

King Vittorio Emanuele II preferred hunting to politics. He also preferred sex to politics, and had a lover in every palace. Stupinigi was the King's favourite palace, and so it was here that he installed his favourite mistress, Rosa Vercellana. Vittorio first set eyes on the voluptuous farmer's daughter when she was only 14 and he was not yet king. Passionately in love at first sight, Vittorio had Rosa kidnapped and brought to a cottage at the far end of the gardens. Eight months later, Rosa gave birth to a baby girl, Vittoria. Vittorio's wife Maria Adelaide was livid. She was even more furious when the affair became common knowledge after the birth of Rosa's second child, a son named Emanuele Alberto. King Vittorio eventually made an honest woman of his Rosa when he married her in a civil ceremony after the Queen's death.

Castello di Rivoli

Piazza Mafalda di Savoia, 10098 Rivoli
011 9565211
www.castellodirivoli.org
Tuesday to Thursday 10.00-17.00, Friday to Sunday 10.00-21.00
Closed Monday, open Easter Monday
admission €6.50, free for under 11
Free guided tours on Saturdays at 15.00 and 18.00;
Sundays and holidays, at 11.00, 15.00 and 18.00
Tours covering the history and architecture of the Castello di Rivoli
are held on Sundays at 16.30.

For those who enjoy contemporary art a visit to the Castello
di Rivoli is well worth the hour-long journey from the
centre of Turin. Founded in 1984, this is Italy's first museum
devoted to contemporary art from 1950 to the present day.

The building's origins go back a lot further. The museum
is in fact made up of the architectural fragments of two
abandoned buildings that were originally part of the Savoy
residency. Some parts date back as far as their function as
a medieval fortress. The visual effect is very dramatic and
gives the air of a Baroque building site, lending itself very
appropriately to the conceptual nature of the contemporary
works it houses. Looking at the external building requires
a leap of imagination – the entrance courtyard would
once have been an internal salon and the reflection in the
mirrored door tricks the eye into believing that the building
is actually symmetrical.

Once inside, enjoy the spectacular juxtaposition of
contemporary art and splendid 18th century interior design.
For those with a hankering for some avant-garde creative
fusion cooking, book into the adjoining restaurant Combal.0
for an unusual dinner experience. Failing that, the cafeteria
is well stocked with lunchtime treats and wine.

Room 1

British artist Richard Long's works involve the natural
world and chart his travels through a mapping of geometric
forms. *Rivoli Mud Circle* is made up from the artist's hand
prints on the wall using local mud. The piece called *Romulus
Circle* is made of stones from the region of Lazio.

Room 5
Michelangelo Pistoletto is one of the maverick artists of the
Turin-based *Arte Povera* movement of the 1970s. His *Venere
delle Stracci* (Venus of Rags) became emblematic of the
movement's interest in using found, ready-made materials.
The classical statue of Venus alongside the colourful,
discarded materials challenges traditional concepts of
beauty.

Room 7
Gerhard Richter's glossy laquers of pure colour in his
Farbtafeln colour charts contrast sharply with the style of the
18th century fresco ceiling with its variations in colour and
technique.

Room 8
This is the King's Apartment of the old castle and it houses
the work of Turin artist Giuseppe Penone. His works discuss
the ideas of artistic processes such as in *Albero di 11 metri*,
which is a plank of wood stretching upwards into a tree. The
fresco in the center of the ceiling is of Diana in a coach drawn
by deer. Another Turin-based artist, Mario Merz, is seen
throughout the museum. A variation of his famous igloo is
in Room 18. He explores ideas of nomadic and temporary
architecture using organic materials.

As the permanent collection is in constant rotation, the rooms
are an eternal attraction themselves, such as **room 24**, with
its geometric painted panels in the shape of a star and
room 27, the 'Chinese Room' with its exotic trompe-l'oeil
painting and meticulous finishings. The adjoining chapel is
also worth a look, with its gilded stucco framing, marbling,
and precious wood inlays, although the altar is no longer in
situ. **Room 31** was the young prince's bedchamber and is
known as 'Room of the Allegory of the Seasons'. The vaulted
ceiling represents Apollo surrounded by Time, Abundance
and Flora. Other artists whose work features are Maurizio
Cattelan, Sol Lewitt, Hannah Starkey and Jannis Kounellis.
The museum also has links with British institutions such as
the Whitechapel Gallery and the Victoria & Albert Museum.

MUSEUMS & CHURCHES

Museums and galleries

Opening times and admission information

The Torino card provides access to more than 120 collections in the Turin region. Otherwise the individual admission is usually around €4 for adults or €2 for children and concessions. Our favourite museums and galleries are reviewed in the main body of the book, but there are other interesting collections to see. They are listed below.

Generally, museums and galleries are closed Monday, some are open late Thursday evenings and smaller institutions close for lunch between 13.00-15.00.

Accademia Albertina
Via Accademia Albertina 6
011 889 020
10.00-18.00 Tuesday-Sunday
map 1-2, F4
Originally the collection of Archbishop Vincenzo Maria Mossi di Morano. Highlights include 60 charcoal cartoons by Gaudenzio Ferrari housed in an eerie, darkened room and two panels from Filippo Lippi's triptych *I dottori della Chiesa Gregorio e Gerolamo (Doctors of the Church, Jerome and Gregory).*

Archivio di Stato
Piazza Castello 209
011 562 4610
map 1-2, E2
One of the most important historical archives in Europe has documents dating back to 726.

Armeria Reale
Piazza Castello 191
011 518 4358
www.artito.arti.beniculturali.it
10.00-19.00 Tues-Sun
map 1-2, E2
Opened in 1837 by King Charles Albert, this museum occupies part of the gallery that linked Palazzo Reale and Palazzo Madama. It contains swords and armour from the medieval and Renaissance periods and follows the development of firearms during the Risorgimento. The collection also includes Napoleonic arms and relics, and oriental weapons.

Biblioteca Nazionale Universitaria
(National University Library)
Piazza Carlo Alberto 3
011 810 1111
09.00-19.00 daily
map1-2, E2
Nearly one million books are housed in the ex-stables of Palazzo Carignano. Vittorio Amedeo II founded the library in 1723 at the Royal University. Just a few steps from here, along Via Cesare Battisti, is a sign marking the house where Friedrich Nietzsche resided in 1888-89.

Biblioteca Reale
Piazza Castello 191
011 453 855
map 1-2 E2
The Savoy library contains numerous drawings by Leonardo

da Vinci. These include a self portrait, architectural plans for defence fortifications, and studies of birds in flight which inspired the artist's designs for an aeroplane.

Borgo Medioevale
see page 91

Fondazione Pietro Accorsi – Museo di Arti Decorative
Via Po 55
011 812 9116
www.fondazioneaccorsi.it
10.00-20.00 Tues-Sun; 23.00 Thurs
admission by guided tour (in Italian)
tours in English can be pre-booked
map 1-2, F3
This museum was conceived as a lived-in home, decorated and furnished according to the 18th century taste of Pietro Accorsi. The interior designer was so well-regarded that he was commissioned to arrange furnishings in Rome's Quirinale Palace. Room 10 reflects Accorsi's taste for French decorative arts and contains a stunning cabinet of Piedmontese design, decorated with painted majolica panels. Baccarat crystal, silverware and porcelain are also displayed, together with a collection of interesting landscape paintings. Original rice paper paintings in the Chinese room reveal the taste for all things Oriental inspired by French Imperialism in the East.

Fondazione Sandretto Re Rebaudengo
011 198 31600
Via Modane 16
www.fondsrr.org
12.00-20.00 Tue-Sun; 23.00 Thur
just off map 1-2, F1
The Foundation is dedicated to providing a venue and context for new generations of artists, critics and curators to meet, exchange ideas and exhibit new work.

Galleria Sabauda
see page 78

GAM – Galleria Civica d'arte Moderna e Contemporanea
see page 80

Museo Civico di Arte Antica
see page 64

Museo Civico di Numismatica, Etnografia e Arti Orientali
Via Bricherasio 8
011 541 557
09.00-19.00 Tue-Sun
map 1-2, B5
This eclectic museum displays sacred and primitive art from Africa, America, Oceania and Asia. The collection is spread over three floors and includes Buddhist sculptures from Gandhara.

Museo della Marionetta (Marionette Museum)
Via Santa Teresa 5
011 530 238
09.30-13.00, 14.00-17.00
visit by appointment only
Sunday puppet shows at 4pm and 5pm by Marionetta Luppi
€3 museum only
€6.50 museum and theatre performance
map 1-2, D3
The best time to see the beautiful marionettes in this collection is preceding or following the Sunday puppet show. The museum houses more than 5,000 hand-painted puppets donated by the Luppi family. They also produce the performances.

Museo della Sindone
see page 58

Museo di Antichità & Porte Palatina
Via XX Settembre 88C
011 521 1106
www.museoantichita.it
08.30-19.30 Tuesday-Sunday
map 1-2, D1
Ancient Roman and Greek pottery, sculpture and other artifacts are displayed in the former conservatory of the Palazzo Reale. The entrance is opposite the ruins of the original Roman gate that once guarded the northern entrance to the city.

Museo di Arte Ammobiliamento
see page 105

Museo Egizio
see page 74

Museo Nazionale del Cinema
see page 49

Museo Nazionale del Risorgimento Italiano
see page 72

Museo Nazionale della Montagna
see page 87

Museo Nazionale dell'Automobile
Corso Unità d'Italia 40
011 677 666
www.museoauto.it
10.00-18.30 Tue-Sun; 22.00 Thurs
map 5-6, H1
The invention and evolution of the Italian car is chronicled through a display of original automobiles. A must-see for car buffs, the museum was opened in 1960 by Carlo Biscaretti di Ruffia, one of the original partners in Fiat and a founder of the Italian Automobile Club. Exhibits include an 1896 Bernardi, an 1899 Fiat, and a Rolls Royce Silver Ghost, as well as Ferrari and Alfa Romeo racing cars.

Museo Pietro Micca
(Pietro Micca Museum)
Via Guicciardini 7a
011 546 317
09.00-19.00 Tue-Sun
map 1-2, A3
Underground tunnels were fundamental to the resistance of 1706 and this museum preserves the memory of Pietro Micca, who exploded the mine that saved Turin. It cost him his life.

Museo Storico Nazionale dell'Artigliera (Artillery museum)
Corso Galileo Ferraris
011 562 9223
09.00-16.00 Mon-Thurs; 13.00 Fri
closed Sat and Sun
map 1-2, B3
Located in the Mastio, the ruin of the fortified citadel, arms from 1300-1900 are dislpayed, including some rare weapons.

Orto Botanico
see page 90

Pinacoteca Agnelli
see page 98

Promotrice delle Belle Arti
Via Balsano Crivelli 11
011 669 2545
10.00-19.00 Tues-Sun
map 3-4, H1
A painting gallery in Parco del Valentino that exhibits early 20th century Piedmontese artists.

Teatro Regio
see page 88
Book in advance for a backstage tour in English or join the Italian guided tour at 3pm Saturday. This can be cancelled for rehearsals so it is wise to phone ahead.

Church hours

Churches open daily at 7am for morning mass, close for lunch at noon, and reopen at 4pm till 7-8pm. Many churches are closed Sunday afternoon.

Madonna della Consolata

Piazza della Consolata
011 436 3235
06.30-12.00 mass every 30 min
Sunday also 18.15 and 19.30
map 1-2, C1

The Consolata is a favourite with locals and much visited by pilgrims in search of healing. A mix of architectural styles, it originated as the 10th century monastery of S. Andrea. The church you see now is primarily the work of Guarino Guarini in 1678. Filippo Fuvarra added the presbytery oval in 1729; a further sumptuous restoration was completed in 1904 by Carlo Ceppi. The high altar features white marble statues of two angels adoring a painting of the *Virgin Maria Consolatrice* by an unknown artist. The painting is said to be miraculous and around the altar are votive offerings from those who have been healed.

Corpus Domini

Piazza Corpus Domini
011 436 6025
map 1-2, D2

The baroque church was built to commemorate the 'Miracle of Turin', said to have occurred at a grain market on 6 June 1453. As a soldier was trying to sell stolen relics, a host fell from his bag and rose up in the sky like a vision.

La Crocetta
Via Marco Polo 3
011 582 992
map 3-4, D1
The district is named after this church. In the square is a clothing market, held each morning and on Saturday. Close by is the gelateria Testa and the bar L'aperitivo.

San Carlo e Santa Cristina
Piazza San Carlo
011 539 281
map 1-2, D3
The baroque churches occupy both sides of Via Roma on the south side of Piazza San Carlo. Santa Cristina's concave facade was designed by Filippo Juvarra.

San Domenico
Via San Domenico
011 522 9711
map 1-2, D3
Turin's only Gothic church dates from 1260. Inside, the church has three naves and an ornately carved pulpit. In the Cappela del Rosario is the 17th century painting *Madonna of the Rosary and the Saints Dominic and Catherine of Siena* by Guercino. An Inquisitor once lived in the nearby convent when one of the rooms was used as a jail.

San Filippa Neri
Via Maria Vittoria 5
011 538 456
map 1-2, E3
San Filippa contains Turin's longest nave at 226 ft. It has six side chapels. Antonio Bettini began the church in 1675, but when the dome collapsed Filippo Juvarra was commissioned to finish construction. Over the main altar is a painting of the *Virgin and Child* by Carlo Maratta. Exhibitions and musical events take place in the oratory.

San Giovanni Evangelista
Corso Vittorio Emanuele II 13
011 659 0511
map 1-2, F5
A pretty 19th century church built by Edoardo Arborio Nella. Enrico Reffo's wax pictures in the central nave, the presbytery, and the apse are stunning.

San Massimo
Via Mazzini 29
011 812 6703
map 1-2, F4
Highlights of this neo-classical church are the baptistry by Cesare Reduzzi and the apse frescoes depicting San Massimo giving a sermon in the church.

Sant'Agostino
Via Sant'Agostino
011 436 8833
map 1-2, C1
Saint Augustine believed that the beauty of art inspired the soul. This early baroque church might inspire yours. It contains a beautiful altar by Carlo Ceppi and other interesting paintings and frescoes.

Santissima Annunziata
Via Po 45
011 817 1423
map 1-2, E3
Designed by Carlo Morello in 1648 and refurbished in 1900, the church has a fine sculpture group of the *Addolorata* by Stefano Clemente that is worth seeing.

Santissimi Martiri
Via Garibaldi 25
Capella della Pia Congregazione
011 562 7226
15.00-18.00 Sat 10.00-12.00 Sun

11.00 Sun Mass, closed July and Aug
map 1-2, C2

Decorating the Capella vault are the beautiful frescoes *Triumph of Paradise* by Stefano Legnani. On the walls are 11 paintings depicting the birth of Jesus, the visit of the Magi and the Star of Bethlehem that guided them. The star theme appears in the perpetual calendar by Antonio Piana, one of only three in the world. The Capella was commissioned in 1662 by bankers and merchants who were members of the congregation.

Santissima Trinità
Via Garibaldi
011 515 6340
map 1-2, D2

This circular church is light and airy with a luminous dome. Inside the dome are delightful 19th century frescoes by Luigi Vacca and Francesco Gonin. The marble interior was decorated by Filippo Juvarra.

Chiesa Valdese
(Waldensian Church)
Corso Vittorio Emanuele II 23
011 669 2838
map 1-2, E5

The Waldese are Protestants who have been present in Italy since the Middle Ages. In 1848 King Carlo Alberto granted religious freedom to the Waldese. They commissioned this church to honour the victory of their battle for religious freedom. When the church was inaugurated in 1853, shepherds from far out in the valleys gathered here for the first Sunday service. The church later became the centre of the Protestant movement in Turin.

In Piedmont, the Waldensian heartland is the area southwest of Pinerolo. Torre Pellice is considered to be the capital of the Waldensian church. Those with an interest in their history and culture should travel there and visit:

Museo StoricoValdese
Via Roberto d'Azeglio 2
0121 932 566
Opening times vary, call ahead.

Tempio Israelitico
(Jewish Synagogue)
Via San Pio V 12
011 669 2387
open by appointment only
map 1-2, E5

This synagogue was built by Enrico Petiti in 1884 after the Jewish community felt compelled to abandon the increasingly out-of-control Antonelli and his Mole. This building has been restored after it was seriously damaged by WWII bombings. The piazza in front is dedicated to Piedmontese writer Primo Levi.

Lingotto and Beyond

Abbazia di Vezzolano
below Albugnano
34 kilometres from Turin
011 436 1577, 011 436 1512
off map

Charlemagne granted the land to build the abbey and Frederic Barbarossa donated the income received from his tenant farmers. There are interesting statues of the Archangels Michael and Raphael. Of special interest is the bas-relief *The Ancestors of the Virgin Mary*, depicting her lineage. The most ancient part of the cloister dates from 1110, with beautiful frescoes and bas-reliefs.

MOUNTAINS

VIEW FROM SAUZE D'OULX

Piedmont's alpine playground has received a huge boost from the 2006 Winter Olympics. Summer visitors will also find a wide range of activities.

The area is now an all-season recreational paradise. Skiers can test their skills on Olympic runs and hikers have plenty of options. Europe's highest golf course is also found here. Those interested in history should visit the monastery at Sacra di San Michele and the fortress at Fenestrelle.

SKIING IN PRAGELATO

Modane
Aiguille de Scolette
△ 3508
△ Punta Lunella 2772
Venaria

V a l l e   d i   S u s a

Susa

Bardonecchia Exilles
Dora Riparia
Salbertrand

Monte Orsiera

Sacra di San Michele
Rivoli
Turin

Avigliana
Grugliasco

Lago Grande
Lago Piccolo

Oulx
Valle del Chisone
Usseaux Fenestrelle
Pragelato
△ Monte Albergian 3043

Giaveno

San Sicario
Sauze d'Oulx
Chisone

Orbassano

Cesana
Sestriere
P I E D M O N T

Claviere
Ripa
△ Punta Rognosa 3280
Perosa Argentina
None

enèvre
iançon

Chisola

Prali

Pinerolo

Grand Pic de Rochebruna 3325
△
Bric Froid △ 3302

Bric Bouchet △ 3216
Torre Pellice
Luserna San Giovanni
Vigone

R A N C E   Abriès
Bobbio Pellice
Pellice
Cavour

Sestriere
• Agnelli's premier resort
Sauze d'Oulx
• a British favourite
Pragelato
• ski station with the most improvements
Bardonecchia
• classic Italian ski resort
Sacra di San Michele
• symbol of Piedmont
Forte di Fenestrelle
• largest fortress in Europe

restaurants p.242
shopping p.275
nightlife p.133, 243-44

Golf Club Sestriere
Play 18 holes in a stunning alpine setting.

Oulx
Charming mountain town.

The Milky Way
An enormous interlinked ski area.

Did you know that..?
Pragelato has an annual beauty contest for cows.

Introducing Sestriere

Tourist office: 0122 755 444
www.sestriere.it, www.montagnedoc.it

It is fitting that the most successful of the pioneering purpose-built ski resorts, established in the early 1930s, has experienced a renaissance courtesy of helping stage the 2006 Winter Olympics.

Sestriere was named by Roman legions who made camp on this high mountain plateau during epic marches through the Alps. The name is derived from the phrase *pietra sistrari*, meaning 'sixth mile stone'. Until the 1920s, this was a barren alpine landscape at 2000m above sea level, with nothing more than a rugged trail and a road keeper's hut. But the all-powerful Agnelli family had a vision for its future: to build the most modern, sophisticated winter sports resort the world had ever seen.

In early days, ski stations were old alpine villages like St Moritz and Davos in Switzerland, with ski lifts simply added on to the town. In the eyes of the ambitious Agnelli, this did not constitute a functional resort. They wanted to create a something new and splendid, a place that would keep their many wealthy friends skiing in Italy. It would be bigger and better than the other purpose-built resorts in France and Switzerland, though some were excellent for their time. In Sestriere, everything would be dedicated to the needs of skiers, with accommodation, ski shops, and lifts all within a moment's walk. This was the first planned ski resort to enjoy instant success. Many other purpose-built ski stations in other countries subsequently used the planning model of Sestriere to foster their own success stories.

It remains unclear as to whether Mussolini had any influence on the Agnelli's decision to build a ski resort. Some reports have it that Mussolini was sick of Italians venturing to St Moritz for ski holidays and dearly wanted a winter sports resort for his people. No matter, the project was a perfect fit for the Agnelli. The family had the finances and clout to gain permission for such a venture, and the determination to complete the project. Giovanni Agnelli was a revered industrialist and a powerful figure in the Senate. His son Edoardo was already a passionate and very able skier. He served as a sounding board for the architects and planners of the new resort, before dying tragically at the age of 35 in a plane crash. The Agnelli carried on, using top quality engineers, designers and architects already employed by Fiat for their motor cars.

The choice of site for Sestriere remains brilliant in itself. It is located at the head of two huge valleys, Susa and Chisone, on a plateau which later proved easy to link to other ski stations to create a vast skiable network. The Agnelli reportedly had a mountain retreat somewhere between the valleys close to Sestriere, so the choice of site was more than likely a well informed and personal one.

When the resort first opened its ski lifts to the public, and unveiled two vast cylindrical hotels looming from a natural amphitheatre in an alpine setting, Sestriere was the talk of not just the close-by city of Turin, but of the entire alpine world. From the very minute the enormous buildings (seen by many as a fascist symbol) appeared, they caused praise and controversy in equal measure, a polarisation that persists right up to the present day. Such was the contrast of the new structures with the natural landscape, and so different were they from the local chalet-style that they came as something of a shock. However, the buildings, the resort and its infrastructure did win massive critical acclaim from the likes of architect Le Corbusier, who admitted that he used elements of the Sestriere model for his Col de Vars summer and winter resort project. Laurent Chappis, the Frenchman who designed Courchevel, now one of the world's leading ski stations, also drew inspiration from Sestriere.

The other great vision of the Agnelli was to make Sestriere accessible to the masses, who might afford a Sunday outing, as well as the elite, who would travel from far and wide to enjoy a whole week's holiday. This is what you would expect from a family who had not just made luxury automobiles for the money-no-object crowd, but also developed popular affordable cars for the public at large.

Just after the unveiling of the controversial hotel blocks in the 1930s, Giovanni Agnelli immediately commissioned the building of a grand, traditional hotel. The Principi di Piemonte still ranks today as one of the finest chateau or palace-style alpine accommodations in Europe. But although the hotel is luxurious, it is not conveniently located for the rest of the facilities in the main part of Sestriere.

Masses of cheap condominium-style apartment blocks and complexes have sprung up over the decades, and whole new sectors of Sestriere have emerged. The town system is now something of a sprawl, including a satellite village called Borgata. Opinion on the aesthetic charm of the town is no longer mixed – it is now seen as categorically unattractive. However, the resort remains thoroughly functional.

Olympic success

Since its inception, the town has been successfully linked to other nearby ski resorts, most notably as part of a vast interlinked ski area called the *Via Lattea*, or Milky Way. The entire area received a huge boost to its economy and image after winning the bid to host the 2006 Winter Olympics. Investment poured in from local and international sponsors and developers. Most important is the construction of an impressive new infrastructure, making the region once again a world class destination. New lifts have been installed, making access to the interlinked resorts of the Milky Way that much better.

In town, many of the shop and apartment complexes had facelifts in the run-up to the Olympics and the two cylindrical towers underwent major refurbishment. The biggest new development is the Olympic Village, which is now an accommodation opportunity for holidaymakers.

2006 Winter Olympics
www.torino2006.org

Sestriere
Men's Downhill, Slalom,
Giant Slalom, Super-G;
also Women's Slalom

Sauze d'Oulx
Freestyle Moguls,
Freestyle Aerials

Pragelato
Ski Jumping,
Nordic Combined,
Cross-country skiing

Cesana San Sicario
Biathlon

Cesana Pariol
Bobsleigh, Skeleton, Luge

San Sicario Fraiteve
Women's Downhill,
Super-G, Combined

Bardonecchia
Snowboarding

Pinerolo
Curling

Turin
Ice Hockey
(Palasport Olimpico &
Torino Esposizione)

Speed Skating
(Oval Lingotto)

Short Track Speed Skating
and Figure Skating
(Palavela)

SKIING IN SESTRIERE

Skiing

Sestriere's main attraction is its altitude, which makes it as snow-sure as skiing gets in northwest Italy. Coupled with the highest skiable mountains in the whole of the Milky Way (rising to 2825m) is a new modern snow-making capacity on the lower slopes, creating a reliable destination for dedicated skiers. New lifts, including a state-of-the-art gondola, have vastly improved links to neighbouring Sauze d'Oulx and San Sicario – two of the pivotal points in the Milky Way system – thus greatly enhancing Sestriere as a skiing holiday base.

Sestriere also has the longest and most exciting slopes in the Milky Way, which is why it was selected to stage the most famous of all Winter Olympic events: the Men's Downhill. When you take the two lifts required to reach the start of this run, known locally as Kandahar Banchetta-Giovanni Nasi, you have a fine view down to the town. Further down to the right is the finishing point of the race in Borgata. It is stomach-churning to think that the world's best skiers achieve this entire descent in about two minutes. This is a must-ski run for intermediate level skiers and above, with some steepish stretches, some rugged terrain in the middle (when the piste has not been prepared for racing), a long banking curve carved through the trees, and a schuss section at the end.

Of the two main skiable sectors, Sises and Motta (the latter is where the Men's Downhill competition began in 1931), Motta has the most challenging runs on its peak. There is a wealth of easier terrain for intermediates to discover before venturing further afield into the Milky Way system.

Summer in Sestriere

A plethora of hiking and biking trails exist in Sestriere. But the resort's main claim to fame in the warm season is the 18-hole golf course, which lies at a higher altitude than any other in Europe.

Golf Club Sestriere

Piazzale G. Agnelli 4
0122 76234
season: daily 17 June-2 September
circuit: 18 holes, Par 66
facilities: driving range, putting green, trolley hire, bar & restaurant

The front nine is in fact quite tiring, with most of the holes lying on a heavily cambered slope. This means that pulling a trolley can be a strain on the wrist, since it is always threatening to tip over. Also, this mountain course has water permanently draining down on to it from the higher slopes, so wheels can get bogged down. A better system (and far less arduous) would be to select the clubs you really need and use a bag with shoulder-straps to carry them. The back nine is far flatter, and being generally above the front section, it is drier. Some of the holes are surprisingly long and challenging, but the main drama is well above you. The mountains cascade in splendid form right down to the fairways. This is an incredible setting for a golf course, and highly recommendable.

Trucioli d'Autore

Another must-visit is the studio workshop of wood carver and designer Carlo Piffer. He has lived in Sestriere for many years, and the locality is cleverly reflected in his work. Carlo was commissioned to design the wooden plaque which dedicates the golf course to the Agnelli family. His shop is situated on Via Louset in the centre of the town.

Via Lattea (Milky Way)
www.vialattea.it

The breadth of the Milky Way interlinked ski area is simply enormous. It consists of five Italian resorts in the Piedmont region: Sestriere, Sauze d'Oulx, San Sicario, Cesana and Claviere. There is also a connection to the French resort of Montgenevre.

The whole area offers 214 ski runs, covering a total of 400 kilometres of pisted slopes (120 of which are equipped with artificial snowmaking), and a wealth of off-piste skiable terrain for good measure. The slopes are linked together by 88 ski lifts. The altitude ranges from 1350m above sea level at the lowest point in Cesana, to 2800m at Mount Motta peak in Sestriere. Many of the key lifts providing the links were upgraded for the 2006 Winter Olympics and to capitalise on future use. The above statistics do not yet comprise the addition of Pragelato's new slopes, which make the interskiable region even bigger.

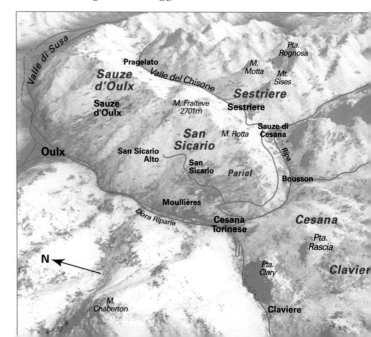

The natural layout of the slopes makes the Milky Way ideal for intermediate level skiers (the bulk of skiers worldwide), with more than 300km of blue or red-graded runs and 80km of black slopes to keep experts well challenged. It is possible to ski to all points of the Milky Way, skiing just the connecting lifts and runs, and return to your base in a single day. But this is a challenge, even for a strong intermediate skier, given the unpredictability of ski lift queues and how many falls one might have en route, not to mention the temptation to stop for numerous *aperitivi* along the way. It is better to target a different area each day, giving enough time on your daily ski adventures to sample more than just the link runs in each resort and, of course, to make liquid and lunch stops.

The Via Lattea website (see above) is excellent, with an English language option. The site has webcams positioned on the slopes and lists special offers on hotel/lift pass combinations.

MILKY WAY MAPS ARE FREE AT ALL TOURIST OFFICES

Sauze d'Oulx

Italians pronounce the x, so the name sounds like *sow-zee dooks,* whereas English speakers usually say *sow-zay dool.* Some locals still insist that Sauze was created for the British ski market. Without doubt it attracts more British holidaymakers than any other Piedmont ski station, but you will also find a lot of New Zealanders and Australians here for seasonal work. In the early days, this was a wild party town known as much for cheap booze as for skiing. It attracted a certain crowd which in turn earned the resort a bad reputation. Much has been done to counter that image and in certain respects Sauze d'Oulx has priced itself out of the problem. The resort is still extremely popular with younger British skiers and snowboarders.

If you stuck to the liveliest bars and clubs you'd be forgiven for believing this was a strictly British resort. There are signs advertising full English breakfasts, and the most popular British lagers and bitters – all to be found on draught in British-style pubs. However, alongside and below the mainly modern resort centre is the atmospheric old town

of Sauze. Here you will find narrow cobbled streets lined with shops selling clothing, local culinary specialities and traditional woodcrafts. There is also the occasional old family-run chalet or hotel, some of which have been lovingly converted into sumptuous upscale accommodation for holidaymakers.

For the first time in the resort's history, an Englishman has been voted on to the Town Council. Originally from Liverpool, Vincent Hawkins (dubbed *Vincenzo* now) has been running one of Sauze d'Oulx's finest hotels and restaurants for 20 years. With his abundant enthusiasm for the resort and region, he naturally became involved in local politics. Vincenzo now has a pivotal role in marketing the resort, but more importantly he is steering it in the direction of sophistication without alienating its youthful core market. Sauze still enjoys a reputation for being one of the few good value mainstream ski resorts in Europe.

Getting around

Tourist Office
0122 858 009
www.montagnedoc.it

In town most of the accommodation and the best bars are easily accessed on foot. Further down the hill, some areas are dependent on shuttle bus connections which are not always reliable. Many visitors opt to bring a car here. This means that you can access different areas without having to ski to them, as well as having the opportunity to explore sights that are off the beaten track. See Travel Basics (p.284) for information on car hire and the best vehicle to use in these mountains.

Skiing in Sauze d'Oulx

Although facilities have received an Olympic upgrade, more could be done to modernise the ski lifts. The slopes, while plentiful, tend to be wide and not that long, making them ideal for intermediates. They are quick to ski so you may get frustrated, especially if you find yourself on a slow lift which in turn makes queue times longer as well.

New lifts have already relieved this problem, but even more are required.

A very popular run is the Gran Pista, which has one of the longest, steepest drops of all Sauze's slopes (650m). The curves and undulations make for some rewarding non-stop cruising on what used to be a Downhill race course. Another benefit of hosting Olympic events has been an injection of funds to expand snowmaking facilities on lower-lying, more vulnerable slopes. Big decisions still need to be made on the future use of the very expensive freestyle slope, lined with snow cannons and flood lights. Due to limited road access in and out of the resort, Olympic guidelines forced Sauze to build this slope below the main part of the town. It is disappointing that it is not connected to the main slopes or ski lifts.

Nightlife

The liveliness of Sauze is no longer in the realm of the lager-lout infested 'Benidorm of the Alps' that it became in the 1980s. Prices have gone up and the most disreputable pubs and clubs have been knocked down. More sophisticated venues like **Cotton Club** are always full after midnight. **Osteria dei Vagabondi** has live music and dancing. The **Queen's Lounge** is a good choice, found in the newly refurbished four-star hotel **Relais des Alpes**.

Summer activities

There are mountain biking and hiking trails galore, but the adventure camp on woodland adjacent to the top of resort is second to none. Here you will find breathtaking entertainment for any child or adult with a head for heights. A network of fitted cables, linking the tree tops of a large area, provide 'flying fox' routes, where you traverse wide-open spaces at considerable height, using harnesses and trapeze wires. There is also tyre swinging, net climbing and many other energetic and challenging exercises, all with safety harnesses and supervision.

Jouvenceaux

Below the town of Sauze d'Oulx, on a level with the freestyle slope, is the charming little village of Jouvenceaux. Look for the medieval church of **Sant' Antonio**. There are frescoes on two outside walls: one has scenes depicting the Last Judgement; the other has a rendering of St Anthony in the centre, the Archangel Michael on the left and St Christopher on the right.

VIEW FROM OULX

Oulx

A bus or car trip down to the small town of **Oulx** (a ten minute drive) is well worth it for local flavour. On summer days the main square is often bustling with a market where woodcarvings, clothes, ready-to-eat meals, fine cheeses and hams are on sale. By night the area is lit up and alive with residents having a casual drink, or strategising over a giant chess board with enormous chess pieces fitted with handles for easy manoeuvrability. Feel free to challenge the winner.

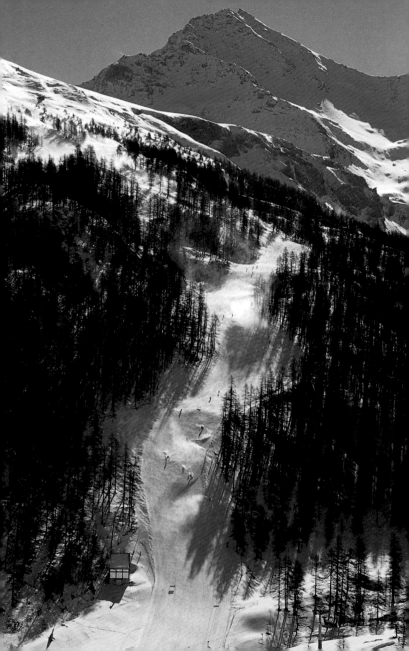

Pragelato

Tourist Office
Piazza G. Lantelme
0122 741 728
www.comune.pragelato.to.it

Just a few years ago, this sleepy little village – unconnected to the downhill ski slopes of Sestriere and the Milky Way – offered only a few kilometres of attractive cross-country ski terrain. Despite its idyllic setting and pleasing traditional architecture it had only a handful of antiquated lifts, and so the place was not rated very highly.

With the advent of Olympic funds came additional cash injections from sharp-eyed developers who never doubted the potential of this beautiful location. Pragelato is now the most exciting destination in the Piedmont mountains, with exceptional facilities for winter and summer alike. Key to its success has been the installation of a new cable car service, which links the heart of Pragelato to Sestriere. This provides easy access to the vast ski terrain of the Milky Way, and to hiking and mountain-biking trails in summer. Locals campaigned for more than 20 years to get this cable car link, but funding did not arrive until the Olympic bid was won and Pragelato was earmarked to host ski jumping and cross-country ski events. All facilities have been upgraded to support these two sports for many years to come.

Between the old town and the ski jumps lies a large prairie with a brand new building erected on it. There are several piste-bashing machines on the lower floors. Conference rooms, bar and restaurant are above, with everything connected by ramps and a lift for the disabled. Built to accommodate the administration needs of officials and athletes during the Olympics, it now provides all the maintenance required for the vastly increased amount of cross-country ski terrain, as well as a sophisticated snow-making station capable of providing cover for cross-country ski routes. In summer, this building is the club house for the new nine-hole golf course (opened in 2006), named after the Agnelli family, which provides visitors to this part of Piedmont with a superb extra facility.

Pragelato New Village has to compete with the very best developments in the entire region. A complex of 205 beautifully appointed apartments is next door to the new cable car station. Built in local stone, wood and slate, everything is in keeping with the natural surroundings. Two and three-floor apartment clusters are linked by little bridges crossing streams. In summer the gardens are filled with more than a thousand different plant varieties. The whole complex, incorporating three bars, a restaurant, modern spa centre and supervised children's area, is run like a hotel from a main reception. Visitors have the choice of self-catering accommodation or half/full board.

The jump site

Super-modern ski jump towers have hydraulic jacks which adjust the ramp gradient. These are floodlit for evening use, providing quite a spectacle when viewed from the old town of Pragelato. A new hotel has been erected on the side of the jump site with state-of-the-art sports facilities to attract youth clubs and competition teams for training purposes.

Cross-country skiing

Aficionados claim that the long ski trails, still maintained, through the forest from the rear of Pragelato, are one of the greatest cross-country itineraries in the world. They offer stunning natural scenery and 'secret' views of the surrounding mountains along the way. During the summer they also attract hundreds of hikers.

Downhill

Pragelato also harbours some off-piste skiing gems, especially the 2.2km run from the Clot de la Soma, accessible via existing local ski lifts, which is considered to be one of the best back-country ski runs in Piedmont.

Other sights

Museo del Costume

(Costume Museum)
Via San Giovanni (Rivet Hamlet)
Saturday 15.00-18.00
Sunday 10.00-12.30/15.00-18.00

This delightful little museum is contained in a centuries-old farmhouse, with exhibits donated by the long-standing families of Pragelato, who are passionate about their history. As well as showing colourful local clothing, exhibits illustrate how people dressed and survived in bitter winter conditions. Outside the museum's windows you can see the state-of-the-art athletic infrastructure, making for an instant and striking contrast of cultures.

The Hurdy-Gurdy Man

Villa San Giovanni 1 (Pragelato)
01220 8959 (call before visiting)
Open daily except Thursday
Guido Ronchail is a local wood sculptor who also makes musical instruments, most notably the *ghironda*, an Italian version of the hurdy-gurdy. If you're lucky he'll play a few tunes for you.

Miss Moo

A sight to behold is the Miss Moo competition which usually takes place on the third Saturday of July. This is the alpine cows' version of Miss World. Local farmers turn out their top breeds in full regalia. The assembled judging panel vote on best horns, udders, coats, and bulk for edibility. Then they taste each cow's cream and milk produce. The final vote is on the all-round turnout of the cows. The bovine beauties are often dressed elaborately, with chandelier-style contraptions on their horns. The outright winner is gifted a garland à la Miss World, and taken on a parade of honour. It has been suggested that the victorious Miss Moo should be officially interviewed, but this has yet to happen.

San Sicario & Cesana

Tourist Office
0122 89202

Dedicated skiers who want to get up early and ski hard all day, and explore the extremities of the Milky Way without needing too much in the way of resort ambience and après-ski life, will do well to stay at San Sicario. Cesana is another small resort, more traditional in style than San Sicario, but with an invasive main road running through it. If the atmosphere of a well-equipped resort attracts you, then Sestriere, Sauze d'Oulx or Bardonecchia represent far better choices.

Skiing

San Sicario is a tiny, modern purpose-built resort and is practically a one-hotel ski station, which has benefited hugely from new lifts. Most important is the cable car link between the resort and the equally tiny resort of Cesana. The ride takes just eight minutes, making for vastly improved links within the Milky Way system.

New parallel ski lifts at Fraiteve guarantee a link between San Sicario, Sauze d'Oulx and Sestriere, so although small in base terms the area has a pivotal role in the Milky Way. The best run on the local slopes is the Women's Olympic Downhill course. From San Sicario's base at 1700m it takes two chairlifts and a drag lift to reach the Fraiteve peak at 2700m. The initial section of the piste is steep before widening out into a series of exhilarating bends mixed with steep drop-offs and flatter sections, making it ideal for high speed cruising.

Bobsleigh

The two resorts now share the most modern and ecologically sound bobsleigh track of any resort in the world. Much care was taken in building the track, as the scale of the work involved would inevitably have a massive effect on the chosen mountainside. When the Olympic bid was won by

Turin, local authorities were sceptical and even considered asking Courchevel in France to host the event on its existing bobsleigh track. But when coherent plans were submitted for what would be the most advanced bobsleigh facility in the world, the decision to build the track on the Pariol slope, off the main road linking San Sicario and Cesana, was taken.

The track is now the envy of bobsleighers worldwide, and it moreover offers post-Olympics visitors the opportunity to ride an Olympic four-man bobsleigh with professionals front and rear, an experience which makes any theme park thrill-ride seem tame. A number of plans are in place to offer tourists a variety of options to ride the track on different styles of sleigh.

From the bobsleigh track there is a view of Europe's highest fortress on top of **Mont Chaberton**. At 3136m, the fort was built at this elevation in the early 1900s to protect against possible French invasion. With its giant cannon, easily able to target armies below, the fort was thought to be invincible and it remained undamaged for 20 years. Unfortunately, when the fortress was attacked for the first time in 1940, the huge guns were destroyed within hours by French specialists using state-of-the-art howitzers from 14km away. The fort is still there, and can be reached by a difficult hike of about three hours. Better to enjoy the spectacle from the top of the bobsleigh track or from nearby Cesana.

Summer fun

The first weekend in July sees Cesana hosting the annual 'Carton Rapid Race', also known as the Cardboard Boat Race. Contestants bring their own cardboard and are given two hours and one roll of sticky tape to make a boat capable of navigating a pre-selected course on a local river. Most craft perish quickly, but as the race has been run for some years now, a class of experts has arisen. You will see some astonishing inventions and some hilarious failures. For more details inquire at the local tourist office.

Claviere

Tourist Office
0122 878856
www.claviere.it

Another small village, Claviere is also part of the Milky Way. You can ski here from Cesana and if you continue on, you'll be skiing into France. Claviere is just across the border from the French resort of Montgenèvre, and there is bus transportation to the train station at Oulx. No Olympic events were held here, but the area was an official training site for alpine and cross-country skiing (16km to Montgenèvre and back). The town lacks a wide variety of ski runs, but the local sports centre has ice skating. In summer there are facilities for golf, hiking and horse riding.

Golf Club Claviere

Strada Nazionale 47
0122 878917
golf.claviere@lavazza.it
season: daily 15 June-15 September
circuit: 9 holes, Par 64
facilities: driving range, putting green, bar & restaurant
Near the French border, this is a small course with an attractive clubhouse.

Bardonecchia

Tourist Office
0122 99032
www.comune.bardonecchia.to.it

Though this resort is not connected to the Milky Way system, its uniqueness of character, challenging ski slopes and vastly improved resort infrastructure – due to hosting the snowboarding events in the Olympic Games – give it excellent winter and summer credentials.

At 1300m above sea level, this is a border town, close by the entrances (rail and road) of the Fréjus tunnels, which link Italy with France. The town claims to be Italy's first ski resort. As local history has it, two Norwegians, the Smith brothers, started building ski jumps back here just after the turn of the 20th century, and by 1909 the first national ski championships took place on the slopes above Bardonecchia. There are earlier reports of ski competitions – but not national events – being staged at nearby Claviere and Montgenèvre. Such is the belief in skiing's origins in Bardonecchia that a marketing slogan for the resort is 'Cradle of Skiing'. One of the vast new hotels built here for the Olympics is called Campo Smith Resort, in honour of the founding brothers. Doubtless the Agnelli, who built nearby Sestriere (arguably the first dedicated ski resort to popularise skiing in Italy) would have something to say about Bardonecchia's claims, but the border resort was an established centre long before Sestriere was an apple in Giovanni Agnelli's eye.

Bardonecchia's plethora of wealthy Torinese, who own second homes here, have been guilty of letting their chalets and town houses remain boarded up during peak holiday times, making the town unappealing to foreign visitors. This clique was largely broken with the arrival of the Olympic Games which brought in new rules for property owners. There are now large hotels with excellent facilities for skiers and summer hikers. One of these comes courtesy of the Olympic Village, which was built to house some 900 athletes in 400 rooms. It is now part hotel, part self-catering centre for holidaymakers.

Skiing and Snowboarding

The 140km of skiing trails is split into four main areas.
These are accessed from separate lifts that leave from
different parts of the resort. The Colomion, Les Arnauds
and Melezet sectors are linked by lifts and ski trails half way
up the mountains. Almost all this terrain is intermediate
level skiing. However, the Olympic half pipe at Melezet
will provide expert trick skiers and snowboarders ample
opportunities to be challenged. The walls to the half pipe,
more than 5m high, are at such an acute angle that this is
one of the most technical half pipes in the world.

From the opposite side of town you can take the chairlift up
to the Jafferau sector which has more challenging descents,
especially from the top elevations which reach 2750m. For
further hardcore skiing, you can hire a guide and take one
of the many off-piste excursions. The most popular involves
a short climb with skis from the top of the Jafferau sector
at Plan delle Selle from where you access the backside of
Jafferau mountain and enjoy a long and rewarding run
down to Rochemolles. Guides can arrange to meet you and
drive you back to the main lifts.

Summer in Bardonecchia

Summer is as exciting as winter if you want an active break. Mountain biking and hiking trails are in more abundance here than most other parts of alpine Piedmont. There is a nine hole golf course in the valley adjacent to the town, pitch-and-putt in size but amply entertaining. You will also find swimming pools and tennis courts in many hotels.

Most of the locals head up the main Colomion chairlift to Plan del Sole where, at 1550m, there is a charming plateau affording excellent views of the surrounding mountains. This is the perfect setting for scores of sundeck loungers, café-style dining tables, and a couple of good quality restaurants and outside barbecues to keep you refreshed all day. There is a good family area with many playground swings, slides, and bouncy castles on site to keep young children entertained too.

Slow Food Trail

During July, the annual **Slow Food Trail** called *Degustando Bardonecchia* is not to be missed. For the price of a few euros you get a five course meal, Piedmont style. Each of the five serving stations is manned by a top local chef, and the route is spread out over an easy hiking trail in the mountains. Each stage is a few kilometres in length, so that your appetite has been restored by the time you reach the next station.

Start with *antipasti* and some appropriately light wines, move on to the *primi pasti* course (normally a pasta with other wines), then to the meat station with heavier full-bodied wines from some of the great Piedmont regions: Barbera, Barbaresco and Roero. Take a long break here and enjoy the walk to the cheese station where the display of whole local cheeses is superb in itself. Try a mixed platter, accompanied by local wines. Buy some cheese to take home, vacuum-packed on the mountain.

The grand finale comes in the form of some delicious dessert wines served up with decadent chocolate canapés.

River Sports on Dora Riparia

335 628 2727
www.okadventure.it

In summer, the fast flowing waters of the Riparia River are used for rafting, canoeing, kayaking and hydrospeed (body rafting with a padded wet suit and plastic float). For the very brave there is canyoning, which involves abseiling the path of a waterfall, leaping into rock pools and some underwater tunneling. All levels of expertise are provided for, including lessons and trips for total beginners. The activities take place at different sites along the river depending on the time of year. Most are based within 20 minutes of Sauze d'Oulx.

Lago Laux

Albergo Ristorante
0121 83 944
www.hotelaux.it

About 30 minutes drive from Sestriere, en route to Fenestrelle, there is a small natural lake near Usseaux. This is a lovely spot to sunbathe during summer. The lake is stocked with trout and you can rent fishing equipment. If you want to take your catch home, the charge is € 8 per kilo.

Summer or winter, this is a great place to stop for lunch. The Albergo restaurant in the lakeside Lago Laux Hotel is well-appointed, serving Piedmont and Provençal specialities. Enquire at the hotel about wildlife photography expeditions in the surrounding nature parks of Troncea and Orsieras.

Il **Forte di Fenestrelle** (Fenestrelle Fortress)

0121 83 600 (times and costs change – check before booking a tour)
www.fortedifenestrelle.com

Commissioned in the 1700s, this monster of a fortress became the biggest single cohesive construction in the world after the Great Wall of China. Built by Piedmontese forces, who wanted to keep the French out of the high Chisone Valley, it comprises three forts built on a steeply rising mountain ridge. The forts are linked by 4,000 steps covering 500 vertical metres – the Empire State Building is only two thirds of this height. The stairs between the forts are covered so that troops could not be seen shifting from one part to the other. A fortress and a prison combined, Fenestrelle was never attacked. Reports of the tough military regime and hostile conditions inside – coupled with its formidable size – kept the fortress safe.

In winter it was a very cold place. An account written by one famous prisoner, Cardinal Bartolomeo Pacca, Secretary to Pope Pio VII, claimed that the cells were often dark for 16 hours a day in winter. At the higher elevations of the fortress, snow would not melt entirely – even in July and August. Aided by fierce howling winds and moisture from snow outside, the inside of the prison walls would sometimes freeze, and prisoners reported they were *'living in a village of crystal'*. Punishment in this fortress was severe: with back packs filled with bricks, prisoners would be made to run up the steps from bottom to top. If they arrived later than the alotted time, they would be made to do it again. Or if they were too exhausted, they might be shot on arrival.

You are required to book a guided tour in order to see inside the fortress. Tours range from one to several hours. Be warned: the tours are physically demanding. The higher you are on Mount Pinaia, the harder it is to breathe. Many of the covered stairways, turrets and cannon rooms are damp, making breathing more difficult.

Avigliana and Lago Grande

Driving from Turin to the mountains will usually involve
the A32/E70, a modern motorway that gets you to the
mountain resorts in about 90 minutes. This is an excellent
road, but high speed driving means that a few important
sights will be missed, notably Avigliana and nearby Sacra di
San Michele.

Avigliana has several buildings, dating from the late
medieval period. These can be seen as you go up towards
the central square, dedicated to Amadeo VII (1360-91), the
Savoy known as the 'Red Count'. The remains of his castle
are found at the top of the hill. The renaissance church of
San Giovanni is also worth a visit.

Nearby **Lago Grande di Avigliana** has superb mountain
views. In peak summer months this is a popular place for
sunbathing, waterskiing and canoeing. Carlo Allais, former
World University Waterskiing Champion, is owner and
instructor at **Club Sport Nautici** (339 6072923). At the height
of the season boats are running from 9am until 9pm. A
good spot for lunch is **Restaurant da Willy** (0119 369049).

Sacra di San Michele

011 939130
www.sacradisanmichele.com
09.30-12.30; 15.00-17.00 Mon-Sat (Oct-Mar)
09.30-12.00; 14.40-17.00 Sun & holidays (Oct-Mar)
open one hour later in summer season
closed Mondays; disabled lift facility
admission €4

FROM AVIGLIANA, FOLLOW THE SIGNS TO THE LAGHI (LAKES) AND
THEN ON TO THE SACRA.

Perched on a mountain top and visible from miles away,
the monastery of Sacra di San Michele is much more than
a beautiful landmark: it is the official symbol of Piedmont.
Any visitor would agree this hallowed place is worthy of that
status. The monastery was built along the great medieval road,
known as the *Via Francigena*, that connected northern Europe
with Rome and the Holy Land. The first Benedictine abbey

was constructed between 983 and 987, above and around three pre-existing chapels dedicated to St Michael. Over the years, several churches were built and rebuilt on the site of the original chapels. The large basilica dates from the 12th century; what visitors see today it the result of a restoration completed in 1937.

The monastery and church have always been the recipients of generous art donations. Inside the church and to the left, the *Great Fresco* (1505) depicts the burial of Christ and the Virgin's death and assumption into heaven. In the Old Choir, look for the 16th century *Tryptych with the Madonna and Child* attributed to Defendente Ferrari. Also by Ferrari is the *Virgin on the throne and Saints*.

In 1991 Pope John Paul II made his own pilgrimage to the Sacra di San Michele. Despite his advanced age and ill health, he managed to climb the 300 steps to the entrance. From the terrace, where the views are spectacular and peaceful in equal measure, the Pope blessed the Susa Valley. In his speech he said: *'Silence, loneliness, attention and prayer, favoured here by natural, artistic and historical surroundings beyond compare, can only arouse good thoughts and feed a man's heart...'*

LAKES

ISOLA BELLA, LAGO MAGGIORE

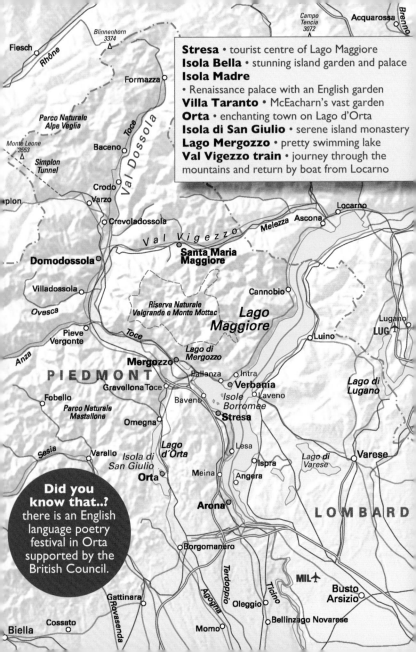

Stresa • tourist centre of Lago Maggiore
Isola Bella • stunning island garden and palace
Isola Madre
• Renaissance palace with an English garden
Villa Taranto • McEacharn's vast garden
Orta • enchanting town on Lago d'Orta
Isola di San Giulio • serene island monastery
Lago Mergozzo • pretty swimming lake
Val Vigezzo train • journey through the mountains and return by boat from Locarno

Did you know that..? there is an English language poetry festival in Orta supported by the British Council.

Lago Maggiore is all about gardens and beautiful scenery.
Lago d'Orta and Isola di San Giulio are both exquisite.

Lago Maggiore is a finger-shaped lake with its northern-most tip located in Switzerland. The sunny western shore is situated in Piedmont, the eastern shore in Lombardy. Of course, being Italy, there is rivalry between the two sides of the lake, but it is the Piedmont shore that has a history of tourism together with the best gardens and a wider choice of sights.

The four main resorts of Lago Maggiore are Stresa and Verbania in the centre, Arona to the south and Locarno (in Switzerland) to the north. There is a ferry service along the lake from Locarno to Arona, a journey that is worth making for the views alone.

Stresa and Verbania are located at Lago Maggiore's widest point. Nearby are three islands: Isola Bella, Isola Madre, and Isola dei Pescatori. The sublime beauty of Isola Bella and Isole Madre's gardens, palaces and views should not be missed. Isola dei Pescatori is an old fishermen's island that now has some excellent shops. A ferry service to all the islands departs from Stresa with stops at Baveno and Verbania.

Lago d'Orta is a smaller lake west of Stresa. The main town of Orta is located on the eastern shore, and is the departure point for Isola di San Giulio. Ringed by mountains, Lago Mergozzo is a tiny lake northwest of Verbania, which is perfect for swimming or playing around in small rowing boats. The water is clear, the air is fresh and it's quiet and peaceful.

Continue in a northerly direction along the motorway from Mergozzo and you will reach the alpine market town of Domodossola – where seven valleys meet.

Stresa

This elegant 19th century resort has been popular with British tourists since the Grand Tour. Many of the original stately hotels still line the promenade facing the lake and Isola Bella. Ernest Hemingway came to Stresa as a young soldier in 1918. His one week's convalescent leave was the inspiration for his bestselling novel *A Farewell to Arms*.

GRAND HOTEL DES ILES BORROMÉES

Stresa lies at the foot of Monte Mottarone on the shores of the central and most populated region of Lago Maggiore. On the opposite side of the mountain is Lago d'Orta. A cable car to the top of Monte Mottarone departs from Piazza Lido at the north end of Stresa.

In central Stresa there is a carpark and ferry terminal at Piazza Marconi, where boats depart every 30 minutes for the Borromean Islands in the centre of the lake. This is also a stop on the Arona-Locarno ferry network that serves all of Lake Maggiore with stops on both sides of the lake (but not the islands).

At the south end of Stresa is Villa Pallavicino, a large park and zoo with animals and exotic birds. It offers a nice day out, with picnic areas and a colourful train for children.

Piazza Cadorna

Stresa's central piazza is full of restaurants with outdoor seating and live music. The different styles of entertainment, from pedal organ to rock guitar can either be amusing or discordant, depending on your point of view. However there is not much to do at night in Stresa: everything closes by 11pm. The town of Orta is more lively at night.

Settimane Musicale di Stresa
August-September
www.settimanemusicale.net
Festival office: Via Carducci 38
0323 31095/30459
concerts €30-60

The world's best conductors, orchestras, soloists and new composers perform in venues around the lake. Inaugurated in 1962 with concerts on Isola Bella, the festival – founded by Venetian lawyer Italo de Daverio to honour his composer father – increases in popularity every year.

Tourist offices
Ferry Terminal, P. Marconi 16
0323 30150
March-October
10.00-12.30, 15.00-18.30 daily
November-March
closed Sat pm, closed Sunday
Book garden and lake tours at the Tourist office. Staff can also help plan your itinerary for the train-boat journey to Domodossola and Locarno.

Villa Pallavicino

0323 31533
www.parcozoopallavicino.it
09.00-18.00 daily March-October
playground, bar, restaurant,
gift shop

A TRAIN FROM STRESA'S
IMBARCADERO SQUARE TO VILLA
PALLAVICINO OPERATES DAILY
FROM 09.30-16.30

The house was built in
1855 as a holiday home for
Queen Margherita and King
Umberto I. The architect
was Ruggero Borghi, a
friend of Manzoni's and
the site chosen is one of the
loveliest on Lago Maggiore.

A later owner, the Duke of Vallimbrosa laid out the park in
naturalistic style and introduced plants such as the Tulip
Tree, *Liriodendron tulipifera*, rare in Europe at that time. In
1862 the villa became the property of the Pallavicino family,
who laid out the gardens as we see them today.

In the grounds there is a zoo, planned by the present Prince
Pallavicino's mother. Here llamas, kangaroos and zebras
mix with flamingos, toucans and many other exotic species
roaming freely through the grounds. This is a good place to
take children, and there are picnic areas and beautiful views
across the lake.

The park also contains numerous old trees, including
majestic sequoias, ginkgos, planes, oaks, magnolias, larches
and a superb Cedar of Lebanon in front of the villa. There
are also vestiges of the formal gardens with open lawns,
azaleas and a large rose garden. At the back of the parterre
there is an enchanting area, a simple path of wildflowers
bordered by cypresses curved so as to create a row of
arches, which give the impression of a cloister opening out
onto water.

Cable car, Funivia

Funivia per Il Mottarone
Piazzale Lido 8
0323 30295
departure every 20 minutes
09.30-17.50 daily
Stresa-Mottarone-Stresa €13, child €7.50 (with garden €13.50)
Stresa-Alpino-Stresa €8, child €5 (with garden €8.50)
Alpino-Mottarone-Alpino €7.50, child €4.50
€9 single ticket with mountain bike

The Stresa-Alpino-Mottarone cable car takes 40 people
per trip to an altitude of 1491m (4,845ft). The Mottarone,
situated between Lago Maggiore and Lago d'Orta, offers
a 360-degree view spanning the Po Valley to the alpine
summits. On a clear day you can see Monte Rosa and seven
lakes: Maggiore, Orta, Mergozzo, Varese, Camabbio, Monate
and Biandronno.

At the top of the Mottarone there are hiking trails in
summer and ski trails in winter. Descend by mountain bike
on properly marked paths, or relax at a table in one of the
restaurants. It is possible to drive to the Alpine Garden (see
below) and continue your journey by cable car to the top of
the mountain.

Giardino Botanico Alpinia

0323 30295
09.30-18.00 daily, April-Oct
€2 garden only

The garden has an altitude of 800m (2,600ft) and stretches
over 9.6 acres (4 hectares) of land. It was founded by Igino
Ambrosini and Giuseppe Rossi in 1934. A speciality of
the garden are the 55-plus species of alpine and subalpine
plants, in addition to species found in the Caucasus,
northern China and mountainous areas of Japan.

Botanico Alpinia has one the finest viewpoints over Lago
Maggiore and the Borromeo Islands.

The Islands

Stresa is the main departure point for ferries to three beautiful islands in Lago Maggiore: Isola Bella, Isola Madre and Isola dei Pescatori. Isola Bella and Isola Madre belong to the Borromeo family and are sometimes called *Isole Borromee*.

Isola Madre is the largest of the three islands, and has a large English garden. Isola Bella is considered the prettiest island because of its beautiful baroque garden. There are also good restaurants and several shops. Jewellery sold here can be less expensive than in Stresa. Isola dei Pescatori belongs to the Italian state. *'Andare a pesca'* means 'to fish', and the island is still populated by fishermen.

Ferry information

Navigazione Lago Maggiore
www.navigazionelaghi.it
800 551 801

stops:
Stresa, Carciano, Isola Bella, Isola dei Pescatori, Baveno, Isola Madre, Pallanza, Verbania (Villa Taranto), Intra

times:
07.10-19.10 Mon-Fri
08.10-19.10 Sat-Sun

cost:
• return ticket to Isola Bella €5.20 adult €2.60 child
• return ticket to Isola Madre €7 adult €3.60 child
• return ticket for 3 Islands €10 adult €5 child
• 3 Islands and Villa Taranto €11 adult €6 child

BEWARE OF TOUTS IN BLUE CAPS WHO OPERATE FROM THE FERRY TERMINAL CAR PARKS – THEY WANT TO SELL YOU A WATER TAXI AND HAVE BEEN KNOWN TO DENY THE EXISTENCE OF A FERRY.

VIEW FROM ISOLA BELLA GARDENS: *FACING PAGE*

Isola Bella

0323 932 483 (visitor office)
www.borromeoturismo.it
09.00-17.30 daily, March-October, Sundays and holidays until 18.00
audio guides available in English
€10 Isola Bella only, €15 including Isola Madre

It must be every garden lover's dream: to own a small island in an idyllic setting where the climate is kind; to build a fairy-tale house and fill it with beautiful objects, and to surround the whole with a magnificent garden. The Borromeo did this not once but twice, when they carved Isola Bella and Isola Madre from bare rock on Lago Maggiore.

The Borromeo are a wealthy and powerful Milanese family who boast cardinals, princes and even a saint amongst their ancestors. The family still use the island as a summer residence, retaining the upper floors of the palace and part of the gardens for their private use.

Named not only after beauty but also after Carlo Borromeo's wife Isabella, the concept of Isola Bella is pure Baroque: a rocky outcrop has been transformed into a monster galleon at anchor on the lake. The solid palazzo on the north of the island represents the prow of the ship, while to the south a magnificent water garden forms the bridge. To reach the bridge, walk from deck to deck up the balustraded terraces until you reach an area bristling with statuary suggestive of masts. From here you have a sweeping view across the lake towards the distant snow-capped Alps.

The dream

It was in 1630 that Carlo Borromeo III conceived his idea to create an island garden to look like a vessel, permanently anchored alongside the town of Stresa. The family lived on Isola Madre, and had been buying up parcels of land on the island known as *Isola Inferiore*. Cesare Borromeo had successfuly petitioned the local bishop to transfer the parish to Isola dei Pescatori; and so Carlo was free to build his vision. He renamed the island *Isola Isabella* in honour of

Family symbols

Three symbols are incoporated into the Borromeo coat of arms: the unicorn on the left standing for purity, the camel on the right symbolising humility and the lemon beneath representing the properties of the family on Lago Maggiore. At the top is the word HUMILITAS, motto of the family's saintly forebear, San Carlo.

Three intertwined rings symbolise the union and loyalty of three noble families: Borromeo, Visconti and Sforza. The rings intersect in such a way that no one ring can be removed. This represents their vow to always remain unified and never descend into petty rivalry.

his wife, Isabella d'Adda and commissioned Bartolomeo Scarione to begin construction. Carlo's original plan called for a modest house in the centre of a large garden. It was Carlo's son Vitaliano VI, with funds from his cousin Cardinal Gilberto III, who enlarged the palace and added to the gardens. The island's name changed over time to Isola Bella.

The palace

Walk through the **weapons room** with its 17th and 18th century armour to reach the **main staircase**, two sets of granite steps covered with a vaulted Wedgwood blue ceiling with white stucco trim. The balustrade is made of reddish Macciavecchia marble.

On the walls are large emblems crowned with portraits of the Borromeo family and prominent Italian families to whom they were related. Look for the Medici balls, Barberini bees and the Farnese lion, and family crests for Popes Pius IV, Urban VIII and Innocent XI.

On the first floor you enter the **medal room**, part of the new wing built by Vitaliano for banquets and important occasions. A large portrait of Vitaliano dominates the room. Off to the side is the **throne room**, used for hearings and named after the monumental carved chair it holds. Look for six large grotesque figures atop the red marble pilasters on the wall, who appear to be supporting the ceiling. Also in the room is an 18th century carved cabinet held aloft by two figures.

The prettiest room in the palace is the **reception room**. It is three stories high and was intended to be the original entrance to the building. Adding to the beauty of the room are the many stunning views from the large windows.

The next room was the music room, but is now known as the **Stresa Conference room**, after a meeting held there in April 1935. Mussolini convened the meeting following Hitler's violation of the Treaty of Versailles. Il Duce met with representatives of France and Great Britain to present a united front against German rearmament. The 'Stresa Front' fell apart after Italy's attack on Ethiopia. As well as a collection of musical instruments, the room displays several works by Flemish artist Pieter Mullier.

Known as 'Il Tempesta', the painter was a friend of the Borromeo family. He was accused in 1676 of the murder of his first wife and three years later was sentenced to 20 years imprisonment. Languishing in a Genoese jail, he wrote letters to the Borromeo and to the Spanish governor of Milan. Mullier's eloquent pleas secured his release in 1685. In gratitude, he painted several works for the palace.

In 1797, after a victorious campaign in Italy, Napoleon and Josephine arrived with a retinue of 60 soldiers. Husband and wife slept in the canopied bed in **Napoleon's room**. Reports of the time tell us that the wife was more courteous than the General, and that everyone was thankful when his stay proved brief. Napoleon left after only two days, and many of the rooms were said to be already dirty and bad-smelling.

Look out for Giovanni Crespi's *St Francis in Ecstasy with two Angels*. In the **library** is a painting of Venice from the school of Canaletto.

Named after a Neapolitan painter, the **Luca Giordano room** displays three of the artist's works, illustrating stories from Ovid's *Metamorphoses*: *The Triumph of Galatea, The Judgement of Paris* and *The Abduction of Europa*. It was said that Giordano painted with both hands simultaneously. In the small study you will find a charming painting of two dogs with a cradle, by Elisabetta Borromeo.

Zuccarelli's room commemorates the 18th century Florentine artist Francesco Zuccarelli. Look for three of his paintings in the room, which are interesting for their historic views of Lago Maggiore.

The extraordinary **ballroom** appears to be constructed of marble, but is an example of trompe l'oeil work. The reason painted plaster was used instead of stone is because it made for better acoustics. Classical guitarist Andre Segovia gave a concert here in 1960.

Below the palace are the **grottoes**, rooms entirely covered in mosaics incorporating black and white pebbles and red and black mirrored marble slabs. The third grotto has a lovely marble statue of *Venus Sleeping,* by Gaetano Monti from the school of Canova. Climb the elliptical stone staircase to return to the first floor.

Walk through the fresco room to **Margarita Medici's room**. Margarita was the sister of Pius IV, wife of Gilberto II Borromeo and mother of San Carlo. In *Portrait of Countess Margarita Medici*, we see her with her children, Federico II, Carlo (holding flowers) and Vitaliano V.

Pass through the octagon to the **tapestry gallery**, essentially a corridor leading to the garden. Take a moment to look at the tapestry closest to the garden. An optical illusion makes the river appear to flow in one direction if you stand on the left, and in the opposite direction if you view the tapestry from the right.

The garden

Emerge from the tapestry gallery into **Diana's atrium**, a rounded lower courtyard containing a statue of Diana. This area 'below decks' connects the palace with the garden. Approach the garden proper by mounting a staircase made up of two asymmetrical flights of steps, which so successfully conceal a twist in direction that you think you are walking into the garden in a straight line. The shape of the island on which the garden is built did not allow for a linear axis from one end to the other, and so the architect Giovanni Angelo Crivelli conceived this clever design strategy.

The garden was begun in 1631 and took 40 years to complete. In Crivelli's design the dominant element is stone, while plants play a secondary role. Crivelli designed the **terraces** on the southern tip of the island to resemble the stern of a galleon. In the area amidships between the palace and the terraced stern, Crivelli built a beautiful fountain, or water theatre, an essential part of all baroque gardens.

The **Massimo theatre** cleverly conceals a reservoir of water pumped up from the lake, and is elaborate in the extreme. The exterior is decorated with shell motifs, pebble-encrusted pilasters, tufa-lined niches containing statues of water nymphs and is topped by a rearing unicorn – the emblem of the Borromeo. Terracotta pots of citrus edge the steps which rise up through five tiers. White peacocks flaunt themselves throughout, and the whole has been compared to the hanging gardens of Babylon.

The intricacy of design and engineering skills involved in creating the garden remind us of the Baroque period's love of the dramatic. Time and the growth of vegetation have blurred the original concept: in the 19th century, magnolias, azaleas and camellias were added to the earlier plantings of grass, low *broderies* and a few clipped evergreens. To the purist, these additions may detract from the original intent, but the beauty of the blue water lilies, large-leaved hydrangeas, palms and roses is quite unforgettable.

ISOLA BELLA TERRACES AND LILY POND

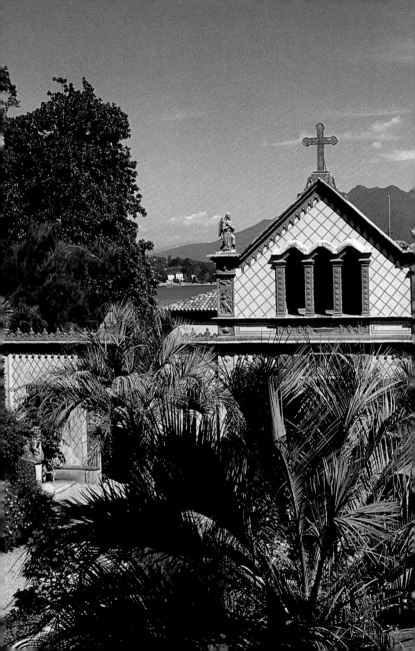

Isola Madre

0323 932 483 (visitor office)
www.borromeoturismo.it
09.00-17.30 daily, Mar-Oct; Sundays and Holidays until18.00
audio guides available in English
€9 Isola Madre only, €15 including Isola Bella

Isola Madre is the largest of Lago Maggiore's islands. It was purchased by the Borromeo in 1501 and became the site of their first home in this region. Unlike the baroque splendour of the palace on Isola Bella, the house here was originally a Renaissance villa dating from the 1500s which the family rebuilt in the 1700s. The rooms are much simpler and decorated with less ornament.

Palazzo del Isola Madre

Begin on the first floor in the **fireplace room**, with paintings by Giovanni Danedi, most notably his *Destruction of Jericho*. Walk through the green and yellow bedrooms to reach rooms containing puppet theatres.

Teatrino delle Marionette

Marionette theatre of the 18th and 19th centuries was an elaborate form of puppetry with stories based on fantasy, but not intended for children. In an age without film or television, puppetry was serious entertainment for grown-ups. The collection of scenery, sets and puppets exhibited in the next three rooms is the highlight of the palace and one of the most important in Europe.

A puppet theatre stage is set up in **room 1**, complete with curtains, wings and movable backdrops. Everything functioned as in a real theatre, and was made to scale. Alessandro Sanquirico was a top stage designer for La Scala in Milan. He worked for the Borromeo at this palace until 1832, painting and building the stages and sets on display. Performances incorporated drawings, painting and special effects of sound and light. Look for the 'cloud machine' and other devices used to create theatrical effects.

In **room 2** are the hand-painted puppets. Each puppet has a different face and a unique expression. You can easily imagine the characters they originally played. **Room 3** has a theatre of horror, a diabolical stage in dark colours where the more frightening performances took place.

A stairway leads down to the ground floor. Proceed through various rooms to the exquisite **Venetian drawing room**. This has a high canopied ceiling supported by columns and decorated with plants and flowers. Suspended in the ceiling is a massive chandelier of Murano glass.

From the window you can see the 19th century **Sepulchral chapel**, where in 2003 the youngest Borromeo married the youngest Agnelli, uniting the dynasty of Lago Maggiore with the dynasty of Turin.

Proceed to the adjoining **reception room**, which also contains a beautiful Murano glass chandelier.

The garden

In contrast to the gardens of Isola Bella, on Isola Madre plants rather than buildings reclaim centre stage. During the 16th century oranges, olives and vines were grown on the island, but the favourable climate encouraged the introduction of exotics. In the 1800s the gardens were laid out to show off the impressive botanical collection which had been accumulated by the Borromeo family. The result is a paradise garden admired by everyone from Napoleon to Queen Victoria.

The south and west sides, which can be up to 4°C warmer than the rest of the island, are made up of terraces where red roses are set off by the blue of the sky and the silver of the lake. Scented and aromatic trees and shrubs fringe the paths, and a pergola hung with wisteria and primrose jasmine leads down to the waterside.

Turning northwards the path winds its way through an English-style woodland. Beyond glades of tree rhododendron and camellias, an amazing old Swamp Cypress stands surrounded by strange 'snorkels' which protrude from the grass, preventing the tree from suffocating. Beyond this is perhaps the most memorable tree in the garden, a huge 200-year-old Himalayan Cypress, the blue-grey foliage of which hangs like curtains to the ground. Almost as impressive however, is a 125-year-old coconut palm on the top terrace which apparently yields 3,000 nuts a year.

At the centre of the garden, between the chapel and the palazzo, is the warmest spot on the island. Taking advantage of the heat is an attractive little Italian-style garden with a grotto and lily pond which, at the right season, is enlivened by the sound of green frogs barking like dogs as they mate.

The harmonious combination of flowery sun-baked terraces with dappled green woodlands makes this garden a wonderful place to spend a couple of hours. Be sure to allow plenty of time to relax and do not rush your visit.

Isola dei Pescatori

The fishermen's island is a summertime tourist
attraction that in the off-season reverts back to its
roots. The small parish church, San Vittore, is light
and airy with beautiful silver candlesticks on the
altar. The island has many excellent fish restaurants
and superb views across the lake to Stresa, Baveno
and Isola Bella.

Gulf of Pallanza

Also known as the Bay of Borromeo, this area is one of the loveliest parts of Lago Maggiore. On the southern shore is the pretty town of Baveno, on the north the Castagnola promontory, a long sunny shoreline where the towns of Suna, Pallanza, Verbania and Intra blend into one another along the water's edge. With a mild and sunny climate, not being too hot or dry, the weather is perfect for plants. The region is rich in semi-tropical trees and flowers; two lush neighbouring gardens, at Villa Taranto and Villa Remigio, are located on the very tip of the headland by Verbania.

Baveno
Along the lake north of Stresa, Baveno is a popular resort with families. The town has a small beach and many campsites in addition to three-star hotels. Baveno has a small ferry terminal and is a stop on the Borromean island route.

The town's 13th century church, dedicated to Saints Protasto and Gervaso, has beautiful frescoes in the octagonal baptistry. Half-hidden among the trees is Villa Branca, a 19th century villa which looks like a fairy castle (not open to the public). The villa is owned by the Branca family, producers of the digestive drink *Fernet Branca*. Queen Victoria used to stay here during her frequent holidays at the lake.

Feriolo
Once a barracks for a garrison of Roman troops stationed here to guard the pass through the Alps, today Feriolo is a town of fishermen and stonecutters. The pinkish granite quarried in the nearby mountains was shipped to Rome for the construction of St Paul's Outside the Walls.

Suna
The first town on the long shoreline promenade to Pallanza has many campsites and shops selling camping equipment.

Pallanza
The waterfront is attractive and south-facing, with the large Piazza Garibaldi situated along the lakeshore. Narrow ochre-coloured shopping lanes lead off the piazza where there is a market and the 15th century church of San Leonardo. Roman

legions were once encamped here, and two statues of ancient goddesses have been excavated nearby.

Verbania
Verbania lies at the tip of a peninsula, directly opposite the gulf from Baveno. The old Roman town is the setting for two magnificient gardens: Villa Taranto founded by Captain Neil McEacharn, Scottish gentleman and soldier, and Villa Remigio, built by a married couple as a celebration of their lasting love.

Intra
Situated at the entrance to the bay, Intra is the region's largest centre of population, with 31,000 inhabitants. The town has a car-ferry terminal and sailing harbour in addition to shops including many department stores. Intra is renowned for its extensive Saturday market. On the lakeshore are two fine old houses, the Villa Barbo and Villa Ada.

Verbania-Pallanza Flower Festival
Floriculture has long been an important industry, with numerous nurseries in the region, and a flower festival has taken place in Verbania-Pallanza since the end of the 19th century. The parade along Pallanza's lakeside is held on the first weekend in September. In the evening the floats, made from many thousands of flowers, serve as a colourful backdrop to the musical entertainment.

Villa Taranto

Via Vittorio Veneto,
Verbania Pallanza
011 55 6667
08.30-18.00 daily,
April-October
restaurant, bar, gift shop
gift shop closed 13.00-15.00
admission €8

'It sounds rather a large
claim to make but is
nevertheless true that at
least 90% of the plants in
Villa Taranto gardens had
never been grown before
I introduced them'

Neil McEacharn

Compared with those of the Borromean Islands, this garden
is very modern. Its 38 acres (16 hectares) contain one of
the largest and most diverse plant collections in the world.
Created in the 1930s by wealthy Scotsman Captain Neil
McEacharn, Villa Taranto was donated to the Italian State
in 1951, and is now the seat of the Prefecture of Verbano-
Cusio-Ossola. The gardens are something of a mixture,
comprising large areas of glorious naturalistic planting,
quantities of extremely rare plants and some formal areas of
bedding plants rather reminiscent of municipal parks.
There are two routes through the garden: a main circular
route that takes you past the main sights, and an off-shoot
that leads you on an alternative winding trail down the hill
to the exit. McEacharn built 7km of avenues, many shaded
by huge conifers. Not far from the entrance is a magnificent
Dahlia garden with more than 300 varieties of flowers. This
part of the garden is a multicoloured feast for the eyes.
Nearby are the tropical greenhouses containing the rare
giant water-lily *Victoria amazonica,* with 2m leaves which
carry sharp needles, keeping the fish at bay.

Beyond McEacharn's mausoleum is a path running up the
hill. At the top, take the bridge across the valley to the
stunning terraced rose garden, which contains an exquisite
fountain. This is the heart of the Villa Taranto – its special
signature garden.

At the far end of the rose garden is a choice of routes. Take
the alternative route to see the waterlily fountain, then
either continue or return to the main (shorter) route.

The plants

Captain McEacharn was assisted by an excellent British head gardener, Kew-trained Henry Cocker.

McEacharn ordered plants from around the globe and these were supplemented by gifts from the neighbours: Prince Borromeo presented him with two *Metasequoia glyptostroboides* – rare fossil trees thought to be extinct until rediscovered in Japan in 1941. Countess Scanni of Rome, founder of *Amici di Fiore*, sent him her irises.

A mild climate and abundant rainfall ensured that plants grow large and lush. Even the most rare and delicate plants have blossomed here. An *Emmenopterys henrii*, a tree related to the coffee tree from the deciduous forests of China, had never before flowered under cultivation, yet several have flourished here.

The garden also boasts a magnolia wood, more than 80,000 tulips, magnificent oleanders, fragrant gardenias and ponds containing lotuses and waterlilies.

DAHLIAS AT VILLA TARANTO

Neil Boyd McEacharn Watson (1884-1964)

In the summer of 1930, Captain Neil McEacharn was on a train to Milan when he read an advertisement for a villa and land at Pallanza on Lago Maggiore. 'La Crochetta' was in his view *a horror*,' but the land seemed ideal for his purpose – to establish a world-class plant collection.

Wealthy from birth, McEacharn had the money to realise his dream. His father, from humble Scottish stock, had emigrated to Australia, married well and made a fortune from exporting lamb to Britain in refrigerated vessels. Neil, who from the earliest age had shown a love of plants, followed the gentlemanly path to Eton and Oxford, serving in the King's Own Scottish Borderers before becoming deputy Lord Lieutenant of Wigtownshire. He had loved Italy from childhood visits aboard his father's yacht, and so was eager for the challenge that Pallanza offered.

McEacharn used military methods to build his garden. A hundred men were employed to cut the dramatic ravine (now crossed by a bridge) which links the Villa with the rose garden. Local people were amazed to see gardeners pouring out of the property like factory workers at the end of each day. Earth was shifted by the ton and the site cleared of everything except a few large trees. McEacharn wrote in his autobiography, '*I…installed a Deccaville railway…the sort used in the 1914 war to bring supplies to the troops, for carting stones and removing trees…*'

At the outbreak of World War II, McEacharn was obliged to leave Italy. He appointed his lawyer, Antonio Cappelletto to take charge of the property. Villa and grounds were variously occupied by Partisans, Fascists, German troops and a South African regiment, but Cappelletto managed to keep the garden going with careful diplomacy and the help of one gardener, Beppo Mazzola. McEacharn returned to the villa and after the death of his second wife Irma (aunt of Queen Elizabeth II) in 1947, he threw himself into experiments with seeds collected from all over the world. He died on the terrace overlooking his beloved garden.

FOUNTAIN AT VILLA TARANTO

Villa San Remigio

Via San Remigio, Verbania Pallanza
0323 504 401
10.30 Saturday and Sunday, May - October
€4 admission by guided tour (in Italian)

One of those who gave plants to McEacharn was his next-door neighbour, the Marchese Sofia della Valle di Casanova. Sofia and her husband Silvio built their garden to celebrate their love. Plaques in the courtyard are inscribed with their vow. Sofia lived to the age of 100, and her daughter sold Villa Remigio to the Piedmont Region in 1977.

The lovers

In 1896 Sofia Browne from Dublin married Silvio della Valle di Casanova, her cousin and childhood sweetheart. It was their dream to build a garden to symbolise their enduring love. Villa Remigio's garden is their legacy.

The garden was a two decade-long labour of love. The couple's aesthetic sense was finely honed. Sofia was a talented painter, and Silvio a poet. Together they created the concept of a series of gardens evoking different moods. To realise their design required the construction of six terraces, because of the sloping site.

The shady lower **garden of Melancholy** contains no flowers and is surrounded by conifers and camphor trees. The sole decoration is a statue of Hercules. On the terrace above is the **garden of Joy** featuring a large shell statue of Diana in a pool, surrounded by roses, sweet-smelling shrubs and clipped box hedges.

Above is the **garden of Hours**, a hot and sunny garden bordered with a balustrade. It contains palms and a large circular sun-dial which bears an inscription translated as: *'Silvio and Sofia ponder why each day the new light laps at the shadows of the hours that have passed.'* The terrace connecting the garden of Hours to the villa also forms the roof of the greenhouse, which contains a vaulted grotto full of ferns, orchids and *Begonia rex*.

The design of the garden is complemented by the planting. Roses, symbolic of love and the brevity of youth, abound as do scented shrubs including *Trachelospermum jasminoides* and *Olea fragrans*. There are also specimen trees including *Castanea crenata*, *Cupressus cashmeriana* and *Libocedrus decurrens*, which have matured to a great size.

A feature of the garden's design is that visitors have no view of the lake until they have reached the top terrace – as rewarding an outlook today as it was when Clara Schumann and other distinguished friends of the couple enjoyed it.

Arona

Arona lies at the southern end of Lago Maggiore. The town
is dominated by Rocca Borromeo, a perfectly preserved
medieval castle that sits atop a spur of rock. Arona is located
at the junction of railway lines to the Alpine passes and to
Milan, Turin and Genoa. The town is also a terminus for
lake steamers and a hydrofoil. Arona has a couple of good
shopping streets parallel to the shoreline.

Rocca Borromeo

Angera, reached by boat from
Arona, 0331 931 300
www.borromeoturismo.it

09.00-17.30 daily, March-October
Sundays and Holidays till 18.00
audio guides available in English €7
adults €7.50, children €4.50

Rocca Borromeo was at first a monastery, but the strategic
importance of the location led to it becoming the property of
the Borromeo and Visconti families, and it remains so to this
day. The castle is worth visiting for the 13th century cycle of
frescoes in the Justice Hall and the wonderful Doll Museum,
the largest collection of hand-painted dolls and doll houses
in Europe. Exhibits have been added that are dedicated to
mechanical dolls of the 19th and 20th century.

CLIMB TO THE TOP OF TORRE CASTELLANA FOR A PANORAMIC VIEW.

ANGERA, SEEN FROM ARONA

San Carlone

Piazzale San Carlo 1
0332 24 9669
08.30-12.30, 14.00-18.30 daily Mar-Oct, 14.00-17.00 Oct-Nov
09.00-12.30, 14.00-17.00 winter weekends and holidays only
€2.50 to top, €1.50 to first platform

A mammoth statue of San Carlo stands in the hills above
the town. It is made of copper plate and is 35m high. Inside
it is hollow with holes cut into the ears and eyes. A circular
stairway takes you up 10m, but the rest must be climbed by
ladder. A safety harness and helmet are provided, with staff
available to show you how to wear them. The ascent is only
for those with no fear of heights.

San Carlo (1538-1584)

Carlo was the devout son of a Borromeo and a Medici. He
was a nephew of Pope Pius IV. Carlo refused a position in
the family banking business in order to help plague victims
and serve the poor of Milan and Lago Maggiore.

Ordained in 1563, Carlo was made archbishop of Milan
in 1564. The man was a contradiction. A hero in times of
plague and war, in times of peace he was a persecutor of
heretics who lobbied for more executions. Carlo died of
plague and was canonised 26 years later.

LAGO D'ORTA

ISOLA DI SAN GIULIO

Orta

A thousand feet above sea level, Lago d' Orta is a glacial lake, enclosed by mountains and high hills covered with chestnut and birch trees. Imported palms also thrive, thanks to a favourable micro-climate. Tiny medieval villages stud the lake's banks, and the island of San Giulio floats in front of the pretty little town of Orta. This is the principal resort on the lake, and one that is well worth a visit.

The flagged square of Orta, walled on three sides by frescoed houses and porticos, its café tables outside in the sun all year round, opens on the west side to the lake. Boats ply back and forth to the island from the jetty flanked by colourful flower beds and shady trees.

On the way into Orta, you can't help but notice the Islamic-inspired confection which is Villa Crespi. From this landmark you can locate the tourist office, train departure point and the car park. The villa was built by textile magnate Cristoforo Benigno Crespi in 1879, and was used to entertain royalty, poets, artists and industrialists. Today it is a hotel and the home of a restaurant whose chef, Cannavaccivolo, has earned a Michelin star.

Roads into Orta are so narrow that cars are not allowed without a special permit. The town can instead be accessed by tourist train or on foot. Park your car in one of three car parks at the outskirts. Opposite the first, near Villa Crespi, is the terminus for the little red and green train (below). Although the train looks as though it belongs in an amusement park, it is a useful means of transport for the journey down to Orta or up to Sacro Monte. Departures are every 20 minutes – more often in peak season – and tickets cost €2.

If you'd like to park closer to town, carry on past the first car park on Via Panoramica and past the second car park until you reach Piazzale Aldo Viglione. From there it's a short walk down the steps and along Via Poli to Orta.

Isola di San Giulio

Boats leave from the main square in Orta
boat €3.00, ferry €2.50

When St Julius (San Giulio) arrived from Greece in the 4th century and stood on the present-day site of Orta, no boatman would take him to the little island in the middle of the lake. Locals claimed that it was populated by dragons and serpents and no one returned alive. The story goes that Julius, guided by his staff, was able to make the journey across the water on his cloak. He promptly rid the island of all reptiles and began to build his hundredth church.

Julius reportedly had many gifts, including prophesy and healing. Once, when he was building a church at Brebia with his brother Julian, a worker accidentally

cut off his own thumb and fainted from loss of blood. Julius put the man's thumb back on, made the sign of the cross over it, and sure enough it stuck there and the worker was healed. Straight away Julius placed the dropped tool in the man's hand and ordered him to get on with his work.

William of Volpiano, the great abbot and founder of monasteries, was born on the island during the seige of 962. At that time the Italian Queen Willa was defending the island and all her kingdom's treasure. She was defeated by Emperor Otto the Great and what happened to the treasure is a mystery. Today, an abbey of enclosed Benedictine nuns occupies part of the island. You might hear the ringing of bells to summon the nuns to prayer, or perhaps the sound of Gregorian chant coming from the Basilica di San Giulio.

You can't visit the abbey but the 12th century Romanesque church is certainly worth a look. It is famous for the immense Gothic pulpit, carved from serpentine stone, incorporating symbols of the four evangelists. Luke is represented by an ox, Matthew by an angel, Mark is the lion and John the eagle. Perhaps more beautiful are frescoes on the right aisle, some of which are attributed to a student of Gaudenzio Ferrari (1480-1546), a famous artist of the Lombard school. There is a lovely painting of St George.

The remains of St Julius are buried in the crypt along with those of four other saints: Elias, Audentius, Philibert and Demetrius. It is believed that St Julius still has the power to heal. A book is kept in the crypt for those who wish to be remembered in the nuns' prayers.

After leaving the church, stroll around the island on the **Way of Silence**, a peaceful walk with signs extolling the virtues of meditation. You will pass the Abbazia Mater Ecclesia. On 30th June, St Julius' day, the mother superior hands out *pane di San Giulio*. The island also hosts classical music concerts and piano recitals in September.

Sacro Monte di San Francesco

Many countries have the tradition of the Sacred Mountain, a holy place found in nature. Piedmont has more of these mountains than other regions in Italy. In 2003, six were named Unesco World Heritage Sites, including this one.

Set amongst the trees are 20 chapels dedicated to the life of St Francis of Assisi. In each chapel a scene is revealed from the life of the Saint using life-size dolls. The idea for this homage to St Francis came from Padre Cieto, a Capuchin monk and architect from Castelleto Ticino.

Construction began in 1590 and there were originally 32 chapels conceived by Padre Cieto. By 1616, only 12 chapels were completed and the Padre's ill health forced a re-think of the plan.

Three years later the Padre died and work was continued by other architects. Non-Catholics may find the scenes rather puzzling and the church of San Nicolao quite sombre.

The mountain has a peaceful atmosphere and there are splendid views of Isola di San Giulio.

Poetry on the Lake

poetryonthelake@yahoo.co.uk

Literary references to Orta are many. Nietzsche's *Thus Spake Zarathustra* was dated *von Orta an*, and it was here that he lost his heart to Lou Salomé. The lake also inspired Robert Browning, George Meredith, Honoré de Balzac and Eugenio Montale. The enchanting little town of Orta is once again a literary centre, at least for a few days a year, when it is alive with poets attending the annual **Poetry on the Lake** event. Poets compete for the *Silver Wyvern*, award supported by Alessi, in an event with the patronage of CICT- UNESCO and the British Council.

The *wyvern*, a two-footed dragon with a serpent's tail, is carved on the splendid Romanesque pulpit in the basilica on the island of San Giulio.

International Poetry Competition for

unpublished poems in the English language opens1st January and closes 30th April.

Awards and Poetry Festival

held the last weekend in September each year, with workshops, readings, and events, including the itinerant
Sacro Monte readings
The Silver Wyvern Award is presented at the festival.

UNESCO World Poetry Day
Readings the weekend nearest to the Spring Equinox, 21st March.

Learning to read the lake

You taught me
the language of the lake. To know
from the fender's thud against the boat,
the frizzle spiralling down the birch,
the thrumming of the palm, which wind
will soon scribble its name across
the open pages of the lake; if we should
fasten the moorings and lock
the shutters close –
or hoist sail and razor through
the colours of the sky.
And hear the bow whine drawn across a saw
of swan wings, with their background beat.

To read, as well, its changing lines.
The precise calligraphy
of the south wind, marking
short, tight strokes, the bold
slashes of Tramontana,
the curling loops a rare west wind
scrawls across the lake. The wayward doodles
of the crazy Cus.
And the notes: the eye ripples
of the plunging grebe, the deltas
drawn by moorhens, the points of light
stippled by oars at dusk.

excerpt from a poem by Gabriel Griffin

VAL DOSSOLA

The Journey

BE SURE TO BRING YOUR PASSPORT

timetable: www.lagomaggioreexpress.com
tickets: day return adult €28, child €14

Make arrangements at the tourist office in Stresa for a delightful day trip that combines a train journey with a relaxed boat ride. Board the train for Domodossola in Stresa (or Arona) at around 8am. Change in Domodossola for the Val Vigezzo train through the mountains to Locarno. Located at the point where seven valleys meet, Domodossola has a lively farmers market on Saturday.

The journey can seem tedious if you don't stop for lunch. Before boarding the Val Vigezzo train, be sure to let the staff know that you wish to stop in Santa Maria Maggiore.

Santa Maria Maggiore

This pretty town is famous for its quality of light. The Vigezzo valley was named the 'painting valley' in the 1650s when many artists established studios here. A school founded in 1850 continues to offer summer art courses.

Contact: Scuola Belle Arti Valentini, 0324 84 213.

Hand-woven cloths and locally made food products are available in the shops. **Miramar,** located near the train station, is an excellent choice for lunch.

Locarno

Re-board the train for the journey to Locarno, Switzerland. You will be subject to a passport check at the border. In Locarno, it's a short walk downhill to catch the ferry. Relax and watch the sunset behind the mountains of Lago Maggiore as the boat returns you to Stresa by around 8pm.

LANGHE

Rolling hills covered in vineyards, medieval towers peeping through the morning mist, truffle hunters walking along the roads at dusk, the smell of chocolate – it must be autumn in Langhe and Roero.

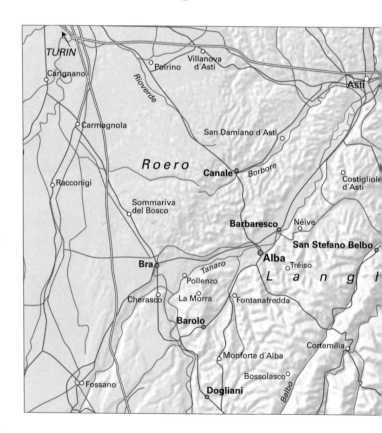

Langhe is wine country, home to Barolo and Barbaresco. Roero has steeper hills and a wilder countryside. More white truffles are found in Roero than in Langhe.

A bustling market town, Alba is the capital of Langhe and home to Ferrero-Rocher. Every October Alba hosts a truffle festival, complete with a palio race and Truffle Queen. The town has a lively bar and club scene.

Slow Food was born in the sedate town of Bra. Acqui Terme is a peaceful spa town with some good art shops.

Alba • relaxed, friendly town with great shopping
Bra • capital of Roero and home of Slow Food
Barolo • the King of wine, the wine of kings
Barbaresco • the Queen of wines
Dogliani • Dolcetta wine country
Acqui Terme
• spa town with hot springs

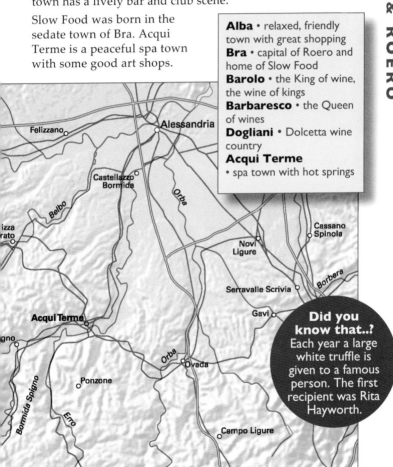

Did you know that..? Each year a large white truffle is given to a famous person. The first recipient was Rita Hayworth.

Langhe & Roero

The Langhe and Roero hills are divided by the Tánaro river, with Langhe situated to the south and Roero to the north. Both Bra and Alba are on the river's banks. They can be covered in dense fog on autumn mornings.

The vine-covered hills around Barolo are coloured red, green and gold in the autumn: what appears to be a patch of sunlight on the hillside is in fact the colour of the vine leaves. Langhe is known around the world for the quality of its wine, and you will hear many different European and American accents in the local enotecas and wine bars during the autumn tasting season. Snap up your 2000 Barolo now and you might even make a profit if you can resist drinking it for a few years.

Barolo is the best known and most expensive of Langhe's wines but it is by no means the only one. The Barolo DOC is south-west of Alba, and the soil in these hills produces a rich red vintage, high in alcohol. Barbaresco is only a short distance away to the northeast, but here the soil is rich in minerals and produces a more gentle, less robust wine.

There isn't much to do in either Barolo or Barbaresco apart from eating and drinking. Barolo has a castle to visit and there are good views from the top of Barbaresco's medieval tower.

Alba, located in the valley between Barolo and Barbaresco, is proud to be one of the world's great wine towns: every window display includes a wine bottle – even shops selling babywear. Alba is also the centre for the world's most expensive foodstuff after caviar: the white truffle, *tartufo bianco*. The annual truffle auction is held in the throne room of the castle at Ginzano Cavour which once belonged to Count Cavour, architect of Italian unification.

Locals in Roero claim that most of the area's white truffles are found in their region. Roero's hills are not rolling and spacious like those in the Langhe. Here they are green, wild and steep. In the autumn dusk you can see the truffle hunters walking with their dogs and their long staffs. When loosened, the earth forms shapes that tantalizingly resemble the precious fungus that is only found here and one other place in the world: Istria, Croatia.

ROERO

Alba

The capital city of Langhe has almost 30,000 citizens. Its economy is fuelled by luxury food products: truffles, wine and chocolate.

Alba is home to Ferrero, makers of Nutella and Ferrero Rocher chocolates. When the autumn fog descends over the city the air smells of chocolate.

October is the best time to visit Alba, when the *tartufo bianco* comes into its short season. It was local chef Giacomo Morra who first determined that the lumpy fungus was good to eat. He used celebrities to promote his discovery and in 1949 sent the best truffle collected that year to the film star Rita Hayworth. She loved the taste and spread the word to her friends and colleagues. In 2004 the prize truffle was awarded to Sophia Loren; and in 2005, to another Italian actress, Sabrina Ferilli.

October is also wine season, when the new vintages are released and local enotecas fill with buyers and collectors from around the world.

ALBA STREET

Resistance

The people of Alba are fiercely independent and there was
a strong resistance movement based here in World War II.
For 23 days in autumn 1944, a thousand partisans held off
Nazi troops. They were led by Franco Centro, aged just 14,
one of many teenagers who fought for the freedom of Alba.
Franco and 24 other partisans were shot in the town square.
Their courage is commemorated by a permanent exhibit in
the town hall.

Palio degli Asini

Ente Fiera Nazionale del Tartufo
Piazza Medford 3
info@fieradeltartufo.org
0173 361 051
numbered seats €23
general seating €12
standing €6

The palio in Siena may be the most famous horse race in Italy but the palio in Alba has got to be the most fun. The race is run on the first Sunday in October with competing *contrade* (boroughs) just like in Siena. Unlike Siena, in Alba the jockey is riding a donkey.

Alba has nine contrade and all participate in the race, each flying their own flag. San Lorenzo has the initials SL on the bottom of its flags.

Palio programme first Sunday in October

10am
donkeys are assigned to each participating borough

11am
all roads are closed to traffic

2.15pm
parade departs Piazza Medford
• along Corso Matteotti
• Corso Bandiera • Piazza Savona • along Via Vittorio Emanuele to Piazza Risorgimento

3pm
• historical re-enactments played by different contrade
• flag-flying • palio races

6pm
awards and celebrations

Alba v Asti

In the 13th century Italy was engulfed in the Guelph versus Ghibbeline conflict, which pitted the Guelph-supported Pope against the Ghibbeline-backed Frederico Barbarossa, the Holy Roman Emperor. Alba sided with Barbarossa, Asti with the Pope. Alba built fortifications and became known as the 'city of the hundred towers'.

Asti was victorious over Alba and chose to celebrate by holding a palio in Alba's town square on the feast of San Lorenzo. To run a race on a saint's day was sacrilege and the citizens of Alba were outraged. The following year, Asti invited Alba to participate in the palio horse race but the Albesi refused. Centuries passed and the Asti palio continued to be an annual event. Jockeys from Alba began to compete and they won the race several times. In fact the Albesi jockeys were so successful in the 1920s they were no longer invited to participate.

When Alba jockeys were refused entry to the 1932 Asti palio, Pinot Gallizio, an eccentric Alba citizen, conceived of the idea for the donkey race to forever poke fun at Alba's overly serious and unpopular neighbours. The Alba palio has become an established event in the autumn calender. It is run for fun, the winner decided by sheer luck and the whims of an ass.

Contrade

San Lorenzo (cathedral)

San Martino (gate)

Brichet (hillock)

Patin/Tesor (slippers/ treasure)

del Fumo (smoke)

delle Rane (frogs)

Moretta (sanctuary)

Santa Barbara (Cherasco)

Santa Rosalia (book)

Truffles

In Alba, there are two types of truffle: *tartufo bianco* and *tartufo nero*, white and black. Both have a pungent aroma of earth and the barnyard.

The scientific name for the white truffle is *Tuber magnatum*. To date, efforts to cultivate them have failed. The white truffle grows wild, several inches below ground near roots of certain trees. Experts claim to be able to identify the type of tree by the taste of the truffle. For instance, one found under an oak or a linden will have a taste of honey.

A truffle hunter is called a *trifolau*. At dusk, in autumn you will see one (always a man) walking with his stick and dog towards a secret place only he knows. Competition is fierce and locations are closely guarded. Dogs take six months to train and are preferred to pigs because they do less harm to the truffle. Many trifolau carry firearms for protection against wild boar and other hunters. Dogs have been shot in disputes over territory.

A black truffle should be eaten within two weeks of harvest and must be stored in absorbent paper (never in rice) that is changed daily. A *tartufo nero* of around 30 grams sells for around €11. *Tartufo bianco* should be eaten within a week of harvest and is also stored in absorbent paper. The value of a white truffle increases with size, so while you may pay €37 for a tiny 17 gram truffle, a 130 gram truffle could cost upwards of €350. At a recent auction, a pair of white truffles sold for €95,000; one weighed 800 grams, the other, 400 grams.

The World Truffle Auction is held in the castle of Grinzane Cavour. The auctioneer must be experienced and discerning as *trifolau* are not above trying a few tricks to raise the prices. One ruse is to glue two or three truffles together with a paste made of egg white and soil from the outside of the truffle. An auctioneer attempting to expose the scam risks destroying a valuable truffle if he is wrong.

Wine

Wine is liquid gold in the Langhe hills and powers the Alba economy. Tasting tours are a primary source of tourist revenue and an enjoyable part of any Langhe holiday. It is not uncommon for visitors to start their day with a tasting at 10am and be well sloshed by lunch. Practice moderation.

Taste and purchase wine at an Enoteca Regionale or Botteghe del Vino. High-quality red wines are produced in Langhe but the region towards Acqui Terme and Asti is better for white. Barbera d'Alba and Langhe Nebbiolo are good red wines that offer a cheaper alternative to Barolo or Barberesco.

Wine tasting tour

Enoteca Barbaresco
Via Torino 8a
0173 635 251
09.30-13.00, 14.30-18.00
closed Wed
Barbaresco

Enoteca Barolo
Barolo castle
0173 56 277
10.00-12.30, 15.00-18.30
closed Thurs
Barolo, Vini rossi DOG

Enoteca Piedmontese
Grinzane Cavour castle
0173 262 159
09.00-12.00, 14.00-18.00
closed Tues
Barolo, Barbaresco, Dolcetto, Barbera, Nebbiolo, Arneis

Bottega del Vino di Dogliani
Piazza San Paolo 9
0173 70 107
09.30-12.30, 15.00-19.00 weekends
15.00-19.00 Fri
Dolcetto

Cantina Comunale La Morra
Via Carlo Alberto 2
0173 509 204
10.00-12.30, 14.30-18.30
closed Tues
Barbera, Barolo, Nebbiolo

Enoteca Roero, Canale
Via Roma 57
0173 978 228
09.30-12.30, 16.00-19.30
closed Wed
Roero, Arneis, Favorita, Barbera

Enoteca Acqui Terme
Piazza Levi 7
0144 770 273
10.00-12.00, 15.00-18.30
closed Mon, Thurs morn
Moscato d'Asti, Acqui Spumante

Barolo

The village itself is small: just a few buildings clustered around Barolo Castle. The castle was first built in the 10th century as a defence tower. It was later purchased by the Falletti, a family of financiers from Alba who transformed it into a residence. Falletti fortunes rose and they became counts and then *marchesi*. Last in the line was Marchese Falletti di Barolo (Carlo Tancredi) who was twice mayor of Turin. He married Giulietta Colbert di Maulevrier. It was Giulietta who first named the wine *Barolo*.

Despite her nobility, Giulietta had liberal ideals and befriended many of the 19th century intellectuals pushing for reform. One of them was Silvio Pellico, a member of the *Carbinari* – a liberal association struggling for Italian independence. Pellico was arrested for subversive activities and served a ten year sentence in a Milan prison. During that time he began to write his classic *Le Mie Prigioni* (My Prisons). After his release, Pellico travelled to Turin where he met Giulietta. Intrigued by Pellico's intellect, she offered him the post of castle librarian.

Today the library has a collection of more than 3,000 books from the 16-19th centuries, including many first editions. The castle is now state property and the cellars house the extensive Enoteca Regionale del Barolo.

In the square in front of the castle is San Donato, a small church that was once the Falletti family chapel.

On the hilltop overlooking Barolo is **La Morra**, a pretty town with lively wine bars and good restaurants.

SAN DONATO, BAROLO

Grinzane Cavour

On a hilltop not far from Barolo is the castle of Grinzane Cavour, former residence of Count Camillo Benzo Cavour, one of the architects of Italian unification. Camillo was sent to live here by his father who disapproved of his son's liberal ideas. It was thought a spell in the country would calm his political fire but instead Camillo was elected mayor of Grinzane and the town was named after him.

The castle is an imposing brick fortress arranged around a cramped courtyard. There is a restaurant on the first floor and the upper floors house a museum of country life featuring exhibits of 17-19th century kitchens, shops and wine-making implements. Grinzane Cavour is now the headquarters of the Order of Knights of the Truffle. They hold the world truffle auction here. The enoteca in the cellar has a range of Piedmont wine including some moderately priced Barolo and Barbaresco. It is smaller and less overwhelming than the enoteca at Barolo.

The municipality of Grinzane Cavour has two centres: Gallo, on the Alba-Barolo road, and Grinzane. Gallo is known for nougat and Grinzane for wine and truffles.

BAROLO

Barolo wine

The King of wines was first produced by a woman. In 1843, Giulietta, Marchesa di Barolo, and her neighbour Camillo Benso Cavour, who both loved the wines of Burgundy, summoned the French oenologist Oudart to Barolo. He applied his methods to the vineyards around Barolo castle and, using the local nebbiolo grape, produced the first wine to be named Barolo. Giulietta sent a gift of 350 barrels to King Vittorio Emanuele II, who quickly purchased vineyards at Fontanafredda near the Barolo estate. In addition to the village of Barolo, the wine region of Barolo encompasses the following villages, and only these can claim to produce Barolo wine: Monforte, Castiglione Falleto, La Morra, Serralunga, Grinzane Cavour, Diano d'Alba, Verduno, Roddi, Cherasco and Novello.

Garnet-red in colour with ruby highlights which turn amber with age, Barolo has an earthy perfume with hints of plum, black cherries, wild rose and/or cinnamon. The acidity and tannins can be rather fierce when the wine is young. This is why Barolo has a minimum age requirement of three years before its release into the marketplace.

Barolo wine is under tight control. Legislation requires that it be produced from 100 per cent nebbiolo grapes grown on authorized vineyards that make only three varieties: Lampia, Michet and Rosé. The wine is aged for not less than 38 months, 24 of which must be in oak barrels. In order to be classed as Riserva, wine must be aged for 62 months with 36 months in oak. Maximum wine production allowed is 80 quintals per hectare (2.4 acres) with a maximum acidity of 0.5 per cent and a minimum alcohol content of 13 percent.

The biggest change in the making of Barolo wine has been the rise of the small independent producer. In the 1960s there were around 12 vineyards, who would vinify their grapes together and sell the result on to large wineries. Today, 150 small vintners dedicate themselves to producing quality Barolo vintages on their own estates.

Barolo producers look to establish a recognised brand – a strategy that is paying off at the auction houses. In 2005 at Zachy's in New York, a Giacomo Caterno Barolo Montfortino Reserva Speciale 1937 sold for $3,290 – the most expensive Italian wine ever sold at auction. Wine buyers were stunned, as the bottle had been valued at around $1,000. At the same auction, a Luciano Sandrone Barolo Cannubi 1997 sold for $1,293. By comparison, a French Chateau Margaux 1995 went for $5,333.

Now is a good time to purchase Barolo, because several excellent vintage years have been followed by three poor ones. The years 1996-2000 produced above-average Barolo, with wine from 2000 considered to be the best in decades. Cold wet weather, including a hailstorm in La Morra, led to a lost harvest in 2002, while drought and heat overripened the crop in 2003. Thus the minimum three-year age requirement means that no Barolo wine was released in 2005 or 2006. One can expect the price of existing bottles to rise as buyers and collectors stock up their cellars. Cannubi, Pio Cesare and Marchesi di Barolo are reputable names.

Barbaresco

The distinctive Barbaresco tower can be seen for miles. It was once part of a medieval defence fortress with walls 3 metres thick. Located between Alba and Asti, Barbaresco endured serious fighting in the Guelph-Ghibbeline wars. Today, all that remains is the tower with a cozy trattoria at its base.

The high street is pretty; on the front of the Town Hall is a large painted sundial. At the end of the street is the desanctified church of San Donato that now houses the Enoteca Regionale Barbaresco.

The wine

Vines have been cultivated here since Roman times. The soil is crumbly and chalky, ideal for growing grapes. In the Barbaresco region, 60 per cent of vineyards are planted with the nebbiolo grape, followed by 15 per cent dolcetto, and 6 per cent each of barbera and chardonnay.

Barbaresco's vineyards are based at an average of 350 metres above sea level, an altitude that brings cooler temperatures and breezes even during the hottest of summers. A pronounced difference between day and night temperatures allows grapes to ripen while preserving the ideal level of acidity.

The Queen of wine was first produced by a man: Domizio Cavazza, professor at the Royal Enological School of Alba. To protect the integrity of the wine he founded a cooperative of Barbaresco wine producers, the very first in Italy.

The microclimate of these hills means that grape varietals grown here do not produce the same results when cultivated elsewhere, not even in the next valley. Barolo and Barbaresco are produced in valleys less than 30 minutes apart by car yet the wine tastes very different. Barbaresco is lighter in texture and flavour than Barolo.

Treiso

In the centre is a good restaurant, with a beautiful view, that has just received its second Michelin star.

Dogliani

Situated on the banks of the
Tanaro river, Dogliani has
some interesting shops and
churches. It is the centre of
Dolcetto, a ruby-red wine that
can claim *superiore* status if
aged for one year.

**SHOPS CLOSE 2 HRS FOR LUNCH,
ALL DAY MON AND WED AM.**

Schellino (1818-1905)

Giovan Battista Schellino was
the local architect responsible
for Dogliani's finest churches.
A lover of rooftops and
towers, he did paid work
from 5am to midnight, six
days per week. On Sunday he
went to mass and did unpaid
work in the afternoon, but
only on churches.

DOGLIANI

San Stefano Belbo

Tucked away in the hills of upper Langhe, on the road to
Acqui Terme, is the birthplace of Cesare Pavese, a famous
20th century author. In the town a museum details his life.

Museum open 10.00-12.30, 15.00-18.30 Mon-Sat except Thurs pm

Born in 1908, Pavese's work concerned the lives of peasants
leaving the land and moving to the city. Pavese himself
moved to Turin where he became a fixture in the local
restaurants. He fell in love with Constance Dowling, a
Hollywood actress, but his passion for her wasn't returned. In
despair, he comitted suicide in August 1950, aged 42. Pavese's
works were translated into several languages (including
English) and are still available in bookshops. His most famous
novel is *La Luna e i Falò* (The Moon and the Bonfires).

216

Bra

The capital of Roero, Bra is situated on the side of a hill that overlooks the junction of the Stura di Demonte and Tanaro rivers. Slow Food originated here and as a result Bra has become a meeting place for food producers from around the world and the location of many food-related events. There is a large farmers market on Wednesday mornings when many of the shops are closed.

Slow Food organises fairs, events and farmers markets that are now important internationally: *Cheese* and *Slow Fish* are events held in Bra on alternate years; *Salone del Gusto*, held in Turin, is the largest food event of its kind in Italy featuring a cornucopia of products.

Slow Food (slowfood.com)

Eating is a political act at Slow Food, an international non-profit association founded by Carlo Petrini in 1986 – in response to the effects of the convenience culture on the planet.

Slow Food wants us to slow down and enjoy our food, to be aware of the true cost of what we eat, and support organic farming, sustainable fishing, and traditional methods of growing and preparing food.

Members are organised into *Convivia*, small locally based groups that plan their own events and initiatives. There are now 750 convivia in 104 countries, with a total of 80,000 members.

BRA

UNIVERSITY OF GASTRONOMY

Pollenzo

Beautifully located on the banks of the river, Pollenzo was first settled in Roman times. The Savoy later established a summer residence here but the Ducal Palace was left to ruin until it was purchased and restored by the University.

University of Gastronomic Sciences

This new fully accredited university offers an undergraduate degree and a masters programme. Founded in 2004, the school now has 150 students but no permanent faculty. Guest lecturers are invited from gastronomic circles worldwide.

Students take courses in the history, science and economics of food production and consumption, in addition to gastronomic literature. The university does not offer cookery courses but does have a library containing thousands of old and out-of-print recipe books, including many English titles acquired from a donor in California. There is also a wine bank containing a sample case of virtually every bottle produced in Italy.

Canale

The distinctive medieval tower on top of the hill (pictured right) belongs to Cisterna Castle. It was once owned by the Bishops of Asti and later by the della Rovere family. Inside is a museum dedicated to traditional work, with exhibits of tools and materials used by cobblers, mattress-makers, printers and other common trades.

Roero's earthy red wine has recently received a DOGC classification. Arneis, the local white wine, is straw-coloured with a greenish tinge. It's fruity but has a slight bitter aftertaste.

Be sure to have lunch in the excellent restaurant based in the Enoteca.

Rocche Valley

Canale is just south of the Rocche Valley, known for its interesting rock formations and wilderness trails. Locals say white truffles are found here and indeed the colour and texture of the soil is similar to the truffle.

Oasi di San Nicolao has a 6.5km nature trail through the wooded rocks. Journey time: three hours.

Acqui Terme

On the banks of the Bromida river is an ancient spa town founded by a Ligurian tribe. Acqui Terme has been famous for its sulphurous thermal hot springs for thousands of years. The marble fountain called the Boiling Spring (*la Bollente*) has become the emblem of the town, gushing waters at 560 litres per minute at a temperature of 75°C.

Ancient Romans appreciated Acqui Terme's waters and built themselves luxurious spa facilities. Two thousand years later, Acqui's spas are still luxurious, with up-to-date facilities supported by qualified medical staff offering a full range of health and beauty treatments.

Water isn't Acqui's only attraction: wines of the region include several DOC and DOCG wines. Be sure to taste a glass of Brachetto and Acqui Spumante. Robellini Palace is the headquarters of the Enoteca Regionale who sell wine made by a variety of Piedmontese producers.

The Spa

Terme di Acqui
Piazza Italia 1
0144 324 390
open year round
book in advance

The waters and mud baths are thought to have therapeutic powers for motor-rehabilitation, arthritis, respiratory dysfunction and circulatory problems.

The spa complex has two centres, one in the town centre and the other across the Bromida river, surrounded by natural parkland.

LA BOLLENTE

The Romans

Aquae Statiellae was popular with Roman legions travelling to and from territories in the north. Gnaeus Pompeius Magnus (Pompey the Great) rested and recuperated here and so did Julius Caesar.

Pliny, Strabone, Seneca and Tacito all wrote about the restorative properties of Acqui Terme's waters. Remains of the town's Roman past can be seen in the ruins of the Roman aqueduct (dating from the first century BC), an old Roman swimming pool, and a Roman Basilica dedicated to St Peter.

Acqui Terme became a duchy under the Longobards and later an earldom. It was allied with the Guelphs against Barbarossa in the medieval wars. In 1278, after hard battles against Genoa, Asti and Alessandria, Acqui came under the protection of the Marquis of Monferrato.

In the 18th century, Acqui Terme was absorbed into the Duchy of Savoy. The dukes regularly came here to take the waters.

FOOD & DRINK

AL BICERIN

The people of Piedmont take food and wine extremely seriously. The region is considered by many Italians to possess the best cuisine in Italy, with Piedmont wines being recognised by connoisseurs as the finest the nation produces. This status has been won thanks to a combination of fertile land and the influence of neighbouring European countries.

Like most regions in Italy, traditional cuisine is based on what grows naturally and in Piedmont the list is impressive. Most of the country is fed on rice, corn and other grains from the Po Valley. Top quality meats and cheeses from the Valle Maira and Valle Grana, high in the mountains, are popular throughout Piedmont. Rivers flowing down from the mountains supply the region with plenty of fresh fish.

The Langhe produces wine, truffles, chestnuts, hazelnuts and mushrooms. It is where the elusive and expensive white truffle is found during late autumn. Truffles are best when eaten close to their source and from October to December, Langhe restaurants are full of gourmands. Hazelnuts appear in cakes and chutneys. They are combined with chocolate to make Nutella, first produced in Alba. Piedmontese *gnocchi* are made with chestnut flour so it is darker in colour and richer in flavour than the standard potato variety. In any restaurant, the cheese board is a feast for the eyes and taste buds.

Piedmont is so abundantly fertile that there is little importing of food from other regions, with the exception of Liguria to the south. Today the journey takes only an hour by car, but it was once necessary to make a pilgrimage to the coast, taking wine, cheese, grain and cured meats, and returning with dried and preserved fish like anchovies, *baccalà* (salted cod) and tuna, as well as capers, olives and olive oil.

The region's position at the foot of the Alps made it a crossroads for many cultures, with a resulting influence on the cuisine. Long ago, the northern valleys comprised a network of salt roads, with traders from Venice travelling across the Alps and onwards to cities in northern Europe. They would return carrying wool and other commodities for sale in Venice and the Levant. In both directions, travellers would rest and eat in Turin, giving the chefs of Piedmont access to a wide variety of ingredients and spices.

During their reign, the Savoy transformed Turin into a glamorous city, attracting chefs, architects and artists from throughout Europe. The chefs of the Savoy courts introduced a French flavour to the cuisine, through the use of sauces and a wide variety of cheeses not common in other regions of Italy. Piedmont was often under Austrian occupation and, although it was an unhappy time for the independently-spirited Piedmontese, there is a legacy of wonderfully rich cakes. The Austrians were masters of the art of dessert, especially the chocolate torte.

National politics played their part as well. With the unification of Italy in 1861, Turin temporarily became the seat of power for all of Italy. Although the capital was later moved to Rome, the cuisine of the region retains sophistication from the days when it was in the spotlight and under the influence of the best international cuisine.

Today, it is restaurateurs who are preserving traditional recipes that are time consuming and difficult to prepare. Dishes like *tajarin* – a remarkably light, hand-rolled and hand-cut pasta – and *agnolotti del plin*, small ravioli filled with pork and lamb, that are closed with a pinch (the Piedmontese word is *plin*).

Families often go out to enjoy many of these dishes rather than take the time to prepare them at home. Fortunately, there is no shortage of good restaurants to choose from. Over the last ten years there has been a steady increase in not only the number of restaurants, but the quality as well. For example, there are nine Michelin-starred restaurants in the Langhe region alone. Increasingly, a growing number of chef-owned restaurants and osterias will serve many of the traditional regional dishes as well as new creations to satisfy a discerning clientele.

Dining in Piedmont

Piedmontese start the day with a *cappuccino* or a *caffelatte* and a pastry. Italians insist that after about 11am, coffee should be an *espresso*. Those who must have milk can ask for a *macchiato* (espresso with a touch of milk) without embarrassment. Stand at the bar to drink your morning coffee, as it can cost an additional two or three euros to sit at a table. In some bars and cafés you pay first and then order.

Lunch can be substantial: a full meal will feature *antipasti* (starter), *primi* (first course) of pasta or rice, *secondi* (second course) of meat or fish, often served with *contorni* (side dish) of vegetables, followed by *dolci* (sweet) or fruit, and finally coffee. Don't feel under pressure to order every course, the trend today is to have only one or two courses at lunch. However, ordering just a single course at dinner is considered bad manners.

Aperitivo has been taken to new heights in Piedmont generally, and in Turin specifically. A sumptuous buffet will accompany your glass of *prosecco*, beer or wine ordered from 6-9pm. There is no additional charge for the food, but sometimes the drinks may be slightly more expensive.

Weekend and holiday meals can be quite long in Piedmont, as dining is a relaxed experience with many courses. Lunch is served from 12.30-2.30pm. If you want a quick lunch, look for a café with meal service. Dinner begins at 8pm and you are expected to occupy the table for the entire night. It doesn't matter if you leave early, and it is not unusual to see empty tables waiting for guests who arrive late.

Coperto (a cover charge) is no longer allowed, but many restaurants charge a few euros for bread. Italians don't tip, especially in family-run places. Often the tip is included in the total without being shown as a separate entry and certainly there is no harm in asking. Five to ten per cent extra is the correct amount to leave for good service.

Degustazione

Many of the better restaurants in Piedmont offer a tasting menu called a *degustazione*. These meals consist of several courses of seasonal and speciality dishes and are usually offered with or without wine. For the best experience choose the degustazione with wine, because each dish and wine will be perfectly matched to bring out all the flavours. But be warned, the meal may last longer than three hours and consist of up to nine courses. With even a small glass of wine per course the alcohol consumed can be substantial. The price for a degustazione may range from €40-€125 depending on the establishment, but if you are hungry this represents good value for money.

Types of establishment

Ristorante

At the higher end of the price range and offering an extended menu. It has become popular for restaurants to call themselves *trattorie* to emphasize the fresh, home-cooked nature of their food.

Trattoria

Usually family-run and serving a limited daily selection, often written on a blackboard. In rural areas these may also be called *osteria* or *locanda*. Credit cards might not be accepted in smaller premises.

Caffè

Often beautifully decorated with period furnishings and lush interiors, cafés in Turin and Piedmont are open throughout the day serving coffee, lunch and *aperitivo*.

Bakeries

Turin's bakeries overflow with chocolate and other delicious tortes. Many of them also sell mini-cakes and pastries.

Enoteca

A place to taste and purchase wine, and in Piedmont they often sell books, corkscrews and other wine accessories.

Bar

In Turin, the typical Italian bar isn't as popular for morning coffee as are the cafés. Many bars offer lavish buffets at *aperitivo* and stay open late, turning into dance clubs and discos.

Coffee

Espresso short and black

Cappuccino espresso with frothed milk

Caffelatte hot milk with espresso added

Caffè doppio a double measure of espresso

Caffè ristretto extra strong espresso

Caffè alto or *caffè lungo* with a little water added

Caffè macchiato espresso with a dash of milk

Latte macchiato a glass of hot milk with a splash of coffee

Caffè americano espresso with a lot of hot water added

Caffè estivo with whipped cream

Caffè freddo cold sweetened black coffee

Cappuccino freddo iced milky coffee

Caffè corretto with a drop of brandy or grappa

Bicerin a Turin speciality made with coffee, chocolate and cream

decaffeinato decaffeinated

bollente boiling (coffee is often served lukewarm)

Typical dishes

antipasti and vegetables

grissini breadsticks

sformato a savoury flan made with vegetables and cheese

bagna càuda hot anchovy and garlic dip served with raw vegetables

filetti di baccalà salt cod fillets

acciughe al verde anchovies in green sauce

insalata russa salad of hard-boiled egg and vegetables

vittelo tonnato cold veal with a tuna sauce

peperoni tonnato peppers with a tuna sauce

pesce carpaccio thin slices of raw fish

primi

agnolotti del plin small hand-made ravioli filled with lamb and pork, and closed with a pinch

tajarin hand-rolled, hand-cut pasta

gnocchi dumplings made with potato and chestnut

burro e salvia butter and sage sauce for pasta

fonduta cheese fondue sauce

tartufo bianco the elusive and expensive white truffle – usually grated on top of pasta or risotto

risotto ai funghi rice with mushrooms

risotto milanese rice with chicken and saffron

secondi

brasato al barolo beef cooked slowly in Barolo wine

fritto misto Piedmontese deep fried mix of savoury and sweet – includes pork, veal, polenta, apples and anything else the cook wants to add

bollito misto boiled meats served with several sauces – tastes better than it sounds

cotechino small pork sausage

coscio di agnello roast leg of lamb

la vignarola artichoke and broad bean stew

spigola al sale salted sea bass

dolci

cugnà or *cognà* chutney made from wine-must and hazelnuts; served with cheese

gianduja chocolate and hazelnut

bonet chocolate biscuits with custard and caramel

torta di nocciole hazelnut cake

Wine

In terms of quality, Italy stands beside France as a dominant player in the global market. Wine produced in Italy can fetch high prices in New York's auction houses and much of the nation's collectable red is produced in Piedmont. Top Italian wines are Brunello di Montalcino, produced in Montalcino in Tuscany, and Barolo, made in the Langhe hills of Piedmont.

Piedmont also produces Barbaresco, another collectable wine sought after by connoisseurs. Prices at the auction houses do not yet attain the lofty heights of a French Chateau Margaux, but nine bottles of 1978 Barbaresco Reserva recently fetched over US $10,000 in New York. In the autumn tasting season, Langhe's *enoteche* are full of collectors and wine buyers from around the globe.

Barolo (p.212) and Barbaresco (p.215) are not the only wines in Piedmont – there are many other less expensive alternatives. Lange Nebbiolo is made from the same nebbiolo grape used in Barolo and Barbaresco. The barbera grape is used for Barbera d'Alba and Barbera d'Asti, with the Alba wine being of better quality. Dolcetto d'Alba is made with the dolcetto grape. Roero reds are produced with locally grown nebbiolo . Dolcetto and Roero wines are drunk young and can be earthy and slightly flinty – good when accompanied by the local spicy salami and strong cheese.

Piedmont produces some good white wines. Cortese and favorita are the most commonly used grapes, with the latter being somewhat sweeter. Gavi, a dry wine made primarily from cortese, is increasing in popularity. The region near Asti is known for producing the fizzy Asti Spumante. The name might conjure memories of cheap bubbly, but the new type of Spumante is dry, light and delicious. Moscato di Asti, a sweet sparkling wine, is perfect after dinner.

There are some quality classifications worth knowing: DOC *(Denominazione di Origine Controllata)* means controlled zone of origin. DOCG *(Denominazione di Origine Controllata e Garantita)* is a higher rating, with the zone of origin guaranteed. Because of the collectability of Piedmont wines, the *DOC* and *DOCG* ratings signify a quality wine. *IGT (Indicazione Geografica Tipica)* is a more recent classification, intended to rate wines from good regions that do not meet DOC and DOCG qualifications. *Vino da tavola* means 'table wine' and these will vary considerably in quality. Some will be good and others should be avoided.

Prosecco A sparkling, dry white wine produced in Veneto, which has become popular throughout Italy. It has a light, fruity bouquet and is often enjoyed as an *aperitivo*. The best ones are *Prosecco di Conegliano-Valdobbiàdene (DOC)*. Prosecco is available in different styles: *secco* (dry) *amabile* (medium-sweet), or *frizzante* (semi-sparkling).

Aperol A bright orange drink that has a sweet tangerine flavour and a bitter grapefruit after-taste. It is made from orange, rhubarb and other ingredients and is one of the most popular Italian drinks.

Campari A bittersweet drink that is cherry-red in colour and often served with orange juice or soda water. A new drink is called a *negroni*, equal parts Campari, Martini rosso and gin – tasty but very strong.

Vermouth (see page 41) With less alcohol than spirits, this is a highly popular drink in Piedmont. It is made locally with alpine herbs and there are two main brands: Cinzano and Martini & Rossi. Vermouth is available as red, rosé or white – in sweet and dry versions.

Beer *Chiara* or *Bionda* is a pale lager; *Rossa* is more like a bitter with a reddish colour; *Scura* is a darker beer similar to stout; *Malto* is malt beer. *Alla spina* is beer from the tap, while *in bottiglia* means 'in the bottle'.

Grappa A strong brandy distilled from grape *pomace* – the skins and seeds of grapes left over after pressing for wine. Juniper berries or plums can also be used to make grappa. The best grappa comes from Piedmont, Tuscany and Sicily. Be careful, grappa will have you walking sideways.

To be listed in The Purple Guide, restaurants must be special in some way, with good food and a friendly atmosphere. We don't like arrogant service even if it comes with a Michelin star or two. For this reason you may not find some restaurants that are listed in other guides. All establishments have been tried by the author or a member of our team. Our reviews are completely independent; we do not accept payment or discounts for our recommendations.

All restaurants are open daily for lunch and dinner unless otherwise indicated.

Restaurant Listings

Restaurants are listed according to price range, signified by the € symbol. Prices are average per person, for 2-3 courses including a glass of house wine. Listings are by district for Turin, and by town for other regions. Restaurants and *trattorie* are listed first, with cafés, bars and nightclubs at the end of each section. Booking is recommended, especially for dinner.

€€€€	€75 and over
€€€	€40 - €75
€€	€20 - €40
€	€20 and under

SMOKING IS BANNED IN ALL BARS AND RESTAURANTS IN ITALY.

Turin Centro

Del Cambio
Piazza Carignano 2
011 54 6690
closed Sun
Michelin-starred
map 1-2, E2
€€€€

Del Cambio has been here since 1757. Furnishings include original red plush benches and gold trimmed chairs, walls are decorated with golden stucco work and the waiters dress in livery. Del Cambio is by far the most luxurious and elegant restaurant in Turin, yet it isn't stuffy. The menu consists of traditional Piedmontese dishes served with creative modern twists and combinations that are so delicious you'll have no trouble eating course after course.

Allow your host to decide both your food and your wine, then sit back and enjoy. Meals here go on for hours, yet the time passes quickly and pleasurably. Count Cavour was a regular here.

Al Garamond
Via Pomba 14
011 812 2781
closed Sat lunch and Sun
map 1-2, E4
€€€

At Al Garamond you'll find classic Piedmontese dishes with some interesting culinary inventions, such as sturgeon carpaccio with foie gras or Jerusalem artichoke *sformato* with anchovy sauce. The fish and wine list are excellent, as is the service. Repeatedly listed as a favourite by local celebs in Torino Magazine.

Babette
Via Alfieri 16/B
011 547 882
closed Sat lunch and Sun
map 1-2, D3
€€€

A modern restaurant set in the rooms of a 17th century baroque palace. Antonio Dacomo and chef Claudio Boretto are continuing the Piedmont tradition of matching the right food with the right wine, and with a cellar of 6,000 bottles there's no shortage of choice.

Mare Nostrum
Via Matteo Pescatore 16
011 839 4543
open daily for dinner
map 1-2, G3
€€€

Mare Nostrum specializes in fish. The young owners create a simple and relaxing atmosphere - the host sits with you while explaining the menu, and tells the story of Mare Nostrum's cuisine as if it were an exciting voyage. The food is outstanding: all the ingredients are fresh and carefully chosen.

Neuv Caval 'd Brons
Piazza San Carlo 151
011 562 7483
closed Sat lunch and Sun
map 1-2, D3
€€€

This restaurant offers three menus: regional, fish, and vegetarian. Interesting items on the regional menu include duck foie gras in Picolit gelatine, and tagliolini with lemon, mint and fresh peas. Neuv Caval 'd Brons also has an excellent selection of cheeses and wines.

Savoia
Via Corte d'Appello 13
011 436 2288
closed Sat lunch and Sun
map 1-2, C2
€€€

The chef and sommelier here pay great attention to detail. Everything brought to the table is made in house: bread, pasta, biscotti. The menu varies according to the season but, if available, try *sformato di crescione all'agretto* (watercress timbale in a sour sauce) or risotto with red wine and toma cheeses. Allow sommelier Luisa Matta to select the wine to accompany your meal. Desserts are excellent, as is presentation.

Torricelli
Via Torricelli 51
011 581 9508
closed Sun and Mon lunch
map 3-4, C2
€€€

A casual trattoria located in La Crocetta just south of GAM. The decor is simple and contemporary, with friendly staff who will carefully describe each dish on the menu. The chef regularly travels the world looking for new dishes and the menu nicely combines tradition and experimentation. The roast pheasant with grappa, truffles, and paté is superb.

Tre Galline
Via Bellezia 37
011 436 6553
closed lunch and Sun
map 1-2, C1
€€€

Tre Galline has been a name in Torinese cuisine for decades - author Cesare Pavese sang its praises. More elegant now than in Pavese's era, but the best dishes are still the classics: *il bollito*, *il*

fritto misto or try the smoked duck breast with nuts.

AB+
Via della Basilica 13
011 439 0618
closed Sun
map 1-2, D1
€€€

A modern Californian-style restaurant with an international menu. William Friedkin and Sherry Lansing held an opening night party here when the former was directing the Turin opera.

Al Gatto Nero
Corso Fillipo Turati 14
011 590 414
closed Sun and August
map 3-4, E2
€€€

A local favourite near Porta Nuova, that serves Tuscan food. The house speciality is *tagliata* made with strips of Chianina steak imported from Tuscany.

Arcadia
Galleria Subalpina
011 561 3898
closed Sun
map 1-2, E2
€€

Arcadia serves fresh high-quality sushi and sashimi at reasonable prices. The large main dining room is impersonal, so request a table in one of the smaller rooms. Service is professional, if perfunctory.

Birilli
Strada Val San Martino 6
011 819 0567
closed Sun
off map 1-2, east of I2
€€

This bustling restaurant is popular with actors and members of the Torino football team. The decor is fun and original, creating a unique atmosphere. Be sure to try the *torta Birilli*.

Hosteria La Vallée
Via Provana 3b
011 812 1788
open dinner only, closed Sun
map 1-2, F4
€€

The ambience is pleasant enough, but it's the extraordinary cuisine that draws the crowds. Dishes are all original inventions, using the best of the past without overdoing modern touches. Duck liver with sweet Muscatel and pan brioche is particularly good.

Le Vitel Etonné
Via San Francesco da Paola 4
011 812 4621
closed Sun and Wed dinner
map 1-2, E3
€€

The name is a pun on the Piedmont dish *vitello tonnato* which is outstanding here.

Osteria Tre Galli
Via San Agostino 25/b
011 521 6027
closed Sun
map 1-2, C1
€€

Tre Galli isn't fancy but it is usually packed with locals who like to banter with the chef. He will gladly make you something vegetarian if you don't eat meat. For antipasti try *sformato* or asparagus topped with eggs. Save room for lavender crème brulée or chocolate lava cake.

Trattoria Valenza
Via Borgo Dora 39
011 521 3914
closed Sun, except market days
off map 1-2, north of C1
€€

An integral part of Borgo Dora, this is the perfect place to eat on a Saturday or after a trip to the market. Walter and his son Luca love to tease and may appear rude, but it's all in good fun. The cuisine is traditional: *agnolotti, pasta e fagioli, bagnet* (meat and vegetable stew). The house coffee is a secret recipe of coffee, liqueur, lemon, and sugar.

C'era una Volta
Corso Vittorio Emanuele II 41
011 650 4589
open for dinner only, closed Sun
map 1-2, E5
€€

A modest sign and entry-phone are the only indication that there is a restaurant on the second floor of this 19th century building. House specialities include a fritto misto served only on Fridays. Prices are reasonable with a tasting menu at only €23.50. Piero Prete will be more than happy to assist you with your dinner selection and wine choice. If you can possibly save room for dolci, try the torrone mousse with dark chocolate or the bonet.

Kipling
Via Mazzini 10
011 812 6883
closed Sun lunch
map 1-2, E4
€€

No surprise that Kipling is popular with English tourists. It is a welcoming restaurant with an unusual mix of Piedmontese and Lebanese dishes. If you're tired of Italian, you may want to share a starter of hummus, falafel and pitta. The risotto with cheese and Nebbiolo wine is delicious.

L'Agrifoglio
Via dell'Accademia Albertina 38
011 83 7064
open late for dinner only
closed Sun and Mon
map 1-2, F4
€€

A pleasant restaurant offering a mix of tradition and comfort. The menu includes creative dishes such as rabbit roasted in oil, onion and cloves or duck liver medallions in wine. The cheese trolley is mouthwatering and there is a good selection of wines.

Spada Reale
Via Principe Amedeo 53
011 8171363
closed Sun
€€
map 1-2, F3

The lighting is bright and the decor a bit tatty, but the food is worth it – especially the *tajarin alla Morcina* with black truffles. The extensive wine list accommodates all budgets.

Dai Saletta
Via Belfiore 37
011 668 7867
closed Sun
no credit cards
map 1-2, E6
€€

With a warm atmosphere, red and white gingham tablecloths and a friendly owner, Dai Saletta is a good place to discover or simply to enjoy the classics of Piedmontese cuisine.

Zafferano Café
Via Sant'Agostino 15
011 521 7356
closed Sat and lunch Sun
map 1-2, C2
€€

Ricky Tognazzi and Simona Izzo have an irreverent take on Piedmontese cuisine and this has led to some unusual and delicious dishes. Seasonal menu.

La Rusnenta
Via Vittorio Andreis 11
011 436 2980
open for dinner only, closed Sun
no credit cards
off map 1-2, north of E1
€

La Rusnenta is located on the second floor of an old building. Here the owners decide your meal for you. Dishes are based on Piedmontese specialities but feature Mediterranean influences.

Societe Lutece
Piazza Carlo Emanuele II 21
011 887 644
map 1-2, F3
€

Pleasant retro-style bistro in a good location with a relaxing atmosphere and good food.

Pizza

Cristina
Corso Palermo 101
011 248 1706
closed Wed
off map 1-2, north of E1

A little out of the way, but locals agree that this place serves the best pizza in Turin. With tomatoes and mozzarella imported from Caserta near Naples, the pizza here tastes authentic. Fish is served too.

Saint Paul
Corso Vittorio Emanuele II 45
011 669 3635
closed Mon
booking required
map 1-2, E5

Tables are packed together in this chic pizzeria that is more New York than Turin. The pizza is cooked on a layer of salt which gives the crust a lively crispness. A complimentary sorbetto follows, and their desserts with melted chocolate are good.

Gennaro Esposito
Via Passalacqua 1/g
011 535 905
closed Sun
map 1-2, A2
Even if you book you may still have to queue at this popular pizzeria, named after the patron saint of Naples.

Cafés (see pages 34-36)

Al Bicerin
Piazza della Consolata 5

Baratti & Milano
Piazza Castello 27

Caffè Fiorio
Via Po 8

Café Lavazza
Via San Tommaso 10

Caffè Platti
Corso Vittorio Emanuele II 72

Caffè San Carlo
Piazza San Carlo, 156

Caffè Torino
Piazza San Carlo 204

Mulassano
Piazza Castello 15

Bars, aperitivo

Centro

Caffè Flora
Piazza Vittorio Veneto 24
011 817 1530
closed Mon
map 1-2, G3
A comfortable bar with a good location overlooking the river Po, it draws an international crowd with many English people.

Caffè Nuovo Nazionale
Via Accademia Albertina 1
011 882 140
map 1-2, F4
The perfect afternoon is spent in this 1950s-style bar gazing out of the large windows at the setting sun reflected in the waters of the Po. It's full of the local art students around aperitivo time.

Caffè Roberto
Via Po 5
011 817 7665
map 1-2, F2
€6 per drink during aperitivo
One of the best aperitivo buffets in the city, and friendly bartenders too.

Lobelix
Via Boucheron 16
011 436 7206
19.00-03.00 Mon-Sat
no credit cards
map 1-2, B2
Large servings of food available throughout the evening. Outdoor seating in summer.

Mood Libri e Caffè
Via Cesare Battisti 3E
011 518 8657
closed Sun
map 1-2, E2
Enjoy a drink in a pleasant bar that is also a new bookstore.

PIAZZA SAN CARLO AT NIGHT

Sfashion Café
Via Cesare Battisti 13
011 516 0085
map 1-2, E2
A bar on the ground floor,
a pizzeria on the first floor.

Xo
Via Po 46
08.30-03.00 daily
map 1-2, G3
In the daytime a bar with sports
on the TV, at night a club full
of university students. Often
has live music and guest DJs on
Friday and Saturday nights.

Imbarchino
Via Montebello 20
20.00-04.00 daily, May-Oct
no credit cards
map 1-2, G6
Located in Parco del Valentino,
the bar terraces descend to the
river Po. End your day watching
the glorious sunset and stay for
cocktails and dancing.

Roman Quarter
Hafa Café
Via Sant'Agostino 23C
011 436 7091

11.00-02.00 daily
map 1-2, C1
An Arabian themed bar with
Moroccan food at aperitivo.

KM 5
Via San Domenico 14/16
011 431 0032
18.00-03.00 Tue-Sun
no credit cards
map 1-2, C2
Mexican bar with aperitivo
buffet.

Live music
Café Proscope
Via Juvarra 15
011 54 0675
22.00-02.00 vary on performance
Wed: live jazz and blues,
Thurs: readings and art exhibitions
Fri: flamenco and tango
Sat: experimental theatre
no credit cards
map 1-2, A2
The venue is connected to the
Teatro Juvarra and offers a varied
programme.

E-lastico Net Café
Via Valprato 76E
011 248 1082

07.30-05.00 Tue-Sat
Jazz, blues and rock bands
off map
A relaxed bar with pool tables
and free internet points. Food
served all day, aperitivo buffet.

Il Magazzino di Gilgamesh
Piazza Moncenisio 13B
20.00-02.00 Mon-Sat
live jazz and blues bands
map 5-6, I6
Still bearing original Asian décor
and has always been a favourite
with music lovers.

Soundtown
Via Claudio Berthollet 25
011 669 6331
11.00-04.00 Mon-Sat
jazz music, cinema
map 1-2, E5
Large bar with intimate spaces
for lunch and tea on the ground
floor. Jazz in the evenings,
film shows and conferences
downstairs. Free internet points.

Discos and dance clubs

Alcatraz
Murazzi del Po 37
349 805 3516

22.00-04.00 Tues-Sat, summer
22.00-04.00 Thur-Sat, winter
drum'n'bass Fri-Sat
no credit cards
map 1-2, G4 parallel to C.Cairoli
Serves a good range of cocktails
to a mixed clientele, small dance
floor but pleasant summer
terrace.

Café Blue
Via Valprato 68
011 28 0251
23.00-04.00 Thur-Sat
21.00-02.00 Sun
rock/hip hop Thur-Sat
tango Sun
The club's entrance is near
the main entrance to the dock
courtyard. Don't be put off by the
grumpy doorman – inside, the
décor is unusual; some seating
and the DJ's console area are in a
railway carriage. The atmosphere
changes on Tango Sundays.

Dock8
Via Valprato 68
011 28 5936
24.00-06.00 Fri-Sat
06.00-12.00 Sun
techno and electric music
A dance club on two levels with
large screen videos.

Docks Home
Via Valprato 68
011 28 5936
24.00-06.00 Tue-Wed, Fri-Sat
house music
A disco on two levels with
choreographed light show in the
lounge. Art is exhibited in smaller
parts of the venue.

Giancarlo
Murazzi del Po 49
011 81 7472
23.00-07.00 May-Oct
no credit cards

map 1-2, G3
Named after the founder, this is more of a pub than a club. A beacon for night owls searching for somewhere open in the wee hours.

Hiroshima Mon Amour
Via Bossoli 83
011 317 6636
21.00-04.00 Tue-Sat
Sat disco admission free
cabaret & theatre admission varies
no credit cards
A cultural centre opened in 1984 to promote Italian and international music, and to present comic and cabaret theatre.

Officine Belforte
Corso Venezia 30
24.00-06.00 Fri,Sat
closed July & Aug
acid techno Friday with DJs
R&B/ hip hop Saturday
Officina has a large main area with a round central bar, a smaller bar and an intriguing Arabian tented room with sofas, cushions and hookahs.

On-Gaia
Via Valprato 68
349 843 0860, 335 42 7935
24.00-06.00 Thur-Sat
hip hop Thursday
techno Friday
rock & pop Saturday
A spacious two-level venue with art exhibits in the White room.

Rock City
Corso Dante 17A
011 319 0884
23.30-05.00 Thur-Sat
house music
admission €10-20
map 1-2, D3
A disco that occasionally presents

interesting events.

The Beach
Murazzi del Po 18-22
011 88 8777
23.00-05.00 Tue-Sun, Feb-Oct
techno and house music
map 1-2, G3 parallel to C.Cairoli
Relax in summer on deckchairs by the riverbank, then dance the night away inside where videos are projected on the contemporary white walls.

Transilvania
Corso Unione Sovietica 353
011 61 3669
21.00-04.00
Heavy metal
Food and drinks such as Dracula's blood are served on coffins. Gothic, dark and spooky, this club was founded by a director of horror movies.

Zoo Bar
Corso Casale 127
011 819 4347
23.00-05.00 Tue,Fri-Sat
closed July & Aug
live events Tuesday
cabaret Thursday
R&B Friday
house/dance Saturday
admission: free Tue, €9 Fri, €10 Sat
map 1-2, H2
The décor of Zoo's upper level is like a that of a loft venue in New York. The lower level is like a Hard Rock Café, filled with memorabilia.

Lingotto and beyond

La Pista
Via Nizza 262 (arriving on foot)
Via Nizza 294 (arriving by car)
011 631 3523
closed Tues
€€€

Elegant and modern, La Pista is located on the Lingotto roof and offers a great view of the city. There is a choice of a meat or fish set menu or à-la-carte. The cheese board is superb with a long list of dessert wines to accompany both pre-dessert and dessert. Arrive by car and be driven to the top on the unique spiral ramp designed for Fiat by Mattè Trucco.

Ristorante Torpedo
c/o Le Meridien Lingotto
011 664 4200
Via Nizza 262
no closed days
€€€
map 5-6, G2

The chef gives local ingredients a modern twist: ricotta *sformato* with a pumpkin chestnut sauce; *tajarin* with spinach, pine nuts and saffron; lamb with mustard and Cuneo peppers. A two- or three-course set menu is offered.

Antiche Sere
Via Cenischia 9
011 385 4347
open for dinner only, closed Sunday
no credit cards
€€

The Rota family's popular trattoria is a drive or taxi ride from the city centre, but the food is worth the effort. The menu rarely changes – long-standing favourites include *tomini al verde* (small toma cheese balls in anchovy sauce) followed by gnocchi with sausage ragù, and for secondi *tapulon* (meat stewed in spiced wine). For dessert try the panna cotta. In summer, they open a vine-covered patio.

Rivoli
Combal.Zero
Piazza Mafalda di Savoia
011 956 5225
closed Mon and Tues
Michelin-starred
€€€€

Chef Davide Scabin's philosophy is concept cuisine: restaurant as theatre. One example is the *Hambook*, ultra-thin slices of prosciutto and strips of melon paste served like pages in translucent containers shaped like books. *Cybereggs* are fried quail-eggs on potato chips with a light peanut sauce, and a deconstructed pizza is served with beer and/or coke.

Superga

Osteria del Paluch
Via Superga 44
011 940 8750
closed Mon, dinner Sun
English menu
€€€

Chef Marina Ramasso collects cookbooks and diaries from the 1800s and these inspire her traditional dishes. She uses fresh Piedmontese herbs and a wood-fired oven in her large kitchen, open to a view of the patio and garden.

Bel deuit
Via Superga 58
011 943 1719
closed Wed, lunch Thurs
€€

Bel Deuit offers simple and nutritious cooking in the warm ambience of an old trattoria. The mountain cured meats and cheeses are excellent.

Susa & Chisone valleys

Bardonecchia

Bardosteria
Via Medail 33
0122 99 862
closed lunch Mon in Summer
€€€

The mountain chalet decor features exposed brick, pine timbers and glass partitions. One of the house specialities is antipasti of veal tartar with raw slices of porcini muchrooms - a veritable masterpiece; or try the small portions of breaded veal escalopes served cold with thin slices of zucchini. The rabbit salad and the fresh cold trout are excellent as are the two types of pasta served in a porcini jus, a sauce as dark as squid ink. As a palate cleanser (or dessert) the vanilla goat's-milk ice-cream is surprisingly delicious.

on the slopes

Bar Colomion
Via Reg. Molino 18
08.30-sunset daily Nov-Apr, Jun-Sept
Open early for a breakfast and coffee, lunch service begins at 12.30 and their sunchairs make for a relaxing afternoon siesta.

pizza

La Filanda
Via Medail 100
0122 999 780
eat in and take away
€

The Sicilian Ferrisi family make outstanding pizza in their wood-fired oven, on which they also grill meat and fish. The wine list features Sicilian wine.

bars, aperitivo

Crot'd Ciulin
Via des Geneys 20
closed Thurs, June and Oct
0122 96 161
This wine bar is located in the old town centre in a 19th century

house. It's managed by Cristina and Massimo Guiffrei, who provide a good aperitivo buffet at around 5pm, with tasty sausages and cheeses.

Sitting Bull
Via Cesare Battisti 1
348 810 8924
11.00-02.00 daily, closed Monday
17.30-18.30 happy hour
A Western-themed bar with 26 types of draft beer and pool tables. Food served includes hamburgers, tortillas and nachos.

Border line
Via Medail 38/B
333 151 8651
09.00-03.00 daily in high season
closed May and Oct
A popular disco-pub with live music.

Fenestrella, Mentoulles

La Meizoun Blancho
Via Granges 10
0121 83 933
no credit cards

€€€
The restaurant is part of an *agriturismo* farm set in the middle of a large park. All the ingredients are organically grown on their farm. The special care taken over the ingredients shows in the tomatoes that burst with flavour, and the subtle garlic toasts with wafer-thin slices of lard drizzled with olive oil that melt in your mouth. The ricotta is fresh (from animal to plate in maximum of two days) and served wrapped in Bresaola drizzled with olive oil. You must try a homemade vol-au-vent filled with speck, tomato and Tome cheese. A house speciality is venison marinated for 24 hours. Beware the after dinner sugar lump: it is pickled in arquebuse alcohol. Suck it hard and your eyes will water for half an hour.

SAUZE D'OULX

Bar Rosa Rossa
Via Umberto I, 86
0121 884 706
07.00-03.00 daily
closed Tues in low season
A historic wine bar with more
than 40 types of grappa as well
as a large selection of white and
red wines. Serves breakfast, and
sausages and cheese at lunch. In
summer there is a large outdoor
patio.

Oulx

Borgovecchio
Via des Ambrois 46
0122 831 017
€
This friendly simple pizzeria with
good quality food and warm local
ambience is located in a cobbled
street just above the old town. The
interior is cosy and comfortable
with a bar area for light snacks.
The main dining room has long
wooden tables shared by groups of
friends and couples. Daily specials
and wood-fired pizzas are washed
down with a carafe of house wine.

La Barrica
Via Faure Rollland 4
0122 830 794
18.00-22.00 daily, closed Mon
A wine bar with more than 450
labels from Piedmont, Trentino
and Sicily. The kitchen offers a
selection of Piedmontese dishes
and platters of salami and cheese
to accompany the wine.

Roxy Bar
Via Monginevro 38
open till 01.00
closed Wed
Good coffee in the mornings,
a large aperitivo buffet in the
evenings and Sky TV with football
on Sunday afternoons.

Pragelato

Antica Osteria
Bivio Val Troncea, Borgata Plan
Via del Beth 26
0122 78 530
open summer and winter
closed Tues
booking required
€€€
Owner and chef, Roberto Jayme,
was born in this modernised 18th
century house. The old cave-style
ovens once used to bake bread for
the winter now make the pizzas
for the restaurant.
Roberto's speciality is a mixed
grill of pork ribs, sausages
and guinea fowl served with
shredded Glore potatoes baked in
milk. The cheese and wine list are
excellent, as is the service. One of
the best restaurants in all of the
Piedmont ski resorts.

Sauze d'Oulx

Chalet Il Capricorno
Le Clotes, Via Case Sparse 21
0122 850 273
www.chaletilcapricorno.it
Michelin-starred
€€€€
This cosy restaurant is situated
2 km from the town centre.
Guests are transported by
skidoo. It is part of a ski chalet
owned by Vincent and Annette
Hawkins, together with Carlo
and Maria Rosa. Chef Maria
works wonders from her kitchen
and her specialities include
aubergine flan with tomato and
basil, mixed peppers with green
beans, followed by handmade
ravioli with julienne of courgette
or *tajarin* with turkey ragu. For
secondi don't miss the roast
ham wrapped with thinly sliced

veal coated with melted Fontina cheese.

Sestriere

La Locanda di Colomb
Frazione Champlas Seguin 27
0122 832 944
closed Mon
€€€
Driving towards Cesana, find the restaurant by turning off the main road from Sestriere at the exit for the village of Champlas Seguin. Be prepared to be entertained by Paolo Columb (above), the charming proprietor. Meat is a speciality: the *carne salata* is made with strips of cured beef. Try the ravioli stuffed with venison and served with butter and sage, or the beef stew with potatoes and polenta. Excellent local wines and cheeses feature strongly on the menu in a great little restaurant.

Grangie Elp
mobile 347 175 2990
Sestriere Area Monterotta
€€€
The name means a refuge, and this attractive restaurant is high up the mountain, in a picturesque setting with spectacular views into France. Take the via Monte Rotta from Sestriere to the road's end, then hike or ski (cross-country) along the 'Balcony Trail' to the restaurant.
The building was hand-built by owners the Scaini family with a giant sundeck where in summer, cows graze only metres away and marmots sit up sniffing the air, as if captivated by the aroma of Mama Scaini's cooking.
Antipasti include fresh anchovies, cheese and garlic bread, salami and ham. Main course specialities are local sausages in polenta and roast rabbit in rich wine ragù. Mama's apricot tart is unforgettable.

Cantini degli Alpini
Cesana Torinese, Via Nazionale 1
Mollieres 1
0122 89 545
closed Tues
€€
This is worthy of a taxi fare from wherever you may be based in the Piedmont mountains. The house specialities are famous and include *mostarda* (boiled fruits pickled with sugar corn syrup, pepper and mustard for one month) served with boiled meats or strong cheeses, gnocchi with the powerful and distinctive flavour of Castlemagna cheese and in the summer season, thin *tajarin* with the freshest porcini mushrooms. For dessert the gently grilled peaches with a baked biscuit topping is a house favourite – which the chef admits is 'almost as good as my grandmother's'. Being a good Italian grandson, he dare not say 'as good,' though it is difficult to imagine peaches ever tasting better.

RESTAURANTS

Lago Maggiore

Arona

Taverna del Pittore
Piazza del Popolo 39
0322 243 366
closed Mon
closed 15 Dec-15 Jan
€€€€
Enjoy a pleasant view of the lake while you relax over a meal. Try courgette flowers filled with lobster, and turbot accompanied by a crisp Pinot Grigio.

Del Barcaiolo
Piazza del Popolo 23
0322 243 388
closed Wed
€€€€
Located in the 14th century Palazzo del Podesta, the restaurant has an open kitchen serving grilled meat and fish.

Al Vecchio Portico
Piazza del Popolo 14
0322 240 108
€€
This rustic cellar-style trattoria is cosy in winter, and in summer there is a large outdoor seating area under umbrellas located across the road in the main piazza with a view over the water. The summer menu is light, with many fish dishes. A perfect vegetarian lunch begins with a hot, flakey vegetable strudel followed by risotto with egg and herbs and topped off with *cassata di ricotta e semifreddi* (ice cream cake). The young staff make a

great show of darting across the road between the piazza and the trattoria kitchen, run by mom who comes out waving if dishes sit waiting.

Trattoria Campagna
Via Vergante 12
0322 57 294
closed Tues and winter Mon
closed 15-30 June and 2 wks Nov
€€
An old-style trattoria that serves pasta, fagioli, grilled meats and fish. There is an excellent cheese board with local mountain and French cheeses.

Vecchia Arona
Lungolago Marconi 17
0322 242 469
closed Fri
€€
The menu changes daily according to the availability of fresh ingredients. The pasta is homemade and the Piedmontese stuffed quail is memorable. There is a tasting menu, a wide selection of French cheeses and a good wine cellar.

Caffè della Sera
Lungolago Marconi 85
closed 2 weeks Jan-Feb
€
The simple menu includes delicious grilled vegetables with smoked cheese.

Cannobio

Del Lago
Via Nazionale 2, Carmine Inferiore
0323 70 595
closed Tues, lunch Wed
closed Nov-Feb
€€€€
Situated by the lake with a beautiful view, and specialises in fish and seafood. Terrine of foie gras with muscatel jelly, duck with sesame, strawberry pastries and other classic cuisine.

Lo Scalo
Piazza Vittorio Emanuele III 32
0323 71 480
closed Mon, Tues lunch
closed 5 wks Jan-Feb
€€€
A superb restaurant where the bread is homemade, the ham is from Val Vigezzo and the cheese board has a vast selection from the local mountains. Try guinea fowl with black truffles, a house speciality.

Domodossola

Albergo Domus
Vicolo Cuccioni 12
0324 242 325
€
A cheap and cheerful family run trattoria that is useful for lunch on market Saturdays.

Bar Moderna/Portico
Piazza Mellerio 4
Located opposite the train station and serving great coffee.

Isola Bella

Elvezia
Via Vittorio Emanuele 18
0323 30 043
€€
Sandwiches and snacks are served downstairs, meals are on the terrace upstairs with good views of Stresa. Try pasta with wild sage followed by lake perch with almonds.

Isola dei Pescatori

Hotel Verbano/Ristorante Unione
0323 30 381 Unione
closed Thursday

0323 30 408 Verbano
Booking required
ring 0336 240 630 for private boat
€€-€€€

Verbano is a restaurant, Unione is a trattoria: both are operated by the same family who provide free transportation in their private boat to and from the island in the evenings. Both establishments serve excellent fish with good homemade pasta. In summer, eat on the terrace with views of Lago Maggiore and Isola Bella.

Isola di San Giulio

San Giulio
Via alla Basilica 4
0322 90 234
€€€

In winter, meals are served in the 18th century dining room, in summer enjoy your meal on a large terrace overlooking the lake. In the evenings private ferry transport is provided from Orta. The chestnut gnocchi is superb as is *penne al capricco*, and trout all'isolana (with butter and basil). The cooking has improved since the arrival of a new chef.

Lesa

L'Antico Maniero
Via alla Campagna 1
0322 74 11
closed Mon, Sun eve
closed 1-15 Nov and 1-15 Jan
booking required
€€€€

An elegant restaurant located in an 18th century castle set in extensive gardens. Tables are beautifully set with silver-trimmed cream damask napkins on pale pink cloths. The food is delicious and meals often go on for four hours. Especially good is the smoked breast of duck carpaccio with a hint of truffle. The wine list is extensive and the service caring and professional.

Pallanza

Milano
Corso Zanitello 2
0323 55 6816
closed Mon eve, Tue
closed mid Nov-mid Feb
€€€

In good weather sit out on the lakeside terrace of this 1920s-style villa. Classic Piedmont dishes are served with an emphasis on ultra-fresh fish from the lake accompanied by organic vegetables. For dessert, try the amaretto bavarois.

Il Torchio
Via Manzoni 20
0323 503 352
closed Wed, lunch Thurs
€€

A rustic trattoria with a warm atmosphere and good Piedmontese cooking.

Caffè Bolongaro
Lungalago Pallanza
0323 50 3346
open daily
€

A popular pizzeria nicely decorated with a large outdoor eating area.

Mergozzo

La Quartina
Via Pallanza 20
0323 80 118
€€€

Chef Laura Perfumo's specialities include pasta filled with braised meat in duck sauce and fillets of white fish. For dessert try and warm pastries filled with apples.

Piccolo Lago

Via Filippo Turati 87
0323 586 792
booking required
closed Sun eve, Mon & January
Michelin-starred
€€€€

Piccolo Lago is the vision of
two brothers from Mergozzo,
Carlo and Marco Sacco. As
children they shared the
same dream: to have the best
restaurant they could imagine,
and they wanted it to be near
their home. Beginning in 1986,
they travelled far and wide to
learn the necessary skills. Carlo
became a sommelier, and Marco
a chef. They returned home,
opened their restaurant in 1995,
improved upon it and earned a
Michelin star.

The restaurant's large main
dining room has wooden floors
and beamed ceilings. It is
perched over Lago Mergozzo,
with large windows looking
over the lake to Mergozzo. There
is also a private dining room.

Marco changes the menu
seasonally, but he always
includes fish caught fresh from
the lake, meat from the region
and selections of fine local
cheeses. His desserts are superb.

The best thing to do is to settle
in for an evening and have the
traditional degustazione menu
(around €60) with wine (an
additional €20). Carlo's choices
are always spot-on, the service
is impeccable, and every dish is
perfect. In a region famous for
its food and wine, the brothers
have made an extraordinary
restaurant.

Vecchio Olmo

Piazza Cavour 2
0323 80 335
closed Thur Sep-Jul, all June
€€

A family-run trattoria located
in the main square on Lago
Mergozzo. The set menu is good
value with excellent fish and
homemade pasta.

Orta

Villa Crespi

Via Giuseppe Fava 18
0322 911 902
closed Jan-mid Feb
booking required
Michelin-starred
€€€€

Set in a luxurious hotel managed
by the Primatesa family. The
fanciful building incorporates
a minaret into the moorish
architecture. Neapolitan chef
Antonino Cannavacciuolo
presides over the restaurant.
Fish is the house speciality but
the loin of lamb with mint and
thyme is worth mentioning. The
extensive wine list has more than
500 labels.

San Rocco
Via Gippini 11
0322 911 912
€€€
A romantic restaurant set in a 17th century monastery on the lakeshore beyond the shopping lanes. Specialities include gorgonzola risotto, fillet of trout and smoked duck breast.

Olina
Via Olina 40
0322 905 656
€€
This modern, friendly restaurant is found on Orta's main street. The set menu is good value, large well-prepared portions and antipasti enough for two. The Val Vigezzo prosciutto and melon starter was delicious, and so large a portion that the waiter packed it to take away. Hand-made pasta is especially good: try pumpkin tortellini or ravioli with asparagus. Fish from the lake is served grilled or pan-fried with almonds, or they do a very nice steak covered with porcini.

Leon d'Oro
Piazza Maria Motta 42
0322 911 991
closed January
€€
Beautifully situated, a vine-covered terrace overlooks the lake and Isola di San Giulio. The restaurant and attached three-star hotel are owned by the Ronchetti family who provide a friendly welcome and good home-style cooking.

Taverna Antico Agnello
Via Olina 18
0322 90 259
closed Tue & Dec-Jan
€€
A rustic old taverna that serves creative regional food including horse with garlic and rosemary and minced donkey, a delicacy.

Venus
Piazza Mario Motta 50
0322 90 259/362
€€
Venus is well-located on the lakefront in a corner of Orta's main piazza, with views out

LAGO MERGOZZO

to the island. Try *tajarin* with lobster, and crumbed lamb cutlets with roast potatoes accompanied by a 2000 Barbera D'Alba, Ornati. The chocolate flan consists of layers of chocolate, almond butter and creme caramel. On summer weekends music is provided by a chap playing requests on keyboards and clarinet.

Osteria al Boeuc
Via Bersani 28
0322 915 854
closed Tue Apr-Dec
closed Mon-Wed Jan-Mar
€
This is a 500-year-old wine bar with barrels for seats. They serve bruschetta, cheese, cold cuts, *salcicia ubriaca* (drunken sausage) together with more than 350 wines. The owners' shop La Dispensa is next door, and sells their sausage.

Arte del Gelato
Via Olina 30
0335 832 9298
Serves the best ice cream in Orta.

Caffe Jazz
Via Olina 13
0322 91 1700
open till 01.00,
closed Monday
A popular jazz bar with good live music and friendly staff.

Sacro Monte
Ristorante Sacro Monte
Via Sacromonte 5
0322 90 220
€€
Located in an old stone farmhouse with three dining rooms and an attached cafe. The atmosphere is quiet and peaceful and the food well-prepared, with an emphasis on meat dishes.

Santa Maria Maggiore
Miramonti
Piazzale Diax 3
0324 950 135
€€
A pretty restaurant serving mountain-cured prosciutto and salami. The pasta with potato, bacon and cheese is a speciality.

Lovely cheese-board with large selection. Desserts are divine.

Da Branin
Piazza Risorgimento
0324 94 933
€€

A pleasant restaurant in the central piazza. Tables spill outside in the summer. Try the carpaccio of meat, game and sea-bass followed by *tajarin* with almonds.

Le Colonne
Via Benefattori 7
0324 94 153
€€

Quail salad, risotto creamed with lard, and fried frog's legs with basil are served in this 18th century dining room.

Stresa

La Scuderia
Villa Pallavicino
0323 32 736
€€€

Stop here for delicious food in a beautifully situated restaurant in the villa's gardens.

Il Triangolo
Via Roma 61
0323 327 36
closed Tues
€€

Airy surroundings and seating on outside terrace in warm weather compensates for the lack of a view. The fish ravioli are excellent.

Lo Stornello
Behind church on lakefront
0323 30 444
closed Tuesday
€

Run by a local couple who serve their own specialities.

Osteria Degli Amici
Via Bolongaro 31
0323 30 453
closed Tuesday
Particularly good pizza is served.

Soriso

Al Sorriso
Via Roma 18
0322 983 228
closed Mon, lunch Tues
Michelin-starred
€€€€

Chef Luisa Valazza was recently awarded her second Michelin star. Be sure to book, as diners come from miles around to this tiny restaurant situated in the hills south of Lago d'Orta. In season, try the ravioli stuffed with pumpkin served with Alba truffles. Luisa's desserts are stunning.

Verbania

Osteria del Castello
Piazza Castello 9
0323 516 579
closed Sun, 1 wk Oct & 1 wk Feb
€€

Traditional Piedmontese cuisine, with mountain-cured salami and cheese from Ossola.

Osteria Boccon Di Vino
Via Troubetzkoy 86, Suna
0323 504 039
closed Tues, Wed lunch & Jan
€€

A small osteria whose assured cuisine belies the basic decor and the menu scribbled on a blackboard. If *maltagliati con i porri* (pasta with leeks) appears, order it; the desserts are equally fine, and as for wine - just order a bottle of Barbera.

Langhe

Acqui Terme

Osteria La Curia
Via Alla Bollente 72
0144 356 049
closed Mon
€€€

Brick-vaulted ceilings, checked tablecloths, a warm fire and the scent of rosemary are all part of the ambience here. The portly owner will enthusiastically recite the menu. Striving for freshness, Piedmont restaurants often prepare only a few dishes each day. Antipasti included *crespelle*, crêpes with pears and melted blue cheese, and *bresaola* with figs and a dip of marmalade. La Curia's chef uses only eggs and flour in his pasta – a dozen eggs for two pounds of fresh pasta – so it's best to keep the sauce simple. Try *burratta* (local cheese similar to mozzarella) fresh basil, tomatoes, and extra virgin olive oil washed down with the local sparkling *Acqui Spumante*. Finish your meal with strudel and fresh figs, or torrone ice cream. The €100 per person *degustazione con tartufo bianco* (when white truffles are in season) is a bargain for five courses including *l'uovo in cocotte* – the absolute best way to eat white truffle. In summer, seating is outdoors in the piazza.

Antica Osteria Bigãt
Via Mazzini 30/32
0144 324 283
closed Wed and Sun lunch
€€

Ancient recipes have been handed down from the founding Cordara family to the present owners Vincenzo Alpa and Ornella Pera. The Osteria specialises in organic beef (butchered according to old methods) mountain cured pancetta, salami and *formaggetta* cheese (made from hill-farmed sheep and goat's milk with added herbs). The traditional dishes include *farinata* – a flat crunchy chickpea bread – vegetables dipped into a hot *bágna cauda*, and *buì* (boiled meats) served hot and dipped into a cold chopped parsley sauce, *el bagnet verd*. The *degustazione della Tradizione* is excellent value for money at €45 for eight courses.

Ca' del Vien
Via Mazzini 14
0144 56 650
closed Mon
€

Located in the centre of town. Chef Gloria serves traditional specials, beef in Barbera, roast peppers with bagna cauda. Together with the Regionale Enoteca, the owners have created a good wine list. If you find a wine you like it's available for purchase at the enoteca.

Pasticceria Voglino
Corso Italia1, Piazza Italia 11
0144 322 412
07.00-20.00 daily
open later in summer

An art nouveau ice cream and pastry shop that dates back to the early 1900s and still uses the old recipes. Voglino is known for its macaroons and rum-flavoured chocolate kisses, called *baci*. The shop's old-style hand-made ice cream parfaits are especially delicious.

Mozart Wine & Coffee
Via Crimea 5
0144 56 482
07.30-02.00 daily
closed August
A stylish café with round booths, marble tables and soft background music. Enjoy the excellent *sacher torte* accompanied by a frothy coffee or a glass of Acqui bubbly.

Alba

Lalibera
Via Pertinace 24a
0173 293 155
closed Sun, Mon lunch
closed in Feb and Aug
€€
One of the most popular restaurants in Alba and a good spot for lunch. Start with *tortino di parmagiano con carciofi* (savoury tart with parmesan and artichoke) followed by chestnut gnocchi with mountain Gorgonzola. The outstanding cheese plate comprises small cuts of eleven cheeses arranged like the numbers on a clock, with a thick paste of fruit jam in the middle for dipping.

Osteria dell'Arco
Piazza Savona 5
0173 363 974
closed Sun, Mon lunch and Aug
€€
This is a comfortable well-located osteria in one of Alba's main squares. The cuisine is traditional featuring handmade pasta and locally reared meat. There is a good list of wines and many are served by the glass. House specialities include: duck breast with fava beans, *tajarin* with tomato and sausage ragu, braised veal, and rabbit cooked in wine.

For dessert, have a traditional hazelnut cake with zabaglione. Prices are reasonable – the five course degustazione menu is only €37.

Da Stefania
Via San Paolo 5
0173 362 768
closed Tues eve, Thurs eve
open in mid-afternoon
€€
A modern trendy restaurant with good pasta.

Vincafe
Via Vittorio Emanuele 12
0173 364 603
closed Mon
€
A popular bistro for lunch with seating outdoors, or inside and downstairs in the brick-vaulted cellar. They have a good selection of Piedmontese sparkling wines.

Osteria del Teatro
Via General Govone 7
0173 34 231
closed Wed
€
This comfortable osteria located in the centre of the old town serves typical local cuisine.

Dance clubs

Caline Club
Corso Bixio 54
0173 441 840

Studio Vu
San Cassiano
0173 285 430

Alto Mondo
Via Tanaro 5
0173 441 972

Albaretto della Torre

Da Cesare
Via Umberto 12
0173 520 141

closed Tues, Wed lunch
€€€

Cesare Giacconi is known for his spit-roasted meats, particularly goat and duck. The restaurant is small and the décor modest. Go in November, during white truffle season, for two or three courses preceded by Cesare's amazing chestnut soup. You may purchase his excellent vinegar here too.

Barbaresco

Antinè
Via Torino 34/A
0173 635 294
closed Wed
booking required
Michelin-starred
€€€€

Chef Andrea Marino opened this restaurant in the centre of Barbaresco in 1998. The décor is minimal but the food is imaginative and the service impeccable. A starter of cod in pastry, with a filling of leeks and tiny capers, is creamy yet tart. The pasta is excellent, especially the *agnolotti*, and the roasted duck drumstick has a delicious crispy skin. The list of Barbaresco wine includes some rare vintages.

Antica Torre
Via Torino 64
0173 635 170
closed Wed eve, Thurs
€€

At the foot of Barbaresco tower, this trattoria is owned by two plump sisters – one cooks, the other serves. The homemade pasta is dished out from large steaming platters – they insist you have seconds.

Outside Barbaresco

Vecchio Tre Stelle
Frazione Tre Stelle
Via Rio Sordo 13
0173 638 192
closed Tues
Michelin-starred
€€€€

Young and talented, the chef aims his menu between modern and traditional cuisine, with an emphasis on meat dishes. In November they offer a *tartufo bianco* menu (€30) with the white truffle topping priced separately at 4.5 euros per gram (20 grams in total provides a good blanketing on each dish). The restaurant is popular with German tourists.

Barolo

Locanda nel Borgo Antico
Via Boschetti 4
0173 56 355
closed Tues, Wed lunch
booking required
Michelin-starred
€€€€

Chef Massimo Camia and wife Luciana are well known amongst wine-buyers from around the world. An autumn favourite is *tajarin* with black truffle, or *gnochetti verdi* (potato dumplings prepared with aged Castelmagno cheese). Massimo offers two wine lists, one is exclusively Barolo. At lunch on sunny days there is limited seating on the terrace.

La Cantinetta da Maurilio e Paolo
Via Roma 33
0173 56 198
closed Wed eve, Thurs
closed Feb
€€

Two brothers, Maurilio and Paolo
Chiappetto, welcome you into
a cosy dining room, with tables
grouped around an open hearth.
In nice weather, book ahead for a
table on the small terrace. A tasting
menu is offered for €30 without
wine. Wonderful house wines
are made from grapes grown on
vines surrounding this delightful
restaurant. There is a bar/enoteca
at the front if you want to sample
a glass.

La Cantinella trattoria
Via Acquagelata 4a
0173 56 267
closed dinner Mon, Tue
€

A traditional trattoria that is good
for a lunch of primi and salad, with
a selection of wine by the glass.

Bergolo
'L Bunet
Via Roma 24
0173 87 013
closed Tues
closed in Jan
€€

Traditional home cooking with a
different set menu each day and a
noteworthy selection of cheeses.

Bra
Osteria Boccondivino,
Via Medicita' Istruita 14
0172 425 674
closed Sun, Mon
10 days in August
€€

The deep yellow décor creates a
warm atmosphere in the osteria
where Slow Food was born.

Badellino
Piazza XX Septembe 4
0172 439 050
closed Tuesday
€€

A family-owned restaurant dating back to the 1900s. If the dessert cart includes an overstuffed chocolate log, be sure to have it. The filling is so delicious another diner was seen to have seconds and then thirds – her plate gladly refilled by the friendly host amidst teasing from the local clientele.

Pasticceria Converso
Via Vittorio Emanuele 199
0172 413 626
closed Mon

An historical café opened in 1902 by Felice Converso whose family of bakers can be traced back to the 1700s. Traditional recipes are still being used by present day owners Renato and Federico Boglione who make perfect croissants and a legendary *panettone* flavoured with sweet Moscato wine.

Cremeria il Chiosco
Piazza Roma 35
0172 412 181
closed Wed

An old-fashioned ice cream and cake shop that serves light meals and sandwiches at lunch. A house speciality is the *bicerin* ice cream.

Canale

All'Enoteca, Davide Palluda
Via Roma 57
0173 95 857
closed Wed & Thur lunch
Michelin-starred
€€€

Chef Davide and his sister Ivana manage this unpretentious restaurant in the same building as the Entoca Roero. A Canale native, Davide was educated in Barolo and achieved his first Michelin star in 2000, aged 29. The atmosphere is warm and comfortable and every dish is outstanding. My companion was a Milan-based food writer who rated it as the best restaurant in Italy. The risotto was divine. I've never had one quite so good, likewise the egg cocotte with white truffle, which was followed by a tender leg of pigeon.

Castiglione Falleto

Le Torri
Piazza Vittorio Veneto 10
0173 62 849
closed all day Tue, Wed lunch
booking advised
€€€

A family-run restaurant with large windows that provide views over the wine-making Barolo region. The cuisine is traditional and chef Maria Cristina makes an excellent Piedmontese *fritto misto* which must be ordered in advance. The wine list is features many local wines including labels from the neighboring Vietti winery.

Diano D'Alba

Trattoria Nelle Vigne
Via Santa Croce 17
0173 46 8503
closed Mon, Tues
€€

This informal trattoria serves well-prepared local dishes including: *anchovies alle nocciole* (anchovies with a hazelnut sauce), tuna in *agrodolce* (sweet and sour sauce), gnocchi of potato and cheese, *agnolotti del plin*, risotto with wine, *bonet*, *torta di miele* (honey cake), *semifreddo al torrone* (torrone ice cream). The wine list includes 200 labels, almost all local.

Grinzane Cavour

La Salinera
Via IV Novembre 13
0173 262 915
closed Tues
€€€
Conveniently located at the bottom of a driveway that leads to Grinzane Cavour castle and enoteca. House specialities are generally meat-based and pasta is home-made. Desserts are excellent, try their *bonet*, (cocoa and coffee blended into a pudding with a lady fingers-type crust and almonds) or *panna cotta* (cooked milk custard).

Nonna Genia
Localita Borzone 1
0173 26 2410
open evenings only
closed Wed and Thur
€€
A friendly trattoria serving local specials. The cheese trolley offers a selection of fresh and ripe cheeses, accompanied by home-made *cognà*. The list has plenty of Piedmont wines, and a good assortment of local grappa.

La Morra

Belvedere
Piazza Castello 5
0173 50 190
closed Sun eve and Mon
€€€
The name means beautiful view. Indeed, the outlook from the baronial dining room perched high above the Barolo vineyards is a reason to visit. The kitchen maintains a high standard that is primarily based around meat dishes. The de-boned rabbit stuffed with herbs is especially good. Belevedere's wine list runs to 83 pages and prices are surprisingly reasonable. Service is generally attentive but can turn brusque when large tour parties fill the function rooms.

Osteria Veglio
Franzione Annunciata 9
0173 509 341
closed Tues, lunch Wed
€€
Chef Franco Gioelli experiments with creative variations on Piedmont cuisine and offers a four course fixed price menu €45.

L'Osteria del Vignaiolo
Regione Santa Maria 12
0173 50 335
closed Wed, Thurs
€€
Local specialities at affordable prices including a four course fixed menu for €30.

Vineria San Giorgio
Via Umberto 1
0173 509 594
11.00-02.00 daily
closed Mon
This wine bar is set in the ancient cellars of the house once occupied by Giuseppe Gabetti, the composer of the Savoy Royal March.

Madonna di Como

Locanda del Pilone
Frazione Madonna di Como 34
0173 366 616
closed Tues, Wed lunch

Michelin-starred
€€€€

An elegant and sophisticated restaurant with windows overlooking Barbaresco vineyards. Chef Maurizio and wife Sabrina Quaranta create imaginative variations on Piedmont cuisine using ingredients home-grown on the farm. The wine list has many labels produced near the Locanda. Specialties include: loin of rabbit with hazelnut, stone ground polenta filled with porcini and white truffle, grilled venison with juniper. For dessert try strawberry cream with Moscato d'Asti sparkling wine.

Monticello d'Alba

Conti Roero
Piazza San Ponzio 3, Localita Villa
0173 64 155
closed Mon, Sun eve
Michelin-starred
€€€€

In August 2004, Chef Siccardi and his wife opened their own restaurant. They have already achieved their first Michelin star. The cuisine is both traditional and creative, combining new approaches with Roero's gastronomical heritage.

Monforte d'Alba

Giardino da Felicin
Via Vallada 18
0173 78 225
open for dinner only
closed Sun eve, Mon
€€€€

An elegantly comfortable restaurant that serves traditional cuisine. *Antipasti* features an excellent fish in a basil sauce, paté made with marsala wine,

spectacular grilled vegetables in a pine nut sauce. House *secondi* include a potatoe *millefoglie* with mushrooms and veal braised in Barolo.

Trattoria della Posta
Loc. Santa Anna 87
0173 78 120
Closed Thurs, Fri lunch
€€€

Gianfranco is the proud owner of this country trattoria. He pays particular attention to seasonal produce and changes the menu and the wine list accordingly. In good weather there is outdoor seating.

Neive

La Cantina del Rondo
Via Fausoni 7
0173 67 9808
closed Mon, Tue
€€

Traditional cuisine and pasta made using organic flour.

Pollenzo

Guido
Via Fossano 19, Pollenzo
0172 458 422
closed Sun, Mon
booking required
Michelin-starred
€€€€

Guido was a chef and father of three boys. Since his death, the boys carry on the family tradition. Mama still makes the pasta and it is her hands in the large black and white photograph above the entrance to the kitchen. Mama's *agnolotti* is so light and thin with a delicious meat filling. Guido is situated on the grounds of the University of Gastronomy, so it is reasonable to expect some

experimental cooking, but the most successful dishes are the simple ones. The dining room is a bit barn-like and noisy with several large tables.

Treiso

La Ciau del Tornavento
Piazza Baracco 7
0173 638 333
closed Wed, Thurs lunch
booking required
Michelin-starred
€€€€
A long-established restaurant with a rather forbidding exterior that conceals a beautiful and warm interior. Inside, the dining room has a panoramic window and terrace with a beautiful view of Barbaresco vineyards. In summer there is outdoor seating on the terrace. The chef and management are new and the restaurant has recently been awarded a second Michelin star. Everything is wonderful but outstanding dishes include a starter carpaccio of smoked

duck and thistles with *fonduta* and quail's egg. For secondi, the Chateaubriand, or Cherasco snails thrice baked are well-known prize-winning dishes. For dessert try the chocolate souffle or the gianduia torte.

Risorgimento
Viale Rimembranza 14
0173 63 8195
closed Mon
Visa only
€€
Risorgimento serves excellent home-made pasta with an emphasis on meat dishes. Save room for peaches in Moscato with zabaglione ice cream.

Osteria dell' Unione
Via Alba1
0173 63 8303
closed Mon, Tues
no credit cards
€€
A traditional osteria that is recommended by Slow Food.

Menu reader

Italian-English
con, alla refers
to how meals are
prepared and/or the
type of sauce

A

**abbacchio alla
scottadito** grilled
lamb chops
acciughe al verde
anchovies in herb
sauce
aceto vinegar
acqua water
affettato misto
cold sliced meats
aglio garlic
agnello lamb
coscio di roast leg
of lamb
agnolotti del plin
lamb ravioli
al forno baked
albicocca apricot
ananas pineapple
anatra duck
anguilla eel
antipasti starters
aragosta lobster
arancia orange
aringa herring
arrosto roast
asparagi asparagus

B

baccalà dried cod
bagna càuda
garlic, anchovy dip
basilico basil
baverese ice-cream
cake with cream
bettelmàt mountain
cheese
birra beer
bistecca beef steak
bollito boiled

bollito misto mixed
meat and sauces
bonet chocolate
biscuits
braciola di maiale
pork steak
brasato al barolo
beef in wine
brodo clear broth
bruschetta bread
slices rubbed with oil
burro butter
burro e salvia butter
and sage sauce

C

cacciatora with a
red wine and
mushroom sauce
caffè coffee
calamari squid
calda hot
calzone folded pizza
canella cinnamon
cannelloni stuffed
pasta
cappelle di funghi
mushroom caps
capretto kid, goat
carbonara with eggs
and pancetta
carciofi artichokes
carne meat
carote carrots
carpaccio sliced raw
meat or fish
carré di maiale pork
loin
castagne chestnuts
cavoletti di Bruxelles
brussels sprouts
cavolfiore
cauliflower
cavolo cabbage
cefalo mullet
cernia grouper
cicoria chicory
ciliege cherries

ciambelle al vino
ring shaped biscuits
cime di rapa
sprouting broccoli
cinghiale wild boar
cioccolata chocolate
cipolle onions
coniglio rabbit
contorni vegetables
coperto cover charge
cotechino small pork
sausage
cotoletta veal, pork
or lamb chop
cozze mussels
crema custard
crespelle pancake
crostata tart
crostini bread
rounds
cugna chutney made
from wine-must and
hazelnuts

D

datteri dates
degustazione tasting
diavola deep fried
digestivo liqueur or
grappa

F

fagioli beans
fegato liver
fettuccine pasta
fichi figs
formaggi cheese
fonduta cheese sauce
fragole strawberries
**fragoline di Nemi
con zabaglione**
Nemi strawberries
and Marsala cream
frittata omelette
**fritto misto
Piedmontese** mixed
fry with meats,
polenta and fruits
frullato milkshake

frutta fruit
frutti di mare mixed
  seafood
funghi mushroom

G

gamberetti shrimp
gamberi prawns
gazzosa lemonade
gelato ice cream
genepì digestif with
  juniper
gianduja chocolate
  and hazelnut
gnocchi potato and
  chestnut dumplings
gorgonzola blue
  cheese
granchio dressed
  crab
granita a drink with
  crushed ice
grissini breadsticks
grigliata grilled

I

indivia endive
insalata salad
insalata russa Russian
  salad
isop digestif with
  mountain thyme

L

lasagne layered pasta
latte milk
lattuga lettuce
legumi legumes
lenticchie lentils
lepre hare
limone lemon
lingua tongue

M

maiale pork
mandorla almond
manzo beef
marroni chestnuts
marsala sweet wine
marzapane marzipan

mascarpone cream
  cheese
mavocchino coffee
  with chocolate &
  foamed milk
mela apple
melanzane
  aubergine
melone melon
menta mint
meringhe meringue
merluzzo cod
**millefoglie al
  cucchiaio** mille
  feuille, pastry
  layered with cream
minestrone
  vegetable soup
mozzarella soft
  white cheese

N

nocciole hazelnuts
noci walnuts
nodino veal chop

O

olio oil
origano oregano
ostriche oysters

P

pancetta bacon
pane bread
panino filled roll
panna cream
pasta noodles
patate potato
pecorino sheep
  cheese
penne pasta quills
peòci mussels
pepe pepper
peperoni peppers
peperoni ripieni
  stuffed peppers
pera pear
pesca peach
pesce fish

carpaccio thin
  slices of raw fish
piselli peas
polenta cornmeal
pollo chicken
polpette meatballs
polpettone meatloaf
pompelmo grapefruit
pomodori tomatoes
  al riso baked whole
  tomatoes stuffed
  with rice
porri leeks
prezzemolo parsley
primi piatti first
  course
prosciutto cured ham
prugne plums
puré di patate
  mashed potatoes

Q

quaglie quails

R

radicchio chicory
ragù tomato sauce
  with meat
rapa white turnip
rapanelli radishes
ravioli stuffed pasta
razza skate
ricotta cottage cheese
**ricotta al forno con
  fiori di zucchina**
  baked courgette
  flowers stuffed
  with ricotta
rigatoni ribbed pasta
  tubes
ripieni stuffed
riso rice
risotto rice dish
risotto al funghi
  mushroom risotto
risotto milanese
  chicken & saffron
  risotto
rosmarino rosemary

S

sagra del frittello
   fried cauliflower
   tops
salame salami
sale salt
salmone salmon
salsiccia sausage
saltimbocca alla
   romana veal escalopes stuffed
   with bacon
salvia sage
sarde sardines
scaloppine veal escalop
sgroppino dessert of lemon
   sorbet, vodka and prosecco
sedano celery
senape mustard
seppie cuttlefish
servizio service
sformato savoury flan
sogliola sole
speck smoked ham
spezzatino stew
spigola al sale salted sea bass
spinaci spinach
stracchino soft cheese
stracciatella soup with beaten eggs
succo juice

T

tacchino turkey
tagliata finely sliced beef fillet
tagliatelle egg pasta
tagliolini noodles
tajarin handmade pasta
tartufo bianco white truffle
tartufo nero black truffle
tavola table
tè tea
tonno tuna
torrone candy made from hazelnut
   and honey
torta tart flan
torta di nocciole hazelnut cake
tortellini stuffed pasta
tramezzini triangular filled
   sandwiches

trippa tripe
trota trout

U

uccelletti small birds wrapped
   in bacon
uova eggs
uva grapes

V

verdura vegetables
vignarola artichoke and
   broad bean stew
vino bianco white wine
vino rosso red wine
vitello veal
vitello tonnato veal with tuna
vongole clams

Z

zafferano saffron
zucca pumpkin
zucchine courgettes
zuppa soup

263

SHOPPING

PORTA PALAZZO MARKET, TURIN

Shopping in Piedmont

Turin

Friendly staff and covered walkways make this city a good place to shop. Prices here are less expensive than in Milan, Florence or Rome. Italy is the best place to buy accessories no matter which city you visit, and Turin is no exception. An abundance of leather and shoe shops offer great deals on belts, bags, scarves, hats and gloves. Turin's proximity to the mountains means there is a wide selection of reasonably priced wool and cashmere knitwear in a variety of colours and styles. With more bookshops than any other city in Italy, Turin is the literary capital of the country. Turin also has an excess of chocolate and sweet shops that pose a great threat to anyone trying to maintain their *bellafigura*.

Mountains

Purchase Italian designed skiwear and sports clothing at shops in the resorts, especially Sestriere. Be sure to buy a pair of the fabulous sunglasses on sale. In spring and summer shops sell hiking clothing and footwear. Somehow Italians are able to design all-weather jackets and outerwear that is fashionable and sometimes even elegant.

Lago Maggiore

Omegna is an industrial town on the north tip of Lago d'Orta. It is the home of Alessi products for home interiors. The road from Mergozzo to Omegna has many discount interior design shops. Santa Maria Maggiore is the place to shop for that gorgeous velvet and lace patchwork quilt of your dreams.

Langhe

Shopping for wine in the Langhe is one of life's most pleasurable experiences, involving much tasting, nibbles of sausage and plenty of laughter. If you have no room in your luggage, go to the post office where you can buy wine carriers acceptable to airlines.

Shops

In Turin, shops are generally open Tuesday-Saturday from around 9am to 7pm. Some shops close for lunch, and most are closed Sunday mornings and all day Monday.

In the mountain and lake resorts, shops will stay open all day everyday during the high season and will close for the low season. During the shoulder seasons shops generally operate limited hours.

Turin

Food and wine

A&G di Claudia Avonti
Via Bertola 26B
011 544 6552
map 1-2, C3
A large variety of organic produce, including baked goods.

Antica enoteca del borgo
Via Monferrato 4
011 819 0461
map 1-2, H3
This wine bar stocks an extensive selection of wines from Piedmont.

Baudracco
Corso Vittorio Emanuele II 62
011 545 582
map 1-2, C4
Homemade local pasta and fine wines, Baudracco's window displays are hard to pass by.

Borgiattino
Corso Vinzaglio 29
011 562 9075
map 1-2, B4
Established in 1927, this cheese shop is one of the best in Turin.

Casa del Barolo
Via Andrea Doria 7
011 532 038
map 1-2, E4
You will be enticed as much by the décor as by the wine.

Markets

Porta Palazzo
Piazza della Repubblica
07.30-13.00 Mon-Fri,
07.30-19.30 Sat
map 1-2, D1
Europe's biggest open air market, selling everything from food and flowers to clothes and home ware.

Balon and Gran Balon
streets north of Piazza della Repubblica
Balon: 07.30-19.30 Sat
Gran Balon: 07.30-13.00 second Sunday of each month (also in Piazza della Repubblica)
Antique and flea market, the Gran Balon is the bigger monthly event.

Confetteria Avvignano
Piazza Carlo Felice 50
011 541 992
map 1-2, D4
Confectionery shop with original
1883 décor that sells regional food
delicacies.

De Filippis
Via Lagrange 39
011 542137
map 1-2, E3
Specialises in pasta, dried and
fresh, all beautifully packaged.

Di per di
Via Santa Teresa 19F
011 549 715
map 1-2, D3
Centrally located supermarket.

Divizia
Via San Tommaso 22B
011 534 918
map 1-2, D3
The shop sells only Piedmontese
products and is supported by the
European Union and the Italian
State.

Enoteca Delsanto
Via Piazzi 5
011 580 7940
map 3-4, C2
Ready-made gift boxes available
or will make to order.

Enoteca Parola
Corso Vittorio Emanuele II 76
011 544 939
map 1-2, C4
Wines from the region and a
range of classic vermouth.

Equamente
Via Fratelli Vasco 6B
map 1-2, E2
Products made by workers who
receive fair pay for their labour.

Gerla
Corso Vittorio Emanuele II 88
011 545 422
map 1-2, D4
Delicious dark chocolate-covered
candied orange peel and pralines.

Gertosio
Via Lagrange 34
011 562 1942
map 1-2, E3
Well-known for pralines.

Giordano
Piazza Carlo Felice 69
011 547 121
map 1-2, D4

Handmade *giandujotti* are the specialty in this tiny shop.

Gobino
Via Cagliari 15B
011 247 6245
map 1-2, F1
They make chocolates from new recipes and are renowned for their *turinot,* a tiny giandujotto.

Il bottigliere
Via San Francesco da Paola 43
011 836 050
map 1-2, E3
You will find many wines from the region here as well as a good selection of champagne.

La Baita del Formaggio
Via Lagrange 36
map 1-2, E3
A fantastic cheese shop selling regional and worldwide varieties.

Menietti
Via Corte d'Appello 22
011 436 9438
map 1-2, C2
A selection of wine accessories are on sale: corkscrews, glasses and even bottling machines.

Paissa
Piazza San Carlo 196
011 562 8462
map 1-2, D3
A historic delicatessen (1884) with a selection of unusual coffee blends and hard-to-find products.

Enoteca Parola
Corso Vittorio Emanuele II 76A
map 1-2, D4
This shop stocks an excellent selection of Piedmontese reds.

Peyrano-Pfatish
Corso Vittorio Emanuele II 76
011 538 765
www.peyrano.com
map 1-2, D4
Opened in 1930, it was originally

the shop of chocolatier Gustavo Pfatish, bought by the Peyrano family in 1963. Chocolates can be purchased online.

Taberna Libraria
Via Bogino 5
011 836 515
open 7 days a week
map 1-2, E3
Turin's most respected enoteca. stocks a number of culinary books and accoutrements.

Tamborini Pasticceria
Via Garibaldi 31/n
011 54 0468
map 1-2, C2
An art nouveau pastry shop that serves the best miniature cakes.

Herbalists

La Recolte
Via Umberto Cosmo 9
011 819 3049
map 1-2, H3
A qualified herbalist, the owner offers remedies and advice on the best use of natural cosmetics, ointments and herbal treatments.

Antica Erborista
Piazza della Consolata 5
map 1-2, C1
An old-fashioned herbalist with a
cornucopia of jars and bottles.

Gifts, toys, handicrafts

Creativity
Via Mazzini 29E
011 817 7864
map 1-2, E4
A great assortment of interesting
gift ideas in all price ranges.

Umbraculum
Via Giuseppe Barbaroux 9
011 561 2992
map 1-2, C2
This shop sells all kinds of candles
and perfumed oils.

Books, stationery, art supplies

Agorà
Via Santa Croce 0E
011 835 973
map 1-2, F3
An excellent photography
bookshop near Piazza Carlina.

Comunardi
Via Bogino 2
011 817 0036
map 1-2, E3
Sells an extensive range of comics
and magazines. Open late.

Feltrinelli
Piazza Castello 17
011 541 627
map 1-2, D2
(also Via Roma 80, map 1-2, D3)
Part of the large national chain,
one of Turin's biggest bookshops.

Fogola Libreria Dante Alghieri
Piazza Carlo Felice 15
011 53 5897
map 1-2, D4
An old-style shop with creaky
floors, books stacked on antique
tables and the owner asleep in an
over-stuffed chair in the corner.

**Hellas International
Bookshop**
Via Bertola 6
011 546 941
map 1-2, C3
A friendly shop with many books
in English.

Libreria Fontana
Via Monte di Pietà 19
011 542 924
map 1-2, D2
Wonderfully located, this
architect-designed bookstore is
bright and contemporary.

Libreria Luxemburg
Via Cesare Battisti 7
011 561 3896
map 1-2, E2
An historical bookshop with
wooden floors; once the heart
of the Risorgimento. Books in
English have a dedicated room
upstairs with a few novels
translated from Italian.

Mondadori Multicenter
Via Monte di Pietà 2
011 577 8811
map 1-2, D2
A multimedia and bookstore on
three floors with a special area for
children. Internet points.

Mood
Via Cesare Battisti 3E
011 566 0809
map 1-2, E2
Browse the wide selection of
books and enjoy a coffee or
a glass of wine in this new
bookstore.

Zanaboni
Corso Vittorio Emanuele II 41
011 650 5516
map 1-2, D4
An eclectic bookshop specialising
in travel, design and art books.

Music

Backdoor
Via Pinelli 45
011 482 855
off map
Worth the trek to find rare and
unusual vinyl and CDs.

FNAC
Via Roma 56
011 551 6711
map 1-2, D3
A book, music and media store
with a box office for event tickets.

Juke Box all'idrogeno
Corso Einaudi 53
011 595 045
map 1-2, A5
Established for 25 years, this shop
specialises in rare vinyl records.

Les Yper Sound
Via Rossini 14
011 812 0152
map 1-2, F2
Close to the University with a
wide variety of used CD's.

Department stores

Langrange 15
Via Lagrange 15
13.00-20.30 Mon
09.30-20.30 Tue-Fri; 21.00 Sat
10.00-20.00 Sun (occasional)
map 1-2, E3

Coin
Via Lagrange 47
13.00-19.30 Mon
09.30-19.30 Tue-Fri; 20.00 Sat
10.00-19.30 Sun (occasional)
map 1-2, E3

Upim
Via Roma 305
13.00-20.00 Mon,
09.30-20.00 Tue-Sat
map 1-2, D3

Clothes, shoes, bags

Arbiter
Piazza Carlo Felice 35
011 547 074
map 1-2, D4
An old shop with a large selection
of leather handbags, umbrellas,
luggage and sports bags. There's
something for everyone at prices
you can afford. Nice staff.

Autopsie Vestimentaire
Via Bonelli 6B
011 436 0641
map 1-2, C1
Women's clothing and accessories
displayed like artworks. Develop
your unique look here.

Bertolini & Borse
Piazza Vittorio Veneto 8-9
011 812 7273
map 1-2, G3
An extensive range of accessories,
from Filofax diaries and designer
pens to stylish shoes and bags.

Carla G
Via Lagrange 7
map 1-2,
also at Via Pietro Micca 9
map 1-2, E3
Young and trendy separates,
dresses and shoes.

Dobhran
Via San Massimo 53
011 883 351
map 1-2, F3
Classic attire for men and women
together with accessories.

Duomo
Piazza Carlo Felice 40
011 517 5127
map 1-2, D4
Sell their own brand of shoes for
men and women.

Fasano
Via Roma 325
011 530 225
map 1-2, D3
One of the largest jewellers in the
city.

Fashion
Via Tiepolo 8
011 631 5105
map 5-6, H5
Designer brands at affordable
prices south of Lingotto.

Genta
Via Corte Appello 2
011 562 1289
map 1-2, E2
A large selection of cashmere and
woollen sweaters for men in many
styles and colours. An equally good
selection of shirts.

Giorgio Monteverdi
Galleria S. Frederico 10-12
Via Roma 316
011 562 5595
map 1-2, D2
The softest most luxurious knitwear
in a myriad of colours for men and
women.

SHOPPING TURIN

Kristina Ti
Via Maria Vittoria 18G
011 837 170
map 1-2, E3
Kristina Tardito's creations are soft
and romantic yet modern.

La Boa
Via Carlo Alberto 24
011 562 2496
map 1-2, E3
Friendly boutique selling stylish
dresses and separates.

La Merceria
Via Villa della Regina 5G
map 1-2, H3
The faded exterior belies the
modern interior with womens'
wear by Alberta Ferretti.

La Terra delle donne
Via San Domenico 18
map 1-2, C2
Vintage clothing and accessories
from 1880-1950.

Marisa Dellachà
Via della Rocca 2
011 812 5314
map 1-2, G4
If you are a fan of vintage attire,
then this is the place to visit.

Mauro
Piazza Castello 75
011 538 525
map 1-2, D2
A tiny shop selling funky shoes
by up-and-coming designers at
incredibly good prices.

Poncif
Piazza Vittorio Veneto 5
011 817 3040
map 1-2, G3
A Florentine company that makes
and sells unisex clothing.

Ruffatti
Via Accademia delle Scienze 4
011 562 9294
map 1-2, E3
Finest quality mens' dress shirts.

Scout
Via Mazzini 1
011 546 589
map 1-2, E4
Trendy clothes and accessories for
women. Young and wacky.

Sebastian
Via Cavour 15A
011 562 9696
map 1-2, E4
Moderately priced, good quality
men's dress shirts.

Shoeco
Piazza Carlo Emanuele II 19
map 1-2, F3
Boutique selling designer shoes .

Soho
Via Rossini 19
map 1-2, F2
Retro 60-70s clothing.

Alternariato
Piazza Vittorio Veneto 16B
011 882384
map 1-2, G3
Jewellery and memorabilia from
the last century, with some lovely
art deco pieces and watches.

Home ware

De Carlo
Via Carlo Alberto 36F
011 543 619
map 1-2, E3
Elegant tableware and cutlery.

Gurlino Arredamenti
Via Carlo Alberto 36
011 562 7442
map 1-2, E3
Home and office interiors.

La bottega del Borgo Nuovo
Via Cavour 41
011 889 325
map 1-2, E4
Soft furnishings and textiles.

Maison
Via San Dalmazzo 26
011 566 0288
map 1-2, C2
Everything for your home.

Marcopolo
Via S Agostino 28
011 436 0037
open late
map 1-2, C2
An elegant shop with a mix of old and new for designed interiors.

Miscellanea
Via San Domenico 6/d
339 797 4016
map 1-2, C2
Selling an eclectic variety of ultra-modern lamps, retro 1950s chairs.

Malls

8 Gallery (Lingotto)
Via Nizza 262
14.00-20.00 Mon,
10.00-20.00 Tue-Sun
PAM Supermarket open
14.00-22.00 Mon
09.00-22.00 Tue-Sun
map 5-6, G2
90 shops, 12 restaurants and bars, 11 cinema halls, supermarket, post office and bank counter.

McArthur Glen
Serravalle Scrivia
0143 609 000
Dedicated bargain hunters would do well to head to this massive designer outlet mall. Catch a train from Porta Nuova station to Novi Ligure (about an hour) then take a regular bus to the village.

Antiques and prints

Fratelli Fogliato
Galleria d'Arte Corniceria
Via Mazzini 9
011 88 7733
map 1-2, E4
Part gallery, part shop. The gallery displays and sells beautiful antique prints and maps. The shop has a large selection of wood and glass picture frames in all shapes and sizes, priced from €8-€50.

Tipolitografia dei Mercanti
Via Mercanti 3/D
011 54 3164
map 1-2, D2
An old wooden sign depicting musicians is found hanging in the window of this charming shop in the Roman quarter. Inside are many old signs and paintings, and the occasional nautical piece.

Galleria Gilibert
Galleria Subalpina 17-19
011 561 9225
map 1-2, D2
Housed in the beautiful Galleria Subalpina and specialising in art nouveau antiques.

Il Cartiglio
Via Po 32D
011 817 9005
map 1-2, F2
Beautiful prints depicting scenes of Turin are the speciality here.

Libreria Antiquaria Piemontese
Via Monte di Pietà 13G
011 535 472
map 1-2, D2
A good range of old advertising posters and shop display items.

L'arte antica di S.Salamon
Via Volta 9
011 549 041
map 1-2, D4
Antique and modern Japanese prints.

Musy Padre e Figlio
Via Po 1
011 812 5582
map 1-2, E2
A historic shop (1707) selling antique jewellery and rare items.

Pregliasco
Via Accademia Albertina 3
011 817 7114
map 1-2, F4
Prints and engravings of Turin.

Stile Floreale
Via Maria Vittoria 19F
011 817 0421
map 1-2, E3
Art nouveau lighting, glass, ceramics, furniture, and jewellery.

Photography

Europhoto
Piazza Carlo Felice 23
011 562 9452
map 1-2, D4
A shop with nooks and crannies stuffed with items to delight any photographer's heart.

Mountains

Bardoneccia

Ugetti
Via Medail 80
0122 99 036
closed Mon in low season
Established in 1921, the shop has a six window display of cakes and chocolate. Hot marmalade and cream *krafen* emerge from the oven at 4pm. Other specialities include *bardonacchiese*, made with rum, hazelnut and chestnuts.

La Vie del Gusto
Via Medail 84
0122 96 981
closed Mon in low season
Riccardo Carena selects the very
best cheese, sausage and wine for
his shop. Stock up on dried pasta,
truffle oil, grappa and honey.

Prodotti da Forno di Federica
Via Medail 66
0122 99 038
closed Mon
Fresh bread, biscuits and cakes
are made on the premises in this
bakery. Especially good are cakes
with nuts, pears and chocolate.

Qukarèn
Via Medail 84
0122 99 9125
Children's clothing and ski
equipment.

Docks Dora
Via Medail 65/A
0122 90 2738
closed Mon & Tues in low season
New and second-hand clothing
for men and women.

Kiriou
Via Medail 56
closed Mon in low season
Guidebooks, maps and popular
novels are stocked here in
addition to small gift items.

Oulx

Piccola Libreria del Merlo
Via Roma 58
0122 831 220
closed Mon
Book shop specialising in alpine
literature and travel guides. Also
hosts literary events.

Lago Maggiore and around

Arona

Il Sito delle Erbe
Corso Cavour 116
Herbal medicines, cosmetic
products and perfume.

Cannobio

Sunday Market
Central squares and side streets
Clothing, food, leather goods,
herbs, and other products found
in markets. With its 200 stalls, it
is a meeting place for locals and
residents of the Swiss shore.

Cavandone

Patricia Piodella
Via del Torchio 6,
0323 557 882
Ceramic lamps, vases and other
pieces, hand-painted on the
premises.

Domodossola

Each Saturday the centre is given
over to a large farmers market
with stalls also selling clothing.

Iperstore GS
Regione Nosere 31
8.30-20.00 daily
Department store

Omegna

Alessi Outlet Store
Via Privata Alessi (Crusinallo)
0323 868 611
14.30-18.00 Mon,9.30-18.00 Tue-Sat
The factory outlet of Alessi,
manufacturers of stylish
household objects for gleaming
kitchens and bathrooms at
discounted prices.

Orta

Penelope
Piazza Motta 26
0322 905 600
Local crafts including hand-
woven kitchen linens printed
with antique wooden stamps and
natural dyes.

Vetroe'
Via Giovanetti 246
0322 905 555
Tiffany lamps, stained glass
windows and furniture designed
and produced by Stefania Berardi
in this artisan shop.

Santa Maria Maggiore

Gioielleria Azzolini
Via Cavalli 7
Garnet necklaces from gems
mined in the local mountains.

Il Portico
Via Rossetti Valentini 12
0324 94786
Various handcrafts and locally
made *Vegezzine* shoes in addition
to stunning velvet patchwork
quilts and damask throws.

Il Telaio di Laura
Via Cavalli 15
0324 94 343
Hand-woven carpets and area
rugs, carry-all bags and car
blankets.

Stresa

Lavrano
Piazza Cadorna 21
0323 304 60
Shoes and accessories, elegant
Bruno Magli and Paciotti and also
casual by Geox and Flexa.

Lunatika
Via Principe Tomaso 9
0323 31212
Designer labels i.e. D&G,
Moschino, Les Copains and
Guess.

Majoli Gentleman
Via Cavour 17
0323 332 85
Suits and accessories with
designer label Cortigiani by
Veneto, a tailor for men.

Odini
Via Garibaldi 7
Young people will enjoy buying
jeans and tops in this modern,
sparsely-furnished establishment.

Proposte
Via Garibaldi 2
Sells sequined evening bags,
original hats, day apparel by
Mariela Burani, Valentino, Fendi
and other designers.

IL TELAIO DI LAURA

Tender
Via P. Tomaso 11
0323 30124
Apparel by Prada, Tod's, Hogan
and Malo shoes, bags and belts.

Zanaboni
Via P.Tomaso 16
0323 30223
Watches and jewellery by Bulgari
and Rolex, silverware, place
cards, frames, tea cutlery sets.

Verbania

Elena Pacchioni
Piazza Garibaldi 22
0323 501 440
Flower essences and natural
foods.

La Cereria del Nord
Via alla Cartiera 52C, Frazione
Possaccio
Artistic beeswax candles.

Coin
Via Mameli 23, Intra
08.00-20.00 Mon-Sat,
09.00-13.00 and 15.00-19.30 Sun
Department store

Langhe & Roero

Alba

Elvira & C. S.n.c.
Di Fascinato Gastone
Via Vittorio Emmanuele 8
0173 44 1154
Purses, small leather goods,
gloves, umbrellas, bags.

Emmendue Calbor S.n.c.
Via Cavour 15B
0174 367 0042
Stoles and scarves for very
reasonable prices.

Nuova G.M.
Via Vittorio Emmanuele 4
0155 411 0062
Cheap sports bags to hold all
your last minute shopping.

Stanga
Via Cavour17A,
0173 44 0438
The very best selection of
corkscrews from Germany and
many other small items for your
kitchen and home.

Tartufi Morra S.R.L
Piazza E. Pertinace 3
0173 36 4271
Fresh white and black truffles
from the most authoritative shop
in Alba. This was where the craze
started. Also sells truffle oils and
other preserves.

Cooperativa Dei Lavoratori
Via Roma 4/6
0173 363 069
07.45-13.00, 15.00-19.30 Tues-Sat,
07.45-13.00 Mon
Supermarket

Oviesse
Corso Langhe 10
0173 363 705
08.00-12.30, 15.30-19.30 Tues-Sat
15.30-19.30 Mon, closed on Monday
morning and on Sundays.
Department store with a
supermarket underground

Basko
Via Roma 8 (in a small indoor
shopping centre)
0173 366 058/443 803
08.30-20.00 Tues-Sat,
14.00-20.00 Mon
Supermarket

Bra

Colleteria silvano Rossini
Via Mendicita' Instruita16, Bra
0172 41 5320
Large selection of cooking knives
and copper utensils, small
appliances and cooking pots.

Cherasco

Barbero, Confetteria e Pasticceria Di Forta Giancarlo
Via Vittorio Emanuele 75, Cherasco
0172 48 8373
Historic chocolate and pastry
shop established in 1884, makes
the best chocolate.

Dogliani

Cillario Alessandra
Via Corte 4
0173 74 2284
Sweaters and jackets for men.

Markets

The main and biggest market in Alba is on Saturday, from early
morning to 1pm in the historical centre.
In addition, there is fruit and vegetable market on Piazza Mercato
Ortofrutticolo and a general small market on Piazza Cagnasso, on
Tuesdays and Thurdays.

TRAVEL BASICS

Climate

Piedmont has a varied climatic range. Dominated by the Alps, the north of the region has a continental climate, whereas the south is influenced by the warm Mediterranean Sea. Winters are cold and dry. In peak months summer temperatures can exceed 30°C. In general, summer temperatures are cooler in the hills, quite hot in the plains and milder on the shores of the lakes. During winter and autumn, banks of fog, which are sometimes very thick, form in the lowlands of the Po valley and in the Langhe. Most of the rain falls between October and April. The best time to visit Turin is between May and October, when temperatures average around 22°C.

Documents

A visa is not necessary for British and EU passport holders. Non-EU citizens should ask their own consulate or the Italian Embassy.
• Passport Agency 0870 521 0410 www.passport.gov.uk
• Foreign & Commonwealth Office 020 7008 1500 www.fco.gov.uk
• Italian Embassy 020 7312 2200 www.embitaly.org.uk

E111 form (changes)

The EHIC (European Health Insurance Card) has replaced the old E111 and from 1 January 2006, E111s are no longer valid. The quickest and easiest way to get an EHIC is to apply online: www.ehic.org.uk
The EHIC entitles UK residents to free medical and dental treatment and to pay local rates for prescriptions.

Arriving and departing

By air
(Turin, Mountains, Langhe)

Turin International Airport (Torino Caselle)

Strada San Maurizio 12
Caselle Torinese
011 567 6361/6362, Fax 011 567 6420
www.aeroportoditorino.it
Located 16km north of the city centre. Flights are occasionally diverted to Genoa in the winter due to fog. If this happens, you will be transferred by bus to Turin.

Cash Point

After you leave the baggage hall, turn right to find two cash points near the end of the main building. One is in the wall, the other is behind sliding glass doors.

From the airport into Turin

The Sadem bus service (www.sadem.it) connects the airport to the centre of Turin from early morning until midnight and takes about 40 minutes. Buses run a stopping service every 30 minutes and tickets cost €5 from automatic machines or the ticket office at the airport. You can pay on board but this will cost 50 cents more. There is a 25 per cent discount for Torino Card holders (p.23). These cards can be obtained at Turismo Torino's Info Points at the airport.
Airport-city: the bus stop is across the street from the Arrivals main exit.
City-airport: at Porta Nuova on the corner of Via Sacchi.

Trains connect the airport to Stazione Dora in Turin every half an hour from about 5am to 9 pm.

The railway station is 140m from the airport and the journey takes about 20 minutes. A ticket costs €3 and is valid for 70 minutes on buses and trams in the city as well. However, Stazione Dora is outside central Turin. More info is found at www.gtt.to.it

Taxis are found in front of the Arrivals main exit. The journey to the city centre takes around 30 minutes and costs about €30.

By air (Lakes)

Milano Malpensa Airport (Milan)

You will need a €1 coin for a baggage cart. The EU queue is on the far right; it's a bit hard to see and it is usually quicker.

Cash Point & Driving

Find a cash point at the end of baggage carousel 6. If you are picking up a car, make sure that you have some change as there are toll fees shortly after you leave the airport.

After driving out of the airport area, be sure to take the motorway entrance for the direction of Genova. It seems strange (since Genova is south) but this is the motorway that takes you northwest to Lago Maggiore. A good road map will make everything clear.

By train

Trenitalia (www.trenitalia.it) runs most of the services in Italy. Other companies that operate are Satti (for Stazione Dora in Turin) and Cisalpino (handling trains coming from Germany and Switzerland).

Turin is on the main Paris-Rome TGV express line.

The main stations in Turin are:
• Porta Nuova: Corso Vittorio Emanuele II, 53 (currently the main station for national and international connections). The service to Milan is the most frequent and takes 80 minutes
• Porta Susa: P. XXVIII Dicembre 8 (covers the regional network)
• Lingotto: Via Pannunzio, I
• Stazione Dora: Piazza Baldissera

By bus

The long distance coach terminal in Turin is at Porta Nuova

By car

Piedmont and Turin have an excellent road network system connecting the city to main national and international destinations. The main tunnels and passes from France and Switzerland link directly to Turin.

Driving in Piedmont

Car Hire

Documentation
• Passport
• Car hire voucher
• Current UK driving licence
• Credit card

It is recommended that UK drivers carry the new EU-style photo licence, including the second paper part. If your licence was issued in another country, you will need to check with the car hire company to see if you require any other documentation.

The credit card is a guarantee and must be the same name as the hirer of the vehicle. Cash deposits are not accepted. You will be asked to sign the conditions of hire. This is the contract between you and the rental company. It is wise to keep a copy of this agreement after your return home in case of any subsequent queries.

Optional Insurances

The optional waiver to cover the CDW excess and to cover the TP excess are a source of commissionable sales revenue for the local car hire office. Charges for these are payable locally and will be added to your credit card. Initial and sign the car hire rental agreement in two places to accept the conditions of these two coverages. Do not initial the rental agreement for any additional insurances (i.e. Super CDW, Super TP, PAI, Super PAI) that you do not require.

Check the spare tyre before embarking on a journey. If this is stolen a police report must be obtained otherwise the cost of the replacement will be charged by the car hire company.

Road fund licence fee

This Registration Fee is a local tax and will be charged to your credit card at a rate of €2 per day, plus tax, to a maximum charge of six days.

A car for the mountains

If you are choosing a hire car for driving in the mountains, the Fiat Panda (four wheel drive version) is a good bet. The small size of the car makes it possible to manoeouvre in the narrow streets and lanes of mountain villages. Four wheel drive is always of benefit if you are driving off the main roads.

In winter, you should carry chains for driving on snowy roads.

Rules of the road

Italians drive on the right-hand side of the road. This means that roundabouts, through lanes, and on and off ramps are located opposite to what British drivers encounter. Check both ways carefully before crossing roads. Also be aware of the local regulations, which are available from the car hire company.

Right of way belongs to main roads only if marked with a yellow diamond on a white background. In all other cases give way to traffic coming from the right. On a roundabout, give way to traffic coming from the left.

You must carry your current driving licence at all times, with an Italian translation (for the second paper part), and another form of identification, preferably with photograph.

Drinking and driving laws are similar to the UK and penalties include on-the-spot fines or, as in the UK, imprisonment for more serious offences. The acceptable blood alcohol level is actually lower in Italy than in the UK.

Seat belts are compulsory and children should travel in rear seats.

The minimum age for driving in Italy is 18 but car hire companies also have their own restrictions.

Dipped headlights should be used in tunnels.

An interior mirror and left-hand side mirror are compulsory.

Sound your horn to give warning of your approach on tiny mountain roads.

Other tips

Road signs in Italy do not indicate which direction the road is taking. Direction of travel is also not indicated on exit signs. Be sure to know the road number you want to travel on, as well as a few key towns on the way, before you make your turn.

In general, Italians like to drive fast and have little patience for the struggling tourist. They will honk, flash their headlights and drive around a vehicle who hesitates. Ignore them, focus on the road, and enjoy driving in Italy.

The motorway

Italy's motorways are well provided with petrol stations, cafés and restaurants. The distance between them is clearly signposted.

Motorway signs are always green and tolls are normally charged. Do not use the lanes reserved for Telepass cardholders unless there is no alternative.

Collect your ticket by pressing the red button at the automatic booth and proceed onto the motorway.

At the exit, hand in your ticket and pay the toll, which will be displayed on an illuminated panel. Short stretches of motorway may display a fixed charge at the entry toll. To pay by credit card, use the channels marked ViaCARD.

Speed limits

• motorways, depending on motor size
110 km, up to 1099cc
130 km, over 1099cc
• open roads 90 km
• built-up areas 50 km
• blue zone in cities 30 km

Fines for speeding are heavy and are payable on the spot or at the local police station (Vigili Urbani). The police must give you a receipt for the amount of the fine paid. Alternatively, fines may be debited to your credit card, having already been forwarded to the car hire company.

Road signs

• *Strada dissetata/Strada deformata* rough or gravel road
• *Senso Unico* - one way
• *a yellow diamond on a white background* - right of way
• *white P on a blue background* designated parking area
• *Zona Disco* - pay and display
• *Yellow lines* - parking prohibited

Security

•Always leave windows closed and doors locked.
•Never leave any valuables in the car.
•If it is absolutely necessary to leave belongings in the car, lock them in the boot.
•Park in guarded car parks.
•Beware of other drivers who 'flash' you to stop.
In the event of car theft, the local car hire agency and the police must be informed immediately.

Breakdowns

If you break down, dial 116 at the nearest phone and tell the operator where you are, the type of car and your registration number. The Italian Automobile Club (ACI) will send someone to fix your car. This not a free service but is cheaper than joining the ACI outright.

Accidents

In the event of an accident involving other vehicles, or

pedestrians, it is vital that the CID form (supplied in car documents), is filled out with full details of all vehicles involved, i.e. number plate and model of car. Both parties need to sign the CID form. Do not move the car until the police arrive.

Getting around Turin

Essential information is found on pages 22-25.

Metro

In February 2006 the first section from Porta Susa to Collegno was opened. With no key sights en route, it is not useful for tourists. Due for completion in 2010, the new underground system will ultimately link Lingotto with the centre and the airport.

Tourist trips

• TurismoBus Torino
free with Torino Card
Discover the main sights of Turin with this service. A conductor announces attractions as you pass and you can get off at any of the 14 stops.
• Touristibus €3.99
This two-hour guided trip leaves from Piazza Carlo Felice every day (except Tuesday) at 2:30pm. It goes through the historic centre of Turin, then out to Stupinigi. There is a multilingual commentary on board.
• Lift to the top of Mole Antonelliana (see page 48)
• Sailing down the River Po
Via Murazzi 65
800 019 152 information and booking
free with Torino Card
The GTT runs a one-hour return boat cruise on the river Po. This begins at the Murazzi dock just below Piazza Vittorio Veneto and travels slowly along the river

beside Parco del Valentino to the Borgo Medioevale, where you may disembark for a walk or a visit before returning.
• Sassi-Superga tramway (see p.101)

Taxis

Legal taxis in Turin are white with an identification name and number, and they all have meters. Unregistered operators may approach you but if you use them you will almost certainly be taken for a very expensive ride. As with the rest of Italy, it is almost impossible to hail a taxi in Turin. Each district has at least one taxi rank, denoted by an orange sign with 'Taxi' in black.

You can telephone in advance (011 5737 or 011 5730). Please note that you will pay additionally for the time it takes for the taxi to reach you from where your call was first received.

Tourist information

Services in the region of Piedmont are excellent, with information in English widely available.

Turin

Turismo Torino Information Points are open every day. Find information on museums, events, shows, restaurants and historic cafés. They also provide a free hotel reservation service.
Tel: 011 535 181; Fax: 011 530 070
info@turismotorino.org
www.turismotorino.org
Information Points:
• Atrium Torino - Piazza Solferino
09.30-19.00 daily
• Porta Nuova railway station
09.30-19.00 Mon-Sat; 15.00 Sun
• Turin International Airport
08.30-22.30 daily

Mountains
Sestriere
0122 755 444
www.sestriere.it www.montagnedoc.it
also see Mountains section for
information in other towns.

Lakes
Stresa
Ferry Terminal, P. Marconi 16
0323 30150
Mar-Oct
10.00-12.30, 15.00-18.30 daily
Nov-Mar
closed Sat pm, closed Sunday

Langhe
Alba
Piazza Risorgimento 2
0173 358 33
www.langheroero.it

Hotels and Restaurants Reservation
Service, Consorzio Turistico Langhe,
Monferrato Roero
Piazza Risorgimento, 2
12051 Alba - Piedmont
0173 362 562; 0173 220 237
info@turismodoc.it
A free reservation service for
booking hotels, B&B, farmhouses,
inns and restaurants in the Langhe,
Roero and Monferrato area.

Disabled travellers

Turin Province
(includes Mountain area)
Two central information offices:
• Centro Informazione Disabilità della
Provincia di Torino
Corso G Lanza 75, Collina
(east side of Ponte Umberto I)
011 861 3141
09.00-17.00 Mon-Fri

• Informa Handicap
Via Palazzo di Città 11, Piazza Castello
011 442 1631
Gradually all buses are being
modified for wheelchair access.

Many routes already are already
adapted but it is advisable to
check with specialist agencies or
the tourist office. The GTT runs a
transport service for the disabled
using equipped minibuses. For
reservations call:
011 568 2315 (08.30-14.00 Mon-Fri)
011 316 1365 or 011 316 0979 (after
hours, Saturdays, public holidays)

Most major sights are wheelchair
friendly with ramps, lifts and
adapted toilets.

For areas outside Turin, contact
the local Tourist Office.

Medical and dental

Medical treatment
• call 118 in an emergency
(ambulance)

Hospitals (Ospedale)
You can obtain treatment at any of
the casualty departments (called
pronto soccorso) in the hospitals
marked on our maps.

Turin
• Ospedale San Giovanni Battista
Molinette (general hospital)
Corso Bramante 88/90
011 633 1633,
• Centro Traumatologico Ortopedico
C.T.O (orthopaedic hospital)
Via Zuretti 29
011 693 3111
• Ospedale Ostetrico Ginecologico
Sant'Anna (gynecological and
maternity hospital)
Corso Spezia 60
011 313 4444
• Ospedale Infantile Regina
Margherita (children's hospital)
Piazza Polonia 94
011 313 4444
• Ospedale Mauriziano Umberto
Primo (general hospital)

Largo Turati 62
011 508 1111
Children's doctor:
day 011 244 411
night 011 562 1606 or 011 549 000

Mountains
• Sauze d'Oulx Hospital (Susa)
Corso Inghilterra 66
0122 621 212
•Ambulatorio Medico (Sestriere)
Piazza Fraiteve 1
0122 754 121
This medical facility provides
services in English and other
languages.

Lakes
• Stabilimento Ospedaliero (Verbania)
Via Crocetta
0323 5411
• Domodossola
Via Giovanni Mauro
0324 4911
• Omegna
Via Mazzini 117
0323 868 111

Langhe
• Ospedale Civico di San Lazzaro
Via Pierino Belli 26 (Alba)
0173 316 111
(doctor on call: 0173 316 316)
• Ospedale Santo Spirito (Bra)
Via Vittorio Emanuele 3
0172 420 111

Chemists (Farmacia)
Many pharmacists speak English
and can assist with minor ailments.
In Italy, medicine is often given
by suppository (*supposta*) to avoid
harming the digestion. Be sure to
ask the chemist. Usual hours:
8.30-13.00, 16.00-20.00 Mon-Sat
Turin
There are three central 24 hour
chemists (closed 12.30-15.00):

• Boniscontro
Corso Vittorio Emanuele 66 (near
Porta Nuova station)
• Nizza, Via Nizza 65
• Comunale 21, Corso Belgio 151B

Embassies
• British Consulate
Via Madama Cristina 99, Turin
011 650 9202
• British Embassy
Via XX Settembre 80A, Rome
06 422 00001
• Irish Embassy
Piazza Campitelli 3, Rome
06 697 9121
• US Embassy
Via Vittorio Veneto 119A, Rome
06 46 741
• Canadian Embassy
Via G.B de Rossi 27, Rome
06 445 981
• Australian Embassy
Via Alessandria 215, Rome
06 445 981
• New Zealand Embassy
Via Zara 28 Rome
06 441 7171

Police and emergencies
There are three types of police in
Italy and it's important to contact
the correct one. Do not approach a
Carabiniere to report a petty theft
or traffic incident.
• Polizia - state police dealing with
general crime, particularly theft
• Carabinieri - military police dealing
with serious crime and state security
• Vigili Urbani - traffic police

Emergency numbers
• **112** Police (English-speaking)
• **115** Fire Brigade (*Vigili d. Fuoco*)
• **118** Ambulance (*Ambulanza*)
• **116** Car breakdown
(*Automobile Club d'Italia*)

Thefts and losses

In the event of a theft, a police report will be required for an insurance claim. Report to the nearest police station. If a passport was lost or stolen, contact your embassy. If only credit cards were stolen, and these have been cancelled, it may not be necessary to make a police report – credit card companies are often satisfied with a telephone report.

Communication

Postage

Stamps are available at post offices or tobacconists. Queues at the post office can be very long. If all you need are stamps to mail postcards or letters, go to a nearby 'Tabacchi' and buy them there. It is much quicker. Most post boxes have two slots, one for city mail (*per la città*), and one for everywhere else (*tutte le altre destinazioni*). Central Post Offices are marked on our maps.

Telephones

The international code for Italy is 39. Include the 0 in all Italian numbers when calling from abroad.

Dial the city code 011 for all numbers in Turin.

Useful numbers
• 12 Italian directory enquiries
• 170 International operator
• 176 International enquiries

To reach a UK operator dial 172 followed by country code 0044.

To call UK mobiles from abroad, dial 0044 and drop the first zero from the number. To ring a local number from a UK mobile within Turin, dial 011 followed by the number.

Internet cafés

• 1pc4you
Via Verdi 20G, 011 835 908
• il Bu.Net – Internet Wine Café
Via San Quintino 13, 011 440 7517
• American Stars
Via Pietro Micca 3A, 011 543 000

Money

Banking hours

08:30-13.30, 15.00-16.00 Mon-Fri Some banks in tourist areas stay open all day. Most banks close on weekends and national holidays.

Cashpoints

Italian *bancomats* vary and some do not accept international transactions from smaller banks. Look for the Cirrus symbol and be sure to bring a card from a globally recognized bank. Cards from internet banks may not work in some machines.

Practical

Tobacconists (Tabacchi)

Purchase cigarettes from licensed tobacconists identified by a white T on a black background. These shops often close by 8pm. Some bars will sell cigarettes after hours and there are vending machines tucked into doorways, but these often charge premium prices.

SMOKING IS BANNED IN ALL PUBLIC BUILDINGS, BARS AND RESTAURANTS.

Toilets

Facilities are variable across the region in both restaurants and bars, and public conveniences are a rarity. In Turin, the lakes and the mountains, facilities are generally good in restaurants and department stores. You will also find well-kept conveniences near major tourist attractions for which you will pay a small charge. The Langhe is not so well set up and toilets can be primitive even in some historic cafés.

Tipping

Tipping is left to your discretion but, as a guide, approximately €5 per week for hotel maids and €6 per week for breakfast in the hotel restaurant.

In other restaurants, the tip is included in the bill. Leave extra if the service was very good. For most bars, just leaving small change is usually adequate.

Entertainment

What's on in Turin

See also pages 88-89
• www.torinospettacoli.it
Events, ticket bookings and prices (Italian)
Events listed in publications:
• Torino Sette
a weekly newspaper supplement in La Stampa on Fridays
• News Spettacolo Torino
free from street stands

What's on in Piedmont

• www.selectitaly.com/events.php
cultural events and ticket bookings (English)
•www.whatsonwhen.com
a good general site in English

Sport

Turin

2006 Winter Olympics

(See also page 125)
Committee for the Organisation of Winter Olympics,
Via Nizza 262/58
011 631 0511
www.torino2006.org

Cycle Hire

There are 70km of cycle routes especially along the rivers and in parks. Cycles can be hired from stands in the parks during the summer months.

Golf

Purchase a Torino golf pass that will admit you to a variety of golf courses located in and around Turin. Passes are valid Mon-Fri. A pass costs €25 for 24 hours and €60 for 72 hours (includes green fee, bag and clubs hire).Visit a Turismo Torino office or email: promozione@turismotorino.org

• Associazione Sportiva I Roveri Rotta
Cerbiatta 24, Fiano nr Turin
011 923 5719
www.iroveri.com, info@iroveri.com
Book in advance, Hcp required
You can only get on to this prestigious course if you take your own clubs. Designed by Trent Jones, it was voted the best in Italy.

Riding

• Ippodromo del Trotto Stupinigi
Via Stupinigi 182, 10048 Vinovo
011 965 1356
Horse riding trail.

Gyms

• Palestra Il Pardo
Via Accademia Albertina 31
011 883 900
09.00-22.00 Mon-Fri; 09.00-18.00 Sat; 09.30-13.30 Sun
www.ilpardo.it
A modern gym and health club that is associated with several hotels in the centre who will book sessions for you.

Ice Skating
• Palaghiaccio Rotelliere
Via Petrarca 39, Lingotto
011 669 9862
12.00-14.00 Tues; 12.00-1300 Thurs;
21.30-midnight Wed and Fri; 15.00-
17.00, 21.00-midnight Sat;
15.00-18.00 Sun
Admission €6, skate hire €5

Jogging
Go to any of Turin's parks outside
of working hours and you will find
joggers aplenty. The most centrally
located is Parco del Valentino. The
Turin marathon takes place in April
each year: www.turinmarathon.it

Swimming
• Centro Nuoto Torino
Corso Sebastopoli 260
011 322 448
An indoor pool for over 16s only.
• Pellerina
Corso Appio Claudio 110
011 744 036
Open-air pool
• Colletta, Via Ragazzoni 5
011 284 626
Open-air and covered pool

Football (spectating)
• Stadio delle Alpi
Strada di Altessano 131
011 738 0081
Turin's two teams, Juventus
and A.C. Torino have their
battleground at the ultra modern
and chilly Stadio delle Alpi, about
30 minutes north of the city centre.
League games are played on
Sunday mornings from September
to May and tickets can be obtained
from the stadium itself or from the
teams' websites: www.juventus.com
www.toro.it
Club stores:
• Juventus/Italia Shop, via Giolitti 2
• Toro Store, Via Allione 3

Mountains, Lakes and Langhe
The main tourist offices in these
regions are very well organised,
with details of all recreational
activities on offer.

Children
Turin has many opportunities
for children to have fun. Parco
Valentino offers cycle hire, river
trips and the Borgo Medioevale,
a reconstruction of a 15th
century village complete with
drawbridge and old workshops.
The Mole Antonelliana Cinema
Museum with its panoramic lift,
360-degree view and interactive
exhibits is a must-see. Also take
a trip on the 1930s funicular,
Tranvia Sassi-Superga, for a ride
through the forest to the top of
the hill. Those with a passion
for cars will enjoy the Museo
dell'Automobile in Lingotto.
Turin has a great tradition of
puppetry with free shows in the
summer at Giardini Reali and a
dedicated museum, Museo della
Marionetta.

Public Holidays
1 January
6 January, Epiphany
Easter Sunday
Easter Monday
25 April, Liberation Day
1 May, Labour Day
 2 June, Republic Day
15 August, Assumption
1 November, All Saints
8 December,
    Immaculate Conception
25, 26 December,
    Christmas Day and Santo
    Stefano

Index

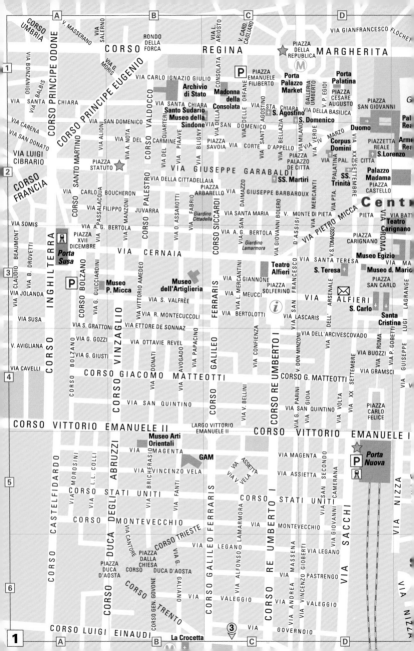

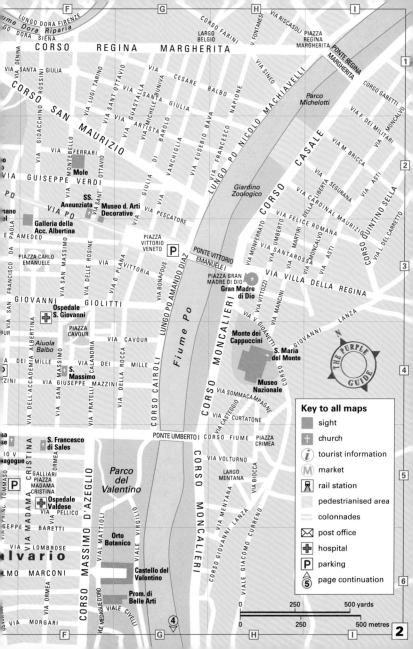

Key to all maps

- ⬛ sight
- ✝ church
- ⓘ tourist information
- Ⓜ market
- 🚉 rail station
- ▢ pedestrianised area
- ▭ colonnades
- ⊠ post office
- ✚ hospital
- Ⓟ parking
- ⑤ page continuation

0   250   500 yards

0   250   500 metres

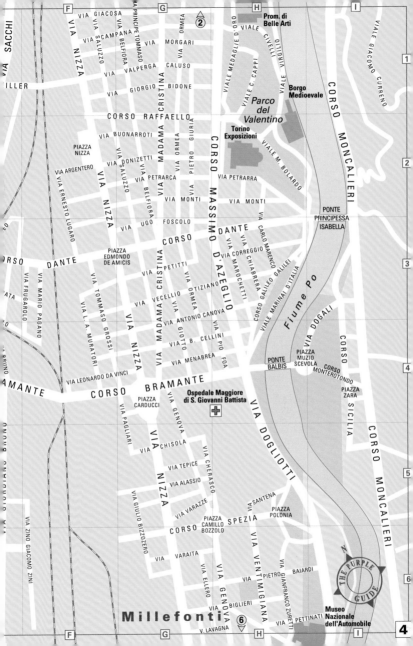

Millefonti

Museo Nazionale dell' Automobile

Lingotto

Oval Lingotto

Stazione Lingotto

Palavela

Giardino Corpo Italiano di Iberazione

Pal. del Lavoro

PIAZZA FRATELLI CEIRANO

PIAZZA BENGAZI

V. ELLERO
VIA BIGLIERI
V. G. ZURETTI
VIA PETTINATI
VIA LAVAGNA
VIA RICHELMY
VIA SPOTORNO
VIA FINALMARINA
VIA GARESSIO
VIA GENOVA
VIA GARESSIO
VIA NIZZA
VIA VADO
VIA GENOVA
VIA VENTIMIGIANA
VIA CORTEMILIA
VIA MILLEFONTI
VIA GIAGLIONE

CORSO CADUTI SUL LAVORO

VIA VALENZA
VIA SOMMARIVA
VIA VINOVO
VIA CANELLI
VIA GENOVA
VIA NIZZA
VIA VENTIMIGIANA

CASORATI
CORSO CAIO
PLINIO
VIA PASSO BUOLE
VIA TROFARELLO
V. FELIZZANO
VIA BARBARESCO
VIA
CANELLI
VIA BEINETTE
VIA TESTONA

STRADA BASSE
VIA CAROLINA INVERNIZIO

CORSO MARONCELLI

AIANO
VIA GENOVA
VIA CORRADINO
SETTE COMUNI
VIA TONALE
STRADA PRACIOSA
VIA ZARA
VIA MONTE BIANCO
VIA GIOVANNI XXII
VIA ROSSINI
VIA PUCCINI
VIA BELLINI
VIA MONCENSIO
V. LEOPARDI

DEI LINGOTTI
VIA PALMA DI CESNOLA
DUINO
VIA TOMMASO VILLA
CORSO ROMA

VORATO
VIGLIANI
VIA ONORATO VIGLIANI
VIA TORRAZZA
VIA MONASTIR
VIA SOMALIA
VIA PININFARINA
VIA SESTRIERE
VIA GRAMSCI
VIA MATTEO
VIA PONCHIELLI
V. SAN
VIA GUIDI
VIA MILLELIRE
VIA CHIALA
VIA F.L. DE MAISTRE
VIA CANDIOLI
VIA BATTISTI

CORSO MONCALIERI
CORSO UNITA D'ITALIA
Fiume Po

P
4

Essential Shopping Italian

English	Italian	Pronunciation
Open	**Aperto**	*ah-***pehr***-toh*
Closed	**Chiuso**	*kee-***oo***-soh*
How much is this?	**Quanto costa questo?**	*kwan-toh* **koh***-sta* **kwes***-toh?*
Can you write down the price?	**Puo scrivere il prezzo?**	*pwo skree-***veh***-reh eel* **preh***-tso?*
Do you take credit cards?	**Prendete carte di credito?**	*pren-***deh***-teh* **kar***-teh dee* **kreh***-dee-toh?*
I'd like to buy . . .	**Vorrei comprare . . .**	*voh-***ray** *kom-***prah***-reh*
Do you have anything . . .?	**Avete qualcosa . . .?**	*ah-***veh***-teh kwahl-***koh***-sah*
larger	**piu grande**	*pyoo* **grahn***-deh*
smaller	**piu piccolo**	*pyoo* **pee***-kohl-oh*
Do you have any others?	**Ne avete altri?**	*neh ah-***veh***-teh* **ahl***-tree*
I'm just looking.	**Sto solo guardando.**	*sto* **soh***-loh gwar-***dan***-doh*

Size Chart

Women's dresses, coats and skirts

Italian	40	42	44	46	48	50	52
British	8	10	12	14	16	18	20
American	6	8	10	12	14	16	18

Women's shoes

Italian	36	37	38	39	40	41
British	3	4	5	6	7	8
American	5	6	7	8	9	10

Men's suits

Italian	44	46	48	50	52	54	56	58 (size)
British	34	36	38	40	42	44	46	48 (inches)
American	34	36	38	40	42	44	46	48 (inches)

Men's shirts (collar size)

Italian	36	38	39	41	42	44	46	48 (cm)
British	14	15	15½	16	16½	17	17½	18 (inches)
American	14	15	15½	16	16½	17	17½	18 (inches)

Men's shoes

Italian	39	40	41	42	43	44	45	46
British	6	7	7½	8	9	10	11	12
American	7	7½	8	8½	9½	10½	11	11½